H

preserving
THROUGH the YEAR

ODED SCHWARTZ

DK

LONDON, NEW YORK, MELBOURNE, MUNICH, DELHI

DORLING KINDERSLEY
Managing Editor Dawn Henderson
Managing Art Editor Christine Keilty
Assistant Designer Jade Wheaton
Senior Jackets Creative Nicola Powling
Production Editor Tony Phipps
Senior Production Controller Jen Lockwood
Creative Technical Support Sonia Charbonnier

Produced for Dorling Kindersley by

SANDS PUBLISHING SOLUTIONS

Editors David & Sylvia Tombesi-Walton
Art Editor Simon Murrell

First published in Great Britain 2012
by Dorling Kindersley Limited, 80 Strand, London WC2R 0RL
2 4 6 8 10 9 7 5 3 1

Material first published in *Preserving* 1996
Copyright © 1996, 2012 Dorling Kindersley Limited, London.
Text copyright © Oded Schwartz 1996, 2012

ISBN: 978 14093 7609 5

Colour reproduction by Opus Multimedia Services, India
Printed and bound by South China, China

See our complete catalogue at
www.dk.com

Contents

Introduction

Being an Israeli, I feel that pickling is in my blood. In the Middle East, the love of preserved food crosses all cultural and religious boundaries and is shared by Jews and Arabs, Muslims and Christians alike. Walk into any Middle Eastern food market, and you will be amazed by the variety of pickles and preserves available: in the cool, dark interiors, you will find a gastronomic Aladdin's cave, stuffed to the brim with exotic spices, oils, fish, and meats.

When I moved to England in the 1970s, I was disappointed by the lack of variety and availability of preserves that I had grown up to believe were everywhere. But the raw ingredients were all there: wonderful fresh fruit and vegetables, and different types of meat and fish. Armed with an extensive knowledge gleaned from my youth, I set out to develop and modify ancient recipes that would work better in the modern, international market and appeal to a Western palate.

The culmination of my endeavours can be seen in this book, which covers a variety of preserving techniques, both sweet and savoury. My aim has been to give these recipes a truly contemporary feel, so that preserving can become as much a part of your life as it is of mine. They are easy to follow and practical, taking into account the constraints and pressures that exist in today's society.

There is a natural and continuous rhythm to the preserving year. Winter is a quiet period when fresh ingredients are often expensive and less readily available. It is the best time to make marmalades, tidy your cupboards, and plan the year ahead. The onset of spring brings young shoots and tender vegetables; and when summer finally arrives, the pace quickens as soft fruit come into season and market stalls are laden with ripened fruit and berries. This is the time to make clear, fragrant jellies, jams, and sweet preserves. During late summer and autumn, your kitchen should exude the delicious, sweet aroma of luscious fruit, spices, and drying herbs. It is also the traditional and most suitable time to cure meats and sausages, smoke fish, and make pâtés.

I sincerely hope that *Preserving through the Year* will encourage you to experience the pleasure and immense satisfaction of preserving your own food. Believe me: there are few things in life more enjoyable than producing your own pickles, relishes, and sauces and consuming the fruit of your labour together with family and friends. Try it for yourself!

Oded Schwartz

Equipment

For successful and efficient preserving, you need good-quality kitchen equipment. Most of the equipment shown here can be found in any well-established kitchen, but a few items – such as the mechanical shredders and grinders, preserving pans, and other specialist utensils – are required to make preserving easier. Most can be found in a good kitchen shop. Top-quality utensils might be expensive but they will last a long time. Equipment such as the dehydrator and smoker is best obtained from specialists.

LARGE COOK'S KNIFE

BONING KNIFE

KITCHEN SCISSORS

PARING KNIFE

HARDWOOD CHOPPING BOARD

CANELLE KNIFE

ZESTER

CORER

FLOATING BLADE PEELER

PEELERS, CORERS, AND ZESTERS
These all make light work of preparing fruit and vegetables.

PESTLE AND MORTAR

FOOD MILL

KNIVES
Sharp knives are essential. Select the best quality you can afford, with solid, well-balanced handles. Sharpen them frequently to maintain them.

HAND GRATER

MANDOLIN

GRATERS AND MANDOLINS
These ease the neat slicing and shredding of vegetables. Choose a good-quality mandolin with an adjustable blade.

GRINDERS
The pestle and mortar is ideal for coarsely grinding small quantities of spices. For fine powders, use an electric coffee grinder or spice mill.

FOOD MILLS
These are ideal for puréeing fruit and vegetable mixtures.

MINCERS
Use a mincer for chopping fruit or mincing meat.

HAND MINCER

MEAT
THERMOMETER

MEASURING SPOONS

SUGAR
THERMOMETER

MEASURING JUG

MEASURING EQUIPMENT
Use glass, china, or stainless steel, and avoid
corrosive metals such as aluminium.

PALETTE KNIVES
These are useful for smoothing surfaces.

WOODEN SPOONS
Keep a separate set
for sweet and savoury
products.

FUNNELS AND SIEVES
Funnels make potting much
simpler; metal sieves should not
be used with acid fruit, as metal
can affect colours and flavours.

JELLY BAG

JAM FUNNEL

FUNNEL

COLANDER

JELLY BAGS AND FILTERS
Unbleached muslin,
cheesecloth, and calico
are ideal for filtering and
straining. Always sterilize
before use (see page 12).
For filtering small
quantities of liquid, use
coffee filter papers.

SLOTTED
SPOON

LADLE

SKIMMER

SKIMMING SPOONS
A crystal-clear jam or jelly is a result
of skimming. Use slotted or perforated
spoons or special skimmers. Always
dip them in cold water before use.

BOWLS

A range of sizes is essential. Use large for steeping and mixing, and medium-sized for measured ingredients. Avoid bowls made out of corrosive materials.

STAINLESS-STEEL MIXING BOWL

GLASS MIXING BOWLS

NON-CORROSIVE PRESERVING PANS

A stainless-steel preserving pan is essential for making chutney and pickles that contain a high concentration of acid.

A thick, heavy base prevents hot spots and protects the preserve from burning

COPPER PRESERVING PANS

A wide preserving pan with a narrow bottom is ideal for making jams and jellies. Always keep it scrupulously clean, and never use it with any acidic foods.

Choose a preserving pan with a capacity of about 9 litres (16 pints)

DEHYDRATORS

Drying can be carried out in a domestic oven, but for large quantities of produce, it is advisable to buy a special dryer. Although relatively expensive, domestic dehydrators are flexible, efficient, consume very little energy, and are easy to use. Always follow the manufacturer's instructions.

These trays allow fast, even drying with no need for rotation and no tainting of flavours

Stackable trays enable you to dry different quantities of fruit and vegetables

SMOKERS

A domestic smoker is a wonderful luxury. Choose a model that is easy to operate and to clean and has an automatic temperature and time control. Make sure your smoker allows you to smoke at low temperatures; in many models, this is an optional extra.

The smoke box controls and directs the flow of smoke; hardwood chips provide the smoke

The steel door is airtight and should be left ajar when the oven is not in use

Containers

For storing moist foods and liquids, use non-absorbent materials such as glazed earthenware, enamel, glass, porcelain, and stainless steel. Avoid vessels made of corrosive material, such as aluminium, or plastic, which tends to stain and absorb flavours. Before using a container, make sure it has no chips or cracks, then wash it well. Sterilize all storage containers before use (see page 12).

Heatproof containers

Pâtés, potted goods, and other preserves that are baked in the oven require glass, earthenware, porcelain, or enamelled heatproof containers. Select dishes that complement the colour of the finished product. Glass is the ideal material to show bottled preserves at their best and is also non-corrosive. Reused glass jars are only suitable for short-term storage. For long-term preservation, it is advisable to use new specialist preserving jars that are suited to high temperatures and have non-corrosive seals.

ENAMELLED RECTANGULAR TERRINE

PORCELAIN RAMEKINS

EARTHENWARE OVAL TERRINE

EARTHENWARE CROCK

Wide-necked jars are essential for recipes using whole fruit or vegetables

Decorative bottles can be used for flavoured oils and vinegars

Hygiene and Safety

It is crucial to follow strict hygiene and safety practices. Make sure all your ingredients are in prime condition, and always keep them at the recommended temperatures. Kitchen surfaces and utensils must be kept thoroughly clean. Wipe down surfaces with a sterilizing solution before you start and as you work. Seal all preserves properly (see opposite) before storing, and discard if they show signs of deterioration (see page 252).

Sterilizing methods

There are two main methods of sterilizing jars and bottles so that they are safe to use in preserving.

BOILING WATER METHOD

Place the washed jars in a deep pan and cover with boiling water. Bring to the boil, and boil rapidly for 10 minutes. Lift the jars out and drain upside down on a clean kitchen towel. Place the jars on a covered tray, and dry in a cool oven. All lids, rubber seals, and corks must be immersed for a few seconds in boiling water. Sterilize muslin, calico, cheesecloth, and jelly bags by pouring boiling water through them.

OVEN METHOD

Place the washed jars on a paper towel-lined tray, and put in an oven preheated to 160°C/325°F/gas 3 for 10 minutes. Allow to cool slightly, then fill with the hot product.

Jars must be without chips or cracks; wash them in hot, soapy water before sterilizing

---

HYGIENE AND SAFETY WITH MEAT

Extra care must be taken when preserving meat. If the following hygiene precautions are observed, you should have no difficulty enjoying the meat products in this book.

- The kitchen must be scrupulously clean. Use separate sterilized utensils for meat, and keep them pristine.
- Sterilize equipment in boiling water. Plastic utensils can be cleaned with sterilizing tablets or in a specialist sterilizing unit used for babies' bottles.
- Warm, moist hands encourage bacterial growth. Wash them frequently with anti-bacterial soap, and always dry them well on a clean towel or kitchen paper. Keep your nails short and well scrubbed.
- Always work in a cool, well-ventilated kitchen, ideally at 10–12°C (50–54°F).
- Always buy the best-quality meat you can afford from a reliable butcher, and tell him what it is for.
- Never allow meat to become warm: keep it refrigerated at 4°C (40°F). Check the temperature of your refrigerator to ensure it is working efficiently.
- Follow the recipes accurately, and always use the recommended quantities of saltpetre, salt, and sugar. Never guess amounts.
- Check your stored products at regular intervals, and discard any that develop an unpleasant smell or show any signs of mould or deterioration (see page 252).

SALTPETRE WARNING

There is some controversy about saltpetre (sodium nitrate). Saltpetre is a naturally occurring substance that, when used in very small quantities, ensures the safety of preserved meats by inhibiting the growth of harmful bacteria. Sodium nitrate (and a similar substance, sodium nitrite) is added to commercially cured meats, and I would not recommend drying or curing meat without it.

- Saltpetre is only available from pharmacists. You will probably have to order it.
- Store it very safely: keep it clearly labelled and out of the reach of all children.
- When using saltpetre, measure it accurately and make sure it is evenly mixed with the other ingredients.
- Recipes in this book that use saltpetre have a clear warning.

Filling and Sealing

Types of Container

Always use sterilized containers with the appropriate lids or seals. For ordinary jars, use vinegar-proof lids to seal pickles and chutneys, and waxed paper discs and cellophane seals for sweet preserves. Special preserving jars are essential if a product is to be heat processed (see pages 14–15).

Cellophane seals *Waxed paper discs* *Corks*

Jam jars *Elastic bands* *Candle wax* *Sealing wax* *Glass bottle*

FILLING AND SEALING JARS WITHOUT LIDS

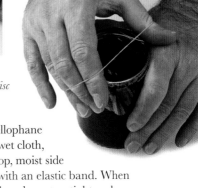

Dampen the cellophane disc before use

1 Use a ladle and a jam funnel to fill the hot sterilized jar. Fill the jar to within 1cm (½in) of the top.

2 Wipe the rim clean with a damp cloth, and carefully smooth a waxed paper disc on to the jam (waxed side down).

3 Wipe the cellophane disc with a wet cloth, place over the top, moist side up, and secure with an elastic band. When dry, it will shrink and create a tight seal.

FILLING AND SEALING BOTTLES

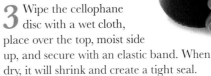

The wax must cover part of the neck of the bottle, as well as the cork

1 Use a ladle and non-corrosive funnel to fill the hot sterilized bottle to within 3.5cm (1½in) of the top. Wipe the rim clean.

2 Soak the cork in hot water for a few minutes. Push it into the bottle as far as it will go, then tap in with a wooden mallet to within 5mm (¼in) of the top.

3 When the bottle is cold, tap the cork down level with the top using a wooden mallet. Dip the top of the bottle several times into melted candle or sealing wax, allowing the wax to set between applications.

Heat Processing

Bottled preserves with low acidity, or a low sugar or salt content, are prone to mould and bacteria contamination. To keep them longer than three or four months, you must heat process them. The preserve is packed into sterilized jars or bottles, sealed, and immersed in water. It is then heated to boiling point and boiled (see box, opposite). On cooling, a vacuum is created. Store in a cool, dry, dark place for no more than two years, checking for deterioration. Discard any preserve with a swollen or damaged seal (see page 252).

Types of Container

Specialized preserving jars come in many shapes and sizes. Select the type that is readily available, for which spare new lids or rubber rings can be found easily. It is always advisable to use new containers that have acid-resistant seals. With one-piece lidded jars, you can see when a vacuum has formed and also if the seal is broken. Bottles without lids require corks to seal them. Always use new lids and corks.

Rubber seal must be new

Bottles must have a ridge so corks can be secured

Rubber seal must be new

CLAMP-TOP PRESERVING JAR

VACUUM ONE-PIECE LIDDED PRESERVING JAR

VACUUM LID AND SCREW-BAND PRESERVING JAR

HEATPROOF BOTTLE

CLAMP-TOP BOTTLE

CLAMP-TOP JAR

1 Place the new, sterilized rubber ring (see page 12) on the edge of the lid. Grip the lid tightly with one hand, and fit the ring over it.

2 Fill the hot sterilized jar to within 1cm (½in) of the top or to the manufacturer's mark. Clamp the lid shut, using a cloth to hold it steady.

LID AND SCREW-BAND JAR

1 Fill the hot sterilized jar (see page 12) to within 1cm (½in) of the top. Wipe the rim, and cover with the sterilized rubber-coated lid.

2 Hold the jar steady with a cloth. Screw the band down until it is tight, then release it by a quarter turn or as directed in the manufacturer's instructions.

SEALING BOTTLES

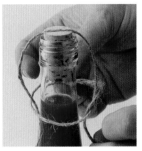

1 Cork the bottle (see page 13), then make a shallow cut in the top of the cork.

2 Cut a piece of string 50cm (20in) long and, keeping one end 10cm (4in) longer than the other, secure it in the cut.

3 Loop the long end of the string around the neck of the bottle, then insert the end of it through the front of the loop.

4 Pull both ends of the string down, to tighten the loop, and tie the loose ends over the cork in a double knot.

HEAT PROCESSING

1 Wrap each jar or bottle in a few layers of cloth or some folded newspaper to prevent them knocking against each other. Stand them on a metal rack placed in the bottom of a large lidded pan.

2 Pour in enough hot water to cover the lids or corks by at least 2.5cm (1in). Cover, bring to the boil, and boil for the stated time (see below). Check the water level occasionally, and top up if necessary.

3 Remove from the heat and lift out the jars with tongs. Place on a rack or cloth-covered surface, immediately tighten screw-bands, then leave to cool completely. As the jars cool, a partial vacuum forms.

4 To check the seal, gently undo the clamp or screw-band and grip the rim of the lid with your fingertips. Carefully lift the jar; if sealed, it will support the weight. One-piece lidded jars dip in the centre if a vacuum has formed.

HEAT PROCESSING TIMES

All times are counted from the moment the water comes back to the boil.

COLD-PACKED PRESERVES		HOT-PACKED PRESERVES	
Weight	Processing time	Weight	Processing time
500g (1lb) jars	25 minutes	500g (1lb) jars	20 minutes
500ml (1 pint) bottles	25 minutes	500ml (1 pint) bottles	20 minutes
1kg (2lb) jars	30 minutes	1kg (2lb) jars	25 minutes
1 litre (1¾–2 pint) bottles	30 minutes	1 litre (1¾–2 pint) bottles	25 minutes

How to make...
Jams

Making jams, conserves, and marmalades is among the simplest ways to preserve; almost any fruit and a surprising number of vegetables can be used. Sugar reacts with pectin and acid to make a jelly, and it also works as a preservative, its high concentration in the jam preventing mould growth. It is crucial to balance the acidity and pectin to create a good set.

Balancing the pectin

Many fruits naturally have the right balance of acidity and pectin, but some need a little help. Do this by adding lemon juice and pectin-rich fruit (such as apples) or a homemade pectin stock or shop-bought liquid pectin. If you have to increase the pectin level by a lot, you must also raise the sugar by the same proportionate amount.

You may reduce the sugar in my jam recipes by up to 30 per cent, but the jam will have a much shorter shelf life; it must be kept in the fridge because there will not be enough sugar to prevent mould growth.

1 After all the ingredients have simmered for 20–25 minutes, add the preserving sugar, and stir well over a medium heat until it has dissolved. Increase the heat and bring to a rapid, rolling boil.

2 Contine to boil the mixture for 20–25 minutes, until the setting point is reached (see box, right). Remove the pan from the heat and leave for a few minutes to allow the jam to settle. Skim if necessary.

TESTING FOR THE SET

A jam is ready to pot when it reaches the setting point, around the time the jam hits a good rolling boil and a sugar thermometer shows 105°C (220°F). Test for the set in one of these ways.

Flake test
Dip a metal spoon into the jam, then turn it so that the jam runs off the side. If the jam is set, the drops should run together and fall from the spoon in flat flakes or sheets.

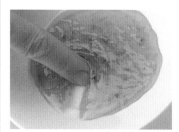

Wrinkle test
Pour a little hot jam on to a cold saucer, and leave it for a few minutes to cool. Gently push the jam with a clean finger; if it wrinkles, it has reached the setting point.

How to make...
Jellies

Jelly-making is a miraculous process: dull and cloudy fruit juice is transformed into a clear, jewel-like substance. Three elements are necessary to achieve this: pectin (which is found in varying degrees in all fruit), acidity, and sugar. Low-pectin fruit such as cherries, peaches, and raspberries are usually supplemented with pectin-rich ones such as apples, cranberries, citrus fruit, or currants.

Key steps

For jellies, wash and chop the fruit, and remove but do not discard the cores of any apples. If you use a food processor for the chopping stage, it will reduce your cooking time, but you will probably have to food-process in batches, due to the quantity of fruit being too large for the bowl.

As with jam-making, cover the fruit (and cores) with water, bring to the boil, and simmer for 20–30 minutes. Before the jelly reaches its setting point and is ready to be ladled into jars, be sure to remove all the froth from the top. The aim is for a beautifully clear end result.

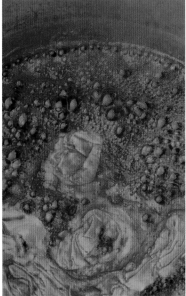

1 Pour the fruit and liquid into a sterilized jelly bag suspended over a large bowl. Leave for 2–3 hours or until it stops dripping. Do not be tempted to squeeze the bag, or the jelly will be cloudy.

2 Return the pulp to the pan, and add water to cover. Simmer for about 30 minutes, then drain as before. Add the juice to the first batch. Heat gently, stirring from time to time, until the sugar has dissolved.

3 Bring the liquid to a rapid boil, then skim well with a slotted spoon to remove the froth. Boil rapidly until the setting point is reached (see page 16), starting to check after about 10 minutes.

How to make...
Fruit Cheeses and Butters

Fruit cheeses and fruit butters date back to pre-Roman times, when the pulp was mixed with honey and dried in the sun. Butters are made in the same way as cheeses, but the cooking time is shorter and sometimes the proportion of sugar is lower, resulting in a softer, more spreadable mixture. A set is achieved by boiling out the moisture, which means that any fruit can be used, since the pectin levels are not an important factor.

Key steps

Cheeses and butters need long, slow cooking and should be stirred frequently towards the end because they burn easily. Quinces, used below, make the best cheese, since they produce a beautifully fragrant dark amber preserve. Both cheeses and butters can be kept for a long time.

The key difference in preparation between fruit cheese and fruit butter is the length of time for which the purée simmers. While for a cheese you reduce the mixture to a dark, thick, glossy paste, a butter is ready when you can leave a clear indent by pressing down on it with a spoon.

1 After chopping the fruit, add some water or cider, bring it to the boil, and simmer for 30–45 minutes, until it is soft and pulpy. Purée it through a food mill or sieve, then add some sugar.

2 Return the purée to the pan, bring slowly to the boil, and simmer for 2½–3 hours, stirring frequently. It will become very thick and start to "plop". Brush a deep baking tray generously with oil.

3 Pour the cheese into the tray in an even layer, 2.5–4cm (1–1½in) thick. Leave to cool, cover with a cloth, and keep in a warm, dry place for 24 hours. Transfer it to baking parchment to cut into squares.

How to make...
Chutneys and Relishes

In India, the word "chutney" refers to a wide range of products – from slow-cooked preserves that are matured for several weeks before use, to simple relishes made from finely chopped raw ingredients that are ready to eat after a few hours' marinating. What they all have in common is the inclusion of acid, spices, and a sweetener. Shown below is the method for making a traditional cooked chutney.

Key steps

The acidity added for both chutneys and relishes comes in the form of vinegar. Although any type of vinegar is suitable, I prefer to use cider vinegar, because its fruity flavour seems particularly appropriate, but white wine vinegar is also a popular choice with many preservers.

Relish differs in preparation from chutney in the length of its cooking time. Depending on ingredients, a relish might cook for only a third as long as a chutney, since the aim is only to take out most of the moisture, rather than to create the thick, glossy end product that is a chutney.

1 Put the produce in a non-corrosive pan with vinegar and salt, and mix well. Bring to the boil, then reduce the heat and simmer until the fruit is soft but not mushy. Add more vinegar or water if it seems dry.

2 Add soft brown sugar to the pan, stirring until it has dissolved. This prevents the mixture from softening any further, so if you prefer a softer chutney, cook the mixture for a little longer before adding the sugar.

3 Cook the mixture for 50–60 minutes, until it is thick and most of the liquid has evaporated. Stir frequently to prevent it sticking. Once poured into jars, the chutney will be ready in 3 weeks.

How to make...
Ketchups and Sauces

Ketchup originally came from China, where, centuries ago, it was the liquid in which fish had been pickled and was popular among seafarers for pepping up their diet of rice gruel. It was brought to Europe at the beginning of the 18th century by merchants returning from the Orient. Ketchup – or tomato ketchup in particular – quickly became the world's most popular condiment. Homemade ketchup is far superior to the bland, sweet commercial varieties.

Key steps

Ketchups and sauces are made in the same way, and you can use many other fruit and vegetables besides tomatoes; especially good are red peppers (as shown in the example below), mushrooms, peaches, apples, pears, and plums. Before you start cooking, skin the produce as necessary, and chop the ingredients finely with a knife or food processor. Make a spice bag and herb bundle (see page 31), and place them in a non-corrosive preserving pan along with the vegetables and enough water to cover. Bring to the boil, then simmer for 25 minutes or until soft.

1 Leave the cooked fruit or vegetables to cool for a little while, then discard the herbs and spice bag that were used. Pass the mixture through a food mill or sieve to turn it into a purée.

2 Place the resulting purée in the cleaned preserving pan, and add the vinegar, sugar, and salt. Bring to the boil, stirring until the sugar has dissolved, then simmer for 1–1½ hours, until it is reduced by half.

3 Mix arrowroot or cornflour to a paste with a little vinegar, and stir it into the sauce. Boil for 1–2 minutes, until slightly thickened. Once it is poured into bottles, heat process them and leave to cool.

How to make...
Pickles and Vinegars

There are two stages to pickling in vinegar. First, the ingredients are salted to draw out excess moisture that would otherwise dilute the vinegar. This is done either by dry-salting or by steeping in a strong saline solution. Vegetables should be soaked for 12–48 hours, depending on size, and kept in a cool place. In hot climates, change the solution daily, since it tends to ferment.

The creative touch

Next, cover the vegetables with vinegar, which can be plain, spiced, or sweet. Flavourings, such as dried chillies and peppercorns, are usually added. If you like crunchy pickles, leave the vinegar to cool before pouring it in; for a softer pickle, use boiling vinegar.

Pickled green vegetables tend to lose their colour with keeping; blanching them briefly will help combat this. You can add a little bicarbonate of soda to the water to preserve their colour (1 tsp for every 500ml/17fl oz water), but it destroys the vitamins in the vegetables.

1 Make enough strong brine to cover the vegetables, using 75g (2½oz) salt for each litre (1¾ pints) water. Pour this over the vegetables, weight down (see page 166), and leave in a cool place for 24 hours.

2 To make a flavoured vinegar, prepare a spice bag (see page 31) and place it in a non-corrosive pan with the vinegar of your choice. Bring to the boil, and boil for about 5 minutes.

3 Pour the boiling vinegar over the rinsed onions, making sure they are completely submerged. Weight down (see page 166) and seal the jars (see page 13). Store in a cool, dark place for 3–4 weeks.

BLANCHING

Blanching plays an important role in preserving because it destroys the enzymes in fruit and vegetables that cause their deterioration and discoloration on exposure to the air (known as oxidation). Green vegetables are usually blanched in salted water (1 tablespoon salt to every 1 litre/1¾ pints water), while fruit are blanched in acidulated water (3 tablespoons vinegar or lemon juice or 2 teaspoons citric acid to every 1 litre/1¾ pints water).

FILTERING

Sometimes, even carefully prepared liquids can become cloudy and need filtering. Pour the liquid through a sterilized jelly bag, or a double layer of sterilized muslin, thin layer of calico, or paper filter (such as a coffee filter or a filter for a home-brewing kit).

Use a sieve to hold a small piece of sterilized muslin or calico, or tie a large piece to the legs of an upturned stool. If using a paper filter, the simplest and most convenient way is to use it to line a funnel.

The best ingredients for...
Jams, Conserves, and Marmalades

Arguably the most popular method of preserving, jam-making is synonymous with fruit – and especially berries. Surprisingly, though, certain vegetables can also be used to make sweet jams. The set of vegetable jams is different – not as firm as a fruit jam – but still perfectly spreadable. Another type of jam, marmalade, is commonly made with citrus fruit, but variants, such as peach, are also known.

CHERRIES
Wonderful jams can be made with cooking cherries (such as morellos) and dessert cherries. However, you will need additional pectin if using the latter.

BLACKBERRIES
Since they are low to medium in pectin, blackberries are best combined with apples or other berries when used for jam.

FIGS
These low-pectin and low-acid fruits can be used to make delicious, exotic-tasting jams that match perfectly with soft cheeses.

BLUEBERRIES
These berries show a great variability in pectin levels and are most commonly combined with other fruit in jams.

RASPBERRIES
Among the most popular fruit for jams, raspberries have a medium pectin level, which helps them achieve a set quite easily.

STRAWBERRIES
Classic summer strawberries are best used as fresh as possible. They are low in pectin so need help in that department to achieve a set.

LEMONS AND ORANGES
Citrus fruit are very versatile and are frequently used in jams, conserves, and marmalades. Being rich in pectin, they help achieve a good set. They are also a good source of vitamin C.

YOU COULD ALSO TRY...

Apples • Aubergines • Gooseberries • Grapes • Greengages • Lychees • Marrows • Melons • Mulberries • Nectarines • Onions • Peaches • Peppers (red) • Pineapples • Pumpkins • Quinces • Squashes • Tomatoes.

PEARS
Low in pectin and acidity, pears are often combined with apples to boost pectin or with citrus fruit to add acidity.

APRICOTS
Jam made from apricots is a real treat. However, because pectin and acid levels vary greatly, some apricots produce a soft set.

PLUMS
Different plums have different pectin levels. Dessert (and ripe) plums are medium-pectin fruit; cooking (and unripe) plums are high in pectin.

BLACKCURRANTS
Even with very ripe blackcurrants, it is possible to make a lovely, fruity jam that captures the pure essence of summer.

DAMSONS
These astringent fruit can make jams with a real kick. They are also high in pectin, so setting is never a problem.

CARROTS
With a higher pectin level than most vegetables, carrots are ideal for jam-making. Their sweetness and colour are also appealing.

The best ingredients for...
Jellies, Fruit Cheeses, and Butters

The key requirement in jelly-making is to use fruit that are juicy or high in pectin – and ideally both. On the other hand, for fruit butters and cheeses, of greatest importance is that the raw produce used is delicious and plentiful. These latter two preserves can also be enhanced through the addition of aromatic liqueurs or other unusual flavourings.

RASPBERRIES
The classic jelly fruit, raspberries give a beautifully clear end product. They can also be used to give a different spin on a curd.

GRAPES
Pectin levels vary in grapes, so add a chopped lemon to boost them when making jellies.

STRAWBERRIES
Delicate jellies can be made from strawberries, but they do have low pectin levels.

CRAB APPLES
These are ideal alternatives to apples to increase the pectin levels when low-pectin fruit are also being used in a jelly.

APPLES
Perfect for jellies and soft butters, apples can also be used in fruit cheeses when combined with damsons or quinces.

LEMONS
Synonymous with fruit curds, lemons are also great pectin-boosting fruit for use in jellies.

YOU COULD ALSO TRY...
Apricots • Blackcurrants • Damsons • Gooseberries • Grapefruit • Guavas • Mangoes • Medlars • Melons • Mulberries • Oranges • Passion fruit • Peaches (ripe) • Peppers (red) • Pineapple • Rowanberries • Sloes • Tomatoes.

BLACKBERRIES
These are an ideal fruit – when combined with apples for a pectin boost – for fruit butters, cheeses, and jellies.

KIWI FRUIT
A lovely, sweet-sour fruit butter can be made from kiwis, with the juice of a lemon providing a little acidity and pectin.

CHILLIES
Add a hint of fire to jellies by throwing some chillies into the mix. Also, try different types of chilli with various fruits.

PLUMS
Lovely jellies can be made from plums, and the different types all give a different result. Experiment with ripeness, too.

PEARS
Fairly firm pears are a wonderful basis for fruit butters and cheeses, especially when combined with quinces, apples, or cranberries.

QUINCES
The best fruit cheese is one made from quinces – and quince butter is also wonderful.

The best ingredients for...
Chutneys, Relishes, Ketchups, and Sauces

A huge number of fruit and vegetables can be used to make chutneys and relishes, but as with all preserving, be sure to use the best-quality ingredients and, ideally, those that are in season. Remember: chutneys improve with age, so don't be in a rush to open them. Ketchups and sauces tend to be drawn from a smaller range of produce, much of which is everyday storecupboard fare.

TOMATOES
The tomato is undoubtedly the ultimate ingredient for chutneys, relishes, ketchups, and sauces.

ONIONS
These are essential in chutneys and relishes. Either colour works equally well, as do the milder shallots.

CHILLIES
As you would expect, chillies add a great little kick, but they might not be to everyone's taste.

PEPPERS
Colour, sweetness, and texture are all benefits afforded to chutneys and relishes by red or yellow peppers.

MARROW
Traditionally, the marrow is a favourite chutney ingredient for the creamy texture it imparts to the end product.

AUBERGINES
This chutney staple is particularly popular with those inspired by Indian, Southeast Asian and Mediterranean dishes.

PLUMS
Delicious sweet-savoury
ketchups can be made with
plums, and they are also
perfect for chutneys.

RHUBARB
The tart flavour of rhubarb
means it tends to blend well with
fruit in chutneys and relishes.

CRANBERRIES
The classic American Thanksgiving
dinner simply wouldn't be complete
without cranberry sauce.

PEARS
When mixed with ginger,
pears are a wonderful
chutney ingredient.

PEACHES
Give peach-based
chutneys a lovely
crunch by adding
walnuts, almonds,
or pecans.

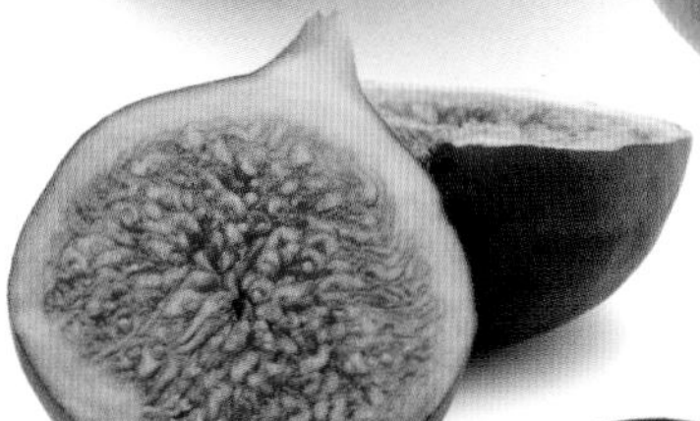

FIGS
Underripe figs are
commonly used in
chutneys and
relishes, adding
an unctuous
texture and a
taste of the
exotic.

APPLES
An apple sauce is the perfect
accompaniment to pork dishes,
but the fruit is also an essential
ingredient in chutneys.

YOU COULD ALSO TRY...
Apricots • Carrots
• Celery stalks • Garlic •
Ginger • Grapes (seedless)
• Green tomatoes •
Kumquats • Limes •
Mangoes • Mushrooms
(flat-cap) • Pineapple •
Pitted dates • Pumpkin
• Raisins • Sweetcorn
(baby or cobs).

The best ingredients for...
Pickles and Vinegars

A good tangy pickle should be a staple in any pantry. It is the perfect accompaniment to hot or cold meats, as well as to cheese and biscuits. The best fruit and vegetables for use in pickling are hard or firm varieties – onions, beetroots, and peppers, for example. Vinegars are not quite so reliant on firmer produce, and delicious ones can even be created with soft summer fruit such as strawberries.

CHILLIES
This perfect pickling ingredient is great on its own but also ideal for adding a kick to other pickled produce.

WALNUTS
Pickled walnuts are a classic of preserving, even though they require a lot of time.

DAMSONS
When pickled, damsons become sweet-sour, and they increase in deliciousness the longer they are kept.

LIMES
Tangy, hot pickles can be made from limes, bringing a taste of India to the table. Add ginger, cumin, and cloves.

CAULIFLOWER
This vegetable works particularly well when pickled with Asian spices and served with Eastern food.

RED CABBAGE
Pickled red cabbage is a longtime classic. Add caraway or cumin seeds for extra flavour.

OKRA
This ingredient makes an interesting textural addition to any pickles inspired by Indian cuisine and flavourings.

YOU COULD ALSO TRY...
Baby purple aubergine • Carrots • Celery stalks • Cucumbers • Fish fillets • Ginger • Gooseberries • Green tomatoes • Horseradish root • Kiwi fruit • Peppers (red and yellow) • Pickling onions • Plums (preferably Switzen) • Radishes • Sorrel • Spinach • Strawberries • Watermelon rind.

DRIED CHILLIES
Vinegars made with dried chillies have a wonderfully warming quality.

PICKLING CUCUMBERS
Gherkins, or pickled cucumbers, are a love/hate food – but they are very popular with preservers.

SHALLOTS
Onions are likely to be the first thing to mind when thinking about pickles, but shallots make for a milder alternative.

GARLIC
When pickled, garlic has an invigorating and refreshing quality. It deserves to be more widely known.

TURNIPS
Good on their own or with beetroot, turnips are a popular pickle ingredient in the Middle East.

BEETROOT
Another staple of the table, pickled beetroot may be pepped up with garlic or tarragon.

Flavourings

The history of good cooking began when people discovered that adding fresh herbs and spices to food turned it into a fragrant delicacy. Since then, achieving the correct balance of flavours has been at the heart of all cuisines. Herbs and spices are valued not only for their flavour and aroma but also because many of them have antiseptic qualities and aid digestion – and they actively help the preserving process.

Spices

Whenever possible, grind spices just before use. Whole spices will keep for up to two years in an airtight container, while ground ones quickly lose their aroma.

GROUND TURMERIC

TURMERIC ROOT

ANISEED

PEPPERCORNS

CORIANDER SEEDS

DILL SEEDS

CELERY SEEDS

GINGER ROOT

CUMIN SEEDS

VANILLA PODS

CLOVES

CHILLI FLAKES

CHILLI POWDER

JUNIPER BERRIES

STAR ANISE

GREEN CARDAMOM PODS

ALLSPICE BERRIES

CINNAMON STICKS

GROUND CINNAMON

NIGELLA SEEDS

FENUGREEK SEEDS

Herbs

Store fresh herbs in a jug of water, or in the bottom of the refrigerator with the stems wrapped in damp paper towels. Fresh herbs can be replaced with dried (except delicate varieties such as basil and parsley), but because the flavour of dried herbs is more concentrated, use half the quantity.

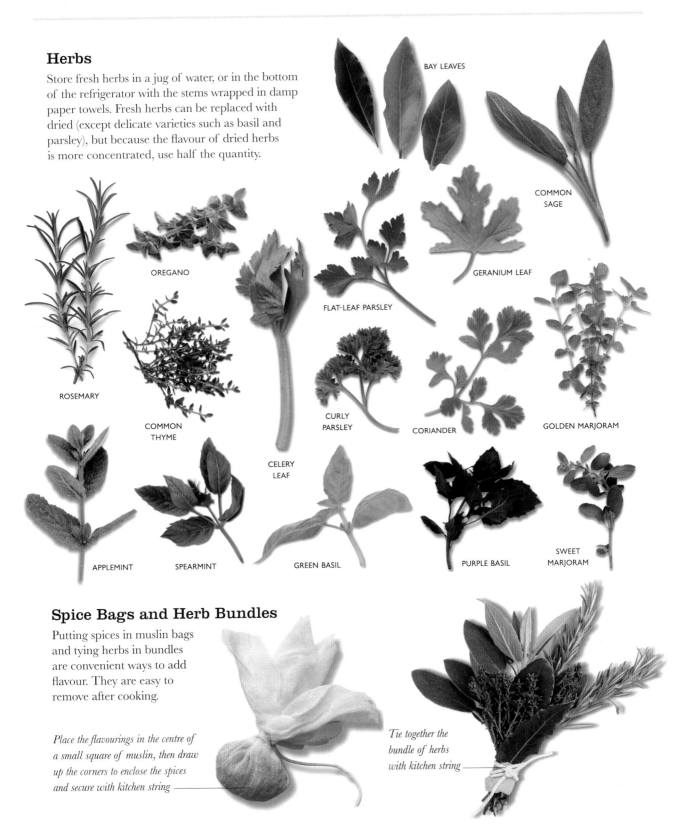

BAY LEAVES

COMMON SAGE

OREGANO

ROSEMARY

COMMON THYME

FLAT-LEAF PARSLEY

GERANIUM LEAF

CURLY PARSLEY

CORIANDER

GOLDEN MARJORAM

CELERY LEAF

APPLEMINT

SPEARMINT

GREEN BASIL

PURPLE BASIL

SWEET MARJORAM

Spice Bags and Herb Bundles

Putting spices in muslin bags and tying herbs in bundles are convenient ways to add flavour. They are easy to remove after cooking.

Place the flavourings in the centre of a small square of muslin, then draw up the corners to enclose the spices and secure with kitchen string

Tie together the bundle of herbs with kitchen string

Late Winter

Seasonal Ingredients

In the latter part of winter, meats are traditionally at their most popular, not least for their warming, homely qualities. The root vegetables are still making their presence known, though, and (depending on quite where you are in the world) citrus-fruit season is upon us. Here is a selection of some of my favourite ingredients for preserving in late winter.

QUAIL
In terms of game, quail has quite a delicate flavour. It is a succulent meat, with a darker-coloured flesh and meatier breast than chicken.

ORANGES
The zingy, zesty quality of oranges is the perfect pick-me-up on a cold winter's afternoon, in whatever form they are served.

PHEASANT
Some say pheasant is very similar in taste to chicken, but it does tend to be a drier meat – and of course, it has a gamey edge to it.

SHALLOTS
These are interchangeable with onions, though they have a milder, more distinct flavour.

RED AND PINK GRAPEFRUIT
This traditional breakfast fruit is probably loved and hated in equal measure, due to its distinctive bitter taste. Use it to make a fabulous curd.

COD FILLET
So popular that there have, in recent years, been calls to choose other fish while reserves increase, cod is a fleshly, versatile, and undervalued fish.

CLEMENTINES
With their high pectin and acidity levels, clementines are ideal for use in jams and jellies but can also be successfully pickled to interesting effect.

VENISON
This low-fat meat can be preserved in a surprising number of ways, including pickling and potting.

Pink Grapefruit Curd

☆☆ **DEGREE OF DIFFICULTY** MODERATE **COOKING TIME** 30–45 MINUTES

SPECIAL EQUIPMENT DOUBLE BOILER; STERILIZED JARS AND SEALANTS (SEE PAGES 12–13)

YIELD ABOUT 1KG (2LB) **SHELF LIFE** 3 MONTHS, REFRIGERATED; 6 MONTHS, IF HEAT PROCESSED

SERVING SUGGESTION USE PINK GRAPEFRUIT CURD TO FILL CAKES, TARTS, AND PAVLOVAS.

INGREDIENTS

grated rind and juice of 1 ruby red or pink grapefruit

segmented flesh of 1 ruby red or pink grapefruit (see steps 2 and 3)

juice of 2 lemons

400g (13oz) preserving or granulated sugar

100g (3½oz) butter, softened

4 eggs and 2 egg yolks (size 3), beaten

3 tbsp orange-flower water

1 Grate the rind of one grapefruit on the fine side of a hand grater, then squeeze the juice.

2 Using a sharp knife, cut off all the peel and pith from the other grapefruit, following the curve of the fruit.

3 Carefully cut out all the segments of flesh from between the membranes, and chop them coarsely.

4 Put the grapefruit juice, zest, and flesh in a saucepan with the lemon juice, sugar, and butter. Heat gently until the butter has melted, then move the mix to a double boiler or a bowl over a pan of barely simmering water.

Add the butter in pieces so that it melts quickly

5 Strain the beaten eggs into the fruit mixture through a fine mesh sieve, stirring constantly with a wooden spoon to ensure they are evenly incorporated.

6 Cook the mixture very gently, stirring frequently, for 25–45 minutes, until it is thick enough to coat the back of the spoon. Do not allow the mixture to boil or it will curdle.

Sieve in the beaten eggs to avoid lumps forming in the curd

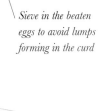

7 Remove the pan from the heat (or the bowl off the water), and stir in the orange-flower water. Ladle the curd into warm sterilized jars; seal immediately with waxed paper discs and cellophane seals.

Orange Marmalade with Coriander

 DEGREE OF DIFFICULTY EASY **COOKING TIME** 1–1½ HOURS **SPECIAL EQUIPMENT** PRESERVING PAN; SUGAR THERMOMETER; STERILIZED JARS AND SEALANTS (SEE PAGES 12–13) **YIELD** ABOUT 2KG (4LB) **SHELF LIFE** 2 YEARS **SERVING SUGGESTION** SERVE ON TOAST FOR BREAKFAST

INGREDIENTS

1kg (2lb) Seville oranges

2 lemons

2 litres (3 ½ pints) water

1.5kg (3lb) preserving
or granulated sugar

3 tbsp coriander seeds, crushed

75ml (3fl oz) dry orange liqueur,
such as triple sec

1 Scrub the oranges and lemons well to remove the wax coating. Halve them crossways, reserving all the pips, then cut each half lengthways. Thinly slice each section to create semi-circles.

2 Place all the pips in a small square of clean muslin. Gather up the ends of the cloth, and secure with string to form a small bag.

3 Place the fruit and muslin bag in a large glass bowl with the water. Weight down with a plate (see page 166) to keep the fruit submerged.

4 The next day, transfer the citrus fruit and water to the preserving pan. Bring to the boil, then reduce the heat and simmer for 45 minutes–1 hour or until the orange rind is just soft and the mixture has reduced by half.

5 Add the sugar to the pan. Slowly return to the boil, stirring until the sugar has dissolved. Skim well, then stir in the crushed coriander seeds.

6 Boil the mixture rapidly for 10–15 minutes or until the setting point is reached (see page 16). Remove the pan from the heat and leave the fruit to settle for a few minutes. Add the liqueur and stir in thoroughly. Ladle the marmalade into the hot sterilized jars, then seal.

This marmalade recipe is flavoured with coriander seeds and orange liqueur. Sweet oranges can be used, but bitter Seville oranges – available only in midwinter – give the best results.

Candied Citrus Peel

☆ **DEGREE OF DIFFICULTY** EASY 🥘 **COOKING TIME** 2¾–3¾ HOURS 🍴 **SPECIAL EQUIPMENT** AIRTIGHT CONTAINER
OR 1 LITRE (1¾ PINT) STERILIZED JAR AND SEALANT (SEE PAGES 12–13) 🏺 **YIELD** ABOUT 1.5KG (3LB)
🏺 **SHELF LIFE** 2 YEARS IN SYRUP; 1 YEAR WITH A CRYSTALLIZED FINISH
🔪 **SERVING SUGGESTIONS** COVER WITH CHOCOLATE OR USE FOR DECORATION

INGREDIENTS

*1kg (2lb) citrus peel, cut
into 5cm (2in) strips*
*1kg (2lb) preserving
or granulated sugar*
350ml (12fl oz) water

1 Put the peel in a non-corrosive pan with enough water to cover. Bring to the boil, then simmer for 10 minutes. Drain, discard the cooking liquid, and cover with fresh water. Return to the boil, then reduce the heat and simmer for 20 minutes. Drain again.

2 Put the cooked peel in a large bowl, cover with cold water, and leave for 24 hours.

3 Drain the peel. Put the sugar and water in a pan. Bring to the boil, stirring until the sugar has dissolved. Add the peel, then reduce the heat and simmer very gently for 2–3 hours or until the peel is translucent and most of the syrup has been absorbed. Stir frequently to prevent sticking.

4 To preserve the peel in syrup, spoon the mixture into the jar, then seal. Alternatively, lift the peel out of the syrup, arrange on wire racks and dry in the oven (see Candied Pineapple Rings, page 228).

5 Dust with caster sugar and store in an airtight container, between layers of waxed paper.

TIP
You can remove some of the outer skin to make the peel less bitter. I find it unnecessary, but it is the traditional method.

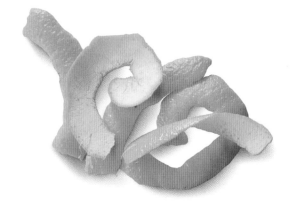

This recipe is a wonderful way to use citrus peel. Any thick-skinned citrus fruit can be used, such as orange, grapefruit, citron, and pomelo. The last two are especially good.

Clementines in Brandy

 DEGREE OF DIFFICULTY EASY **COOKING TIME** ABOUT 1¼ HOURS **SPECIAL EQUIPMENT** PRESERVING PAN; SUGAR THERMOMETER; 2 x 1 LITRE (1¾ PINT) STERILIZED JARS WITH SEALANTS (SEE PAGES 12–13) **YIELD** ABOUT 2KG (4LB)
SHELF LIFE 2 YEARS **SERVING SUGGESTION** SERVE IN THE SYRUP WITH THICK CREAM

INGREDIENTS

2kg (4lb) clementines

*1kg (2lb) preserving
or granulated sugar*

2 litres (3½ pints) water

FOR THE SPICE BAG (SEE PAGE 31)

5cm (2in) piece fresh ginger root

1 tsp cloves

1 clementine leaf (optional)

FOR EACH JAR

2 cloves

a few shreds of fresh ginger root

clementine leaves (optional)

about 250ml (8fl oz) brandy

1 Prick the clementines in a few places with a wooden skewer.

2 Put the sugar and water in the preserving pan with the spice bag. Bring to the boil, and boil rapidly for 5 minutes. Add the clementines. Return to the boil, then simmer very gently for about 1 hour or until they are soft.

3 Lift out the fruit with a slotted spoon. Arrange in the hot sterilized jars with the spices and clementine leaves, if using.

4 Bring the syrup to the boil, and boil rapidly until it reaches 113°C (235°F) on the sugar

thermometer. Allow to cool to 75°C (167°F).

5 Pour in enough brandy to half-fill the jars. Top up with the syrup, then seal. The clementines will be ready to eat in 1 month but improve with keeping.

VARIATION

KUMQUATS IN BRANDY
Use the same quantity of washed and pricked kumquats, and cook for about 25 minutes or until the fruit is just soft. Continue as for the main recipe. Other alcohol, such as vodka, rum, or eau de vie, can be used instead of brandy.

Whole clementines preserved in a brandied syrup make a superb dessert. Choose small, thin-skinned clementines, preferably with some leaves still attached.

TIP
Before using the clementines, wash them well in hot, soapy water to remove the wax coating, then dry thoroughly.

*A few fresh
clementine leaves and
spices add decoration,
as well as flavour*

*The fruit may
have a wrinkled
appearance once
they have matured*

Spiced Whole Oranges

 **DEGREE OF DIFFICULTY** MODERATE **COOKING TIME** ABOUT 1 HOUR **SPECIAL EQUIPMENT** CANELLE KNIFE; NON-CORROSIVE PRESERVING PAN; 2 LITRE (3½ PINT) WIDE-NECKED, STERILIZED JAR WITH VINEGAR-PROOF SEALANT (SEE PAGES 12–13) **YIELD** ABOUT 1KG (2LB) **SHELF LIFE** 2 YEARS  **SERVING SUGGESTIONS** SERVE WITH COLD HAM (SEE PAGE 184 FOR RECIPE), TURKEY, CHICKEN, OR OTHER POULTRY

INGREDIENTS

1kg (2lb) small, thin-skinned oranges, preferably seedless

1 litre (1¾ pints) cider vinegar or distilled malt vinegar

750g (1½lb) sugar

juice of 1 lemon

cloves

FOR THE SPICE BAG (SEE PAGE 31)

2 tsp cloves

2 cinnamon sticks, crushed

1 tsp cardamom pods, crushed

1 Scrub the oranges well, then remove alternate strips of rind from each one with the canelle knife and add to the spice bag.

2 Put the oranges in the preserving pan with enough cold water to cover. Bring to the boil, then simmer very gently for 20–25 minutes or until the peel is just soft. Lift out the oranges with a slotted spoon and drain well.

3 Measure 1 litre (1¾ pints) of the cooking liquid and return to the pan. Add the vinegar, sugar, lemon juice, and spice bag. Bring to the boil, and boil for 10 minutes. Remove from the heat and skim well. Return the oranges to the pan and leave to stand overnight.

4 The next day, return the mixture to the boil, then simmer very gently for 20 minutes. Carefully remove the oranges from the liquid with a slotted spoon and leave to cool slightly.

5 Stud each orange with a few cloves and arrange in the hot sterilized jar. Bring the syrup to the boil, and boil rapidly until it has thickened slightly. Pour the syrup into the jar, making sure the oranges are completely covered, then seal. The oranges will be ready to eat in 1 month but improve with keeping.

Spiced oranges are a classic British preserve. In this elegant version, the oranges are left whole instead of being sliced. They make a welcome addition to a festive meal.

Orange and Tarragon Mustard

 DEGREE OF DIFFICULTY EASY **COOKING TIME** 1–2 MINUTES **SPECIAL EQUIPMENT** SPICE MILL OR COFFEE GRINDER; SMALL STERILIZED JARS WITH VINEGAR-PROOF SEALANTS (SEE PAGES 12–13) **YIELD** ABOUT 500G (1LB) **SHELF LIFE** 6 MONTHS **SERVING SUGGESTION** SERVE WITH COLD MEAT

INGREDIENTS

finely grated rind and
juice of 2 oranges
250g (8oz) yellow mustard seeds
100ml (3½fl oz) white wine vinegar
2 tsp salt
1 tbsp chopped fresh tarragon
or 1 tsp dried tarragon
a little brandy or whisky

1 Put the orange rind and juice in a small pan. Bring to the boil, then reduce the heat and simmer for a few seconds. (This improves the keeping qualities of the mustard.) Remove from the heat and leave to cool completely.

2 Coarsely grind 200g (7oz) of the mustard seeds in the spice mill or coffee grinder. Place in a glass bowl with the remaining whole mustard seeds, add the boiled orange juice and rind, and mix well. Leave to stand for about 5 minutes, then stir in the vinegar, salt, and tarragon.

3 Pack the mustard into the sterilized jars. Cover each one with a waxed paper disc that has been dipped in brandy or whisky, then seal. The mustard will be ready to eat in a few days. (This gives the whole mustard seeds time to swell and soften.)

This coarse-grained mustard is particularly good for coating meat before roasting. The tarragon adds to its spicy sweet aftertaste. If you plan to use it immediately, there is no need to boil the orange juice.

Shallot Vinegar

 DEGREE OF DIFFICULTY EASY **COOKING TIME** 3–4 MINUTES **SPECIAL EQUIPMENT** THERMOMETER; 2 x 500ML (17FL OZ) STERILIZED BOTTLES WITH VINEGAR-PROOF SEALANTS (SEE PAGES 12–13) **YIELD** ABOUT 1 LITRE (1¾ PINTS) **SHELF LIFE** 2 YEARS **SERVING SUGGESTION** USE TO MAKE SALAD DRESSINGS

INGREDIENTS

500g (1lb) shallots

1 litre (1¾ pints) white wine vinegar or cider vinegar

1 Peel and coarsely chop the shallots, and divide among the bottles.

2 Put the vinegar in a non-corrosive pan. Bring to the boil, and boil rapidly for 1–2 minutes. Remove from the heat and leave to cool to 40°C (104°F).

3 Pour in the warm vinegar, then seal. Shake the bottles occasionally during storage to help release the shallot flavours. The vinegar will be ready to use in about 3 weeks, at which point you may decide to filter out the shallot pieces to create a clear vinegar.

VARIATION

CITRUS VINEGAR

Peel the rind from 3–4 oranges or lemons. Remove as much white pith as possible, then thread the peel on to wooden skewers and put one in each bottle. Cover with the warm vinegar and complete as for the main recipe.

TIP
Use this vinegar for dressing salads, or add it to hollandaise sauce instead of fresh shallots.

Shallot Confiture

 DEGREE OF DIFFICULTY ADVANCED **COOKING TIME** DAY 2, 30–35 MINUTES; DAY 3, ABOUT 20 MINUTES; DAY 4, 2¼–2¾ HOURS **SPECIAL EQUIPMENT** NON-CORROSIVE PRESERVING PAN; STERILIZED JARS AND VINEGAR-PROOF SEALANTS (SEE PAGES 12–13) **YIELD** ABOUT 1.25KG (2½LB) **SHELF LIFE** 2 YEARS **SERVING SUGGESTIONS** ESPECIALLY GOOD WITH VENISON AND LAMB

INGREDIENTS

1.3kg (2lb 10oz) shallots

150g (5oz) salt

1.5 litres (2½ pints) distilled white vinegar or white wine vinegar

1kg (2lb) preserving or granulated sugar

FOR THE SPICE BAG (SEE PAGE 31)

4 cardamom pods

2 cinnamon sticks

3 strips lemon rind

1 tbsp caraway seeds

1 tbsp cloves

½ tsp bird's eye chillies

1 Peel the shallots by blanching in boiling water for a few minutes (see page 21). Make sure that the root end remains intact or the shallots will disintegrate during cooking.

2 Place the peeled shallots in a large glass bowl. Cover with cold water and add the salt. Mix well until the salt has dissolved, then weight down (see page 166) and leave for 24 hours.

3 Put the vinegar, sugar, and spice bag in the preserving pan. Bring to the boil, and boil steadily for 10 minutes, stirring occasionally. Skim well.

4 Drain the shallots, rinse well, then drain again. Carefully add them to the boiling syrup. Return to the boil, then reduce the heat to minimum and simmer very gently for 15 minutes.

Remove from the heat and leave to cool, then cover and leave to stand overnight.

5 The next day, bring the mixture slowly to the boil, then reduce the heat and simmer very gently for 15 minutes. Cool and leave overnight as before.

6 The next day, bring the mixture slowly to the boil, then simmer very gently for 2–2½ hours, or until the shallots are translucent and golden brown.

7 Carefully lift the shallots out of the syrup with a slotted spoon, and pack them loosely into the hot sterilized jars. Return the syrup to the boil, and boil rapidly for about 5 minutes. Pour into the jars, then seal. The shallots are ready to eat immediately but improve with keeping.

This spicy, sour-sweet confiture is my adaptation of an ancient Middle Eastern recipe. The slow, careful cooking is important; otherwise, the shallots tend to lose their shape.

Pickled Venison

☆☆ **DEGREE OF DIFFICULTY** MODERATE **COOKING TIME** ABOUT 2½ HOURS **SPECIAL EQUIPMENT** FOOD PROCESSOR; SPICE MILL OR COFFEE GRINDER; STERILIZED, WIDE-NECKED 500G (1LB) JARS WITH VINEGAR-PROOF SEALANTS (SEE PAGES 12–13) **YIELD** ABOUT 1.5KG (3LB) **SHELF LIFE** 5 WEEKS, REFRIGERATED; 1 YEAR, HEAT PROCESSED **SERVING SUGGESTION** SERVE AS A MAIN COURSE WITH RICE

INGREDIENTS

250ml (8fl oz) groundnut or mustard oil

1kg (2lb) boneless shoulder or haunch of venison, cut into 5cm (2in) cubes

300ml (½ pint) red wine vinegar

100g (3½oz) tamarind block

1 tbsp salt

1 tbsp dark soft brown sugar or jaggery

2 tsp green cardamom pods, lightly toasted

1 tsp nigella seeds, lightly toasted

1 tsp cumin seeds, lightly toasted

FOR THE SPICE PASTE

500g (1lb) onions, coarsely chopped

5 garlic cloves, peeled

3–4 fresh chillies, deseeded

5cm (2in) piece fresh ginger root, coarsely chopped

2 tbsp coriander seeds, freshly ground

1 Purée all the ingredients for the spice paste in the food processor. Heat the oil in a pan, add the venison, and brown on all sides. Remove from the pan.

2 Add the spice paste to the pan. Fry over a high heat for a few minutes, then reduce the heat and simmer for 30 minutes or until pale brown. Return the meat to the pan and simmer for 1½ hours or until tender. If it becomes too dry, add 1–2 tablespoons of water.

3 Warm the vinegar and pour it over the tamarind. Leave to soak for 30 minutes. Strain and discard the seeds. Stir the salt and jaggery or sugar into the liquid, and add to the pan. Bring to the boil, then simmer gently for 15 minutes or until the oil rises to the top.

4 Grind the cardamom pods in the spice mill or coffee grinder. Sieve into the pan and add the nigella and cumin seeds. Remove from the heat. Pack into the hot sterilized jars, then seal. The venison is ready immediately but improves after 1 week. Keep refrigerated, or heat process for 35 minutes (see pages 14–15).

TIP
Skim off the fat from the top of the jar before reheating the meat.

Potted Venison

☆☆ **DEGREE OF DIFFICULTY** MODERATE **COOKING TIME** 2½–3 HOURS **SPECIAL EQUIPMENT** FOOD PROCESSOR;

1 LITRE (1¾ PINT) STERILIZED DISH OR 6 x 175ML (6FL OZ) RAMEKINS (SEE PAGES 12–13) **YIELD** ABOUT 1KG (2LB)

SHELF LIFE 1 MONTH, REFRIGERATED **SERVING SUGGESTION** TRADITIONALLY SERVED IN

A RAMEKIN, WITH WATERCRESS, AND ACCOMPANIED BY TOAST

INGREDIENTS

250g (8oz) bacon rashers, rinds removed and tied together with string

750g (1½lb) boned shoulder or leg of venison, trimmed well and cut into 2.5cm (1in) cubes

100g (3½oz) butter

2 garlic cloves, finely chopped

250ml (8fl oz) port or good red wine

1 tsp juniper berries, crushed

1 tsp freshly ground black pepper

2 blades mace

a few bay leaves and cranberries, to garnish (optional)

FOR THE HERB BUNDLE (SEE PAGE 31)

2 sprigs thyme

1 bay leaf

2–3 sage leaves

a strip of lemon rind

FOR THE CLARIFIED BUTTER, TO SEAL

100–250g (3½–8oz) butter

1 Coarsely chop the bacon and put in a deep casserole with the herb bundle and all the remaining ingredients, except the clarified butter and garnish. Cover and bake in an oven preheated to 160°C/325°F/ gas 3 for 2½–3 hours, until the meat is very tender.

2 Remove the mace, herb bundle, and bacon rinds from the dish. Put the meat in the food processor, and process to a smooth paste. Pack into the dish or individual ramekins. Leave to cool completely. Cover and refrigerate for 2–3 hours.

3 Meanwhile, make the clarified butter. Melt the butter in a small saucepan over a very low heat, then let it foam for a few seconds. Skim the froth from the surface and leave the butter to cool slightly. Pour the cooled butter through a muslin-lined sieve, leaving the milky sediment in the bottom of the pan. If you rinse the muslin in cold water before use and wring it out well, this helps catch any remaining froth.

4 Pour the melted clarified butter over the meat until it forms a layer about 1cm (½in) thick, using the larger quantity if covering the individual ramekins. Refrigerate until the butter has set. Garnish with bay leaves and cranberries, if desired. The venison is ready immediately.

Venison makes the most delicious potted meat. The addition of bacon provides moisture. For best results, select dry-cured bacon.

Quail and Pheasant Terrine

☆☆☆ **DEGREE OF DIFFICULTY** ADVANCED · **COOKING TIME** ABOUT 2 HOURS · **SPECIAL EQUIPMENT** FOOD PROCESSOR; 2 x 1 LITRE (1¾ PINT) TERRINES · **YIELD** ABOUT 2KG (4LB) · **SHELF LIFE** 3–4 WEEKS, SEALED WITH LARD, REFRIGERATED · **SERVING SUGGESTION** SERVE WITH ROCKET SALAD AND A PEACH CHUTNEY (SEE PAGE 79)

INGREDIENTS

4 quails, boned, with the skin left on

2 tbsp honey

¼ tsp salt

4 tsp brandy

FOR THE FORCEMEAT

1 large, old cock pheasant, boned, all skin and sinew removed, chopped

300g (10oz) pork tenderloin, cubed

100ml (3½fl oz) brandy

200g (7oz) shallots, chopped

2 garlic cloves, chopped

a little oil or butter

500g (1lb) skinless mild bacon or salt belly of pork, cut into small pieces

250ml (8fl oz) dry white wine

2 eggs (size 2)

1½ tsp freshly ground black pepper

1½ tsp salt

2 tbsp finely chopped thyme

15 juniper berries, coarsely ground

finely grated rind ½ lemon

FOR THE GREEN FORCEMEAT

100g (5oz) baby spinach

2 tbsp finely chopped parsley

FOR THE TERRINES

2 pieces of caul fat or 300g (10oz) streaky bacon rashers, rinds removed

1 Lay the quails skin side down on a board, and spread with the honey, salt, and brandy. Tightly roll up the birds and put in a bowl. Cover and refrigerate for 12 hours.

2 For the forcemeat, combine the pheasant and pork. Add the brandy and mix well. Cover and refrigerate for 12 hours.

3 Soften the shallots and garlic in a little oil or butter for a few minutes. Leave to cool. Combine with the pheasant, pork, and bacon in the food processor. Process for 1–2 minutes, adding some of the wine and any liquid left in the bowl, until smooth. Add the eggs, seasoning, thyme, juniper, and lemon rind. Mix well. Weigh 100g (3½oz) of the mixture and reserve. Cover the rest and refrigerate for 2 hours.

4 For the green forcemeat, blanch the spinach for 2 minutes (see page 21) and squeeze dry. Put in the food processor and purée. Mix with the reserved forcemeat and parsley. Refrigerate for 2 hours.

5 Unroll the quails, skin side down, on a board. Divide the green forcemeat between them, placing it in the centre of each

bird. Fold over the skin flaps to encase it, and reshape the quails.

6 Line the terrines with the caul fat or bacon, leaving an overhang of at least 2.5cm (1in) so it can be folded over to cover the pâté. (If using bacon, stretch the rashers with the back of a knife blade first, and overlap them in the terrine.) Spoon a quarter of the forcemeat into each terrine and smooth it with a palette knife. Arrange the quails on top, pressing them lightly into the mixture. Spoon in the remaining forcemeat, making sure there are no air pockets, then smooth the surface level.

7 Fold over the ends of the caul fat or bacon, and cover each dish with the lid or a double layer of foil. Put the terrines in a roasting tin filled with enough warm water to come halfway up the sides of the dishes. Bake in an oven preheated to 160°C/ 325°F/gas 3, for 2 hours or until each pâté has shrunk from its dish and is surrounded by liquid.

8 Remove the dishes from the roasting tin and leave to cool. Weight down each pâté (see page 166), then refrigerate overnight. The pâtés are ready immediately.

Pickled Fish

☆ **DEGREE OF DIFFICULTY** EASY **COOKING TIME** ABOUT 30 MINUTES **SPECIAL EQUIPMENT** 2 LITRE (3½ PINT) STERILIZED GLASS OR EARTHENWARE JAR WITH VINEGAR-PROOF SEALANT (SEE PAGES 12–13)

 YIELD ABOUT 1.5KG (3LB) **SHELF LIFE** 3–4 MONTHS, REFRIGERATED

SERVING SUGGESTION SERVE WITH A MIXED LEAF SALAD AS A LIGHT FIRST COURSE

INGREDIENTS

1kg (2lb) firm, very fresh fish fillets, cut into 5cm (2in) chunks

5 tsp salt

6–7 tbsp groundnut or refined sesame oil

500g (1lb) onions, sliced into thin rings

1 litre (1¾ pints) red or white wine vinegar

2 tbsp soft brown sugar

1 tbsp mild curry powder

1 tsp ground turmeric

2.5cm (1in) piece fresh ginger root, shredded

2–3 dried red chillies

1–2 bay leaves

1 Put the fish in a bowl. Sprinkle with 3 teaspoons of the salt, mixing well. Leave for 2 hours. Drain and dry on paper towels.

2 Heat 4 tablespoons of the oil in a large, heavy frying pan. Add the fish, a few pieces at a time, and fry over a high heat for 3 minutes on each side or until evenly browned and just cooked through. Drain on paper towels.

3 Put the sliced onions, vinegar, sugar, curry powder, turmeric, ginger, and remaining salt in a non-corrosive pan. Bring to the boil, skim well, and boil for 5–6 minutes, until the onion is cooked but still slightly crunchy. Remove the onion with a slotted spoon and drain well.

4 Arrange the fish and onion in alternate layers in the hot sterilized jar, adding the chillies and bay leaves and finishing with a layer of onion. Bring the vinegar back to the boil and pour into the jar. Add the remaining oil to cover, then seal. The fish will be ready to eat in 2 days.

Spring &
Early Summer

Seasonal Ingredients

Spring is all about rebirth and new growth. The weather starts to improve and get warmer, and slowly but surely we begin to eat lighter, fresher meals – a trend that continues through the summer. The world around us seems more colourful, and that is reflected on our plates, with vibrant reds and greens abounding. Here is a selection of some of my favourite ingredients for preserving in spring and early summer.

GARLIC
Although most commonly used as seasoning, garlic is far more versatile than that. Its cloves can be pickled, used in chutneys, or chargrilled, for example.

ASPARAGUS
This delicious "superfood" is perfect for preserving in oil, allowing you to extend the rather short asparagus season by a few months.

CHICKEN
Preserving chicken helps improve its flavour and adds a different dimension to this Sunday-roast staple. Use the best-quality meat possible.

WILD STRAWBERRIES
Think summer fruit, and strawberries spring to mind. This is the best time of year to pick some and turn them into jams, vinegars, and so on.

PRAWNS AND SHRIMPS
These are fairly interchangeable. However, for a "meaty" option, prawns are the sensible choice, while the smaller shrimps are perfect for potting.

BLACK CHERRIES
With a sharper taste than its red cousin, the black cherry is the ideal fruit to use for preserving – in a confiture, for example.

HERRING
Rollmops is a classic herring recipe, but one of my own inventions – herrings in spiced oil – is fast finding favour among my friends who love a hit of chilli.

LAMB
This meat is closely associated with Easter in many parts of the world. One of the best ways to use it all year round is to turn it into delicious sausages.

Potted Shrimps

☆ **DEGREE OF DIFFICULTY** EASY **COOKING TIME** ABOUT 17 MINUTES **SPECIAL EQUIPMENT** 6 x 175ML

(6FL OZ) RAMEKINS **YIELD** ABOUT 1KG (2LB) **SHELF LIFE** 1 MONTH, REFRIGERATED

SERVING SUGGESTIONS SERVE AS A FIRST COURSE WITH A ROCKET SALAD AND

BROWN BREAD AND BUTTER, OR USE TO FILL SANDWICHES

INGREDIENTS

1kg (2lb) raw shrimps

*300g (10oz) clarified butter
(see page 47, step 3)*

1 tsp salt

*½ tsp freshly ground white
or black pepper*

½ tsp ground mace

*large pinch cayenne pepper
or chilli powder*

1 Cook the shrimps in boiling water for no more than 2 minutes. Drain, refresh under cold water, drain again, then peel.

2 Place the shrimps in a bowl and mix with 200g (7oz) of the melted clarified butter and all the remaining ingredients. Divide between the ramekins and bake in an oven preheated to 190°C/375°F/gas 5 for 15 minutes.

3 Leave to cool, then refrigerate for 2–3 hours. Seal the tops with the remaining melted clarified butter (see page 47, step 4). Cover and refrigerate. The shrimps will be ready to eat in 24 hours.

It is essential to use freshly boiled shrimps, preferably small brown ones, for their fresh, sweet flavour. The shells are usually removed, but I like their crunchiness and therefore remove only the heads.

Smoked Prawns

☆☆ **DEGREE OF DIFFICULTY** MODERATE   **COOKING TIME** ABOUT 20 MINUTES, SIMMERING; 2 HOURS, SMOKING   **SPECIAL EQUIPMENT** SMOKER   **YIELD** ABOUT 1KG (2LB)   **SHELF LIFE** 1 MONTH, REFRIGERATED; 3 MONTHS, FROZEN   **SERVING SUGGESTIONS** SERVE AS A SNACK WITH DRINKS OR AS A FIRST COURSE; ADD TO FISH STEWS, RISOTTOS, AND PASTA DISHES JUST BEFORE SERVING

INGREDIENTS

1.5kg (3lb) raw prawns

2 litres (3½ pints) water

1 tbsp salt

1 bunch of fresh dill or fennel flowers and stems, or 2 tbsp dried dill

2–3 tbsp olive or groundnut oil

FOR THE BRINE

1.5 litres (2½ pints) water

350g (11½oz) salt

1 Remove the heads from the prawns and discard. Wash the prawns well and leave to drain for 30–45 minutes.

2 Make the brine by mixing together the water and salt until the salt has dissolved. Pour over the prawns and weight down (see page 166) so that they are completely submerged. Leave for 30 minutes and then drain well. (This produces mildly salted prawns; for a saltier flavour, leave for up to 1 hour.)

3 Put the first measure of water and salt in a large pan and bring to the boil. Add the dill or fennel and simmer for 15 minutes, then add the prawns. Simmer for 2–5 minutes or until the prawns are just cooked.

4 Lift out the prawns and cool on a wire rack for 1–2 hours or until just dry to the touch.

5 Brush the prawns with the oil and cold-smoke below 25°C (77°F) for 2 hours.

6 Wrap the prawns in waxed or greaseproof paper and refrigerate.

Smoking gives a new dimension to prawns, adding to their flavour and shelf life. I find oak smoke too strong for delicate shellfish and prefer to use lighter, more fragrant woods such as apple or citrus.

ASPARAGUS

It is better to use in-season local asparagus rather than imported varieties. Cook it on a griddle before freezing it – this will retain its delicate flavour and texture. Freshly picked green asparagus is ideal for preserving in oil; simply adapt the peppers recipe on page 119.

Black Cherry Confiture

☆ **DEGREE OF DIFFICULTY** EASY **COOKING TIME** ABOUT 30 MINUTES

SPECIAL EQUIPMENT PRESERVING PAN; SUGAR THERMOMETER; STERILIZED JARS AND SEALANTS (SEE PAGES 12–13) **YIELD** ABOUT 1.5KG (3LB) **SHELF LIFE** 2 YEARS

SERVING SUGGESTIONS SUPERB FOR BREAKFAST OR AS A FILLING FOR CAKES

INGREDIENTS

1.25kg (2½lb) black cherries, pitted

750g (1½lb) preserving or granulated sugar

250ml (8fl oz) blackcurrant or redcurrant juice (see Hot Crab Apple Jelly for method, page 198)

4 tbsp kirsch or cherry brandy

1 Layer the cherries and sugar in the preserving pan. Add the blackcurrant or redcurrant juice, cover, and leave for a few hours.

2 Bring the mixture slowly to the boil, occasionally shaking the pan gently. Skim well, then boil for 20–25 minutes or until the setting point is reached (see page 16).

3 Remove the pan from the heat and leave the fruit to settle for a few minutes. Stir in the kirsch or brandy. Ladle into the hot sterilized jars, then seal.

TIPS
- The juice of 3 lemons can be used instead of the currant juice.
- Any type of sour black cherry can be used, but morello is the best.

This is one of the greatest European preserves — sour-sweet cherries embedded in an intensely flavoured red jelly.

Wild Strawberry Confiture

☆☆ **DEGREE OF DIFFICULTY** MODERATE **COOKING TIME** 25–30 MINUTES

SPECIAL EQUIPMENT PRESERVING PAN; SUGAR THERMOMETER; STERILIZED JARS AND SEALANTS (SEE PAGES 12–13) **YIELD** ABOUT 1.25KG (2½ LB) **SHELF LIFE** 6 MONTHS

SERVING SUGGESTIONS SERVE WITH SCONES AND CREAM, OR USE TO FILL TARTLETS

INGREDIENTS

750g (1½lb) preserving or granulated sugar

1kg (2lb) wild strawberries

250ml (8fl oz) vodka (40% proof)

1 Layer the sugar and wild strawberries in a large glass bowl, starting and finishing with a layer of sugar. Pour over the vodka, cover with a clean cloth, and leave to stand overnight.

2 The next day, drain the liquid into the preserving pan. Bring to the boil, and boil rapidly for a few minutes or until it reaches 116°C (240°F) on the sugar thermometer.

3 Add the wild strawberries. Return to the boil, and boil for 5–7 minutes or until the setting point is reached (see page 16). This recipe produces a soft set.

4 Remove from the heat and leave the fruit to settle for a few minutes. Skim well. Ladle into the hot sterilized jars, then seal.

Wild strawberries are highly aromatic and full of flavour. Marinating the fruit, followed by careful cooking, helps maintain the texture and fragrance of this confection. Use it to fill tarts, or serve with scones and clotted cream.

Strawberry Vinegar

☆ **DEGREE OF DIFFICULTY** EASY ⬛ **COOKING TIME** 3–4 MINUTES 🍴 **SPECIAL EQUIPMENT** THERMOMETER; FOOD PROCESSOR; STERILIZED JELLY BAG; STERILIZED BOTTLES WITH VINEGAR-PROOF SEALANTS (SEE PAGES 12–13) 🫙 **YIELD** ABOUT 2 LITRES (3½ PINTS) **SHELF LIFE** 2 YEARS ⊘ **SERVING SUGGESTIONS** USE TO DRESS SALADS, FINISH MEAT SAUCES, OR SPRINKLE OVER FRESH STRAWBERRIES

INGREDIENTS

*1.25 litres (2 pints) cider vinegar
or white wine vinegar*

*1kg (2lb) ripe, full-flavoured
strawberries*

*a few wild or small cultivated
strawberries and a few basil leaves
(optional)*

1 Bring the vinegar to the boil in a non-corrosive pan, and boil rapidly for 1–2 minutes. Remove from the heat and leave to cool to 40°C (104°F).

2 Hull the strawberries, then finely chop in the food processor. Transfer to a large glass jar or bowl.

3 Pour the warm vinegar over the chopped berries and mix well. Cover with a clean cloth and leave to stand in a warm place (a sunny windowsill is ideal) for 2 weeks, stirring occasionally.

4 Strain the vinegar through the jelly bag, then filter (see page 21). Pour into the sterilized bottles, then seal.

5 To intensify the flavour of the vinegar, thread a few wild or small cultivated strawberries and some basil leaves alternately on to thin wooden skewers. Insert a skewer into each bottle, and seal. The vinegar is ready to use immediately, but the flavour improves with keeping.

VARIATION

BLACKBERRY OR
BLACKCURRANT VINEGAR
Substitute blackberries or blackcurrants for the strawberries, and increase the vinegar to 1.5 litres (2½ pints). Omit the wild strawberries and basil. Follow the method as for the main recipe. Blackberry or blackcurrant vinegar makes a superb salad dressing or can be diluted and served as a refreshing drink.

TIP
Although the flavour of fruit vinegars improves with keeping, their colour will eventually fade and turn brown.

Crystallized Flowers

☆ **DEGREE OF DIFFICULTY** EASY   **SPECIAL EQUIPMENT** ARTIST'S SMALL PAINT BRUSH; AIRTIGHT CONTAINER

SHELF LIFE 3 MONTHS   **SERVING SUGGESTION** USE TO DECORATE CAKES AND DESSERTS

INGREDIENTS

egg white, to coat

pinch of salt

a few drops of rose- or

orange-flower water

perfect flowers

caster sugar

1 Beat the egg white with the salt and rose- or orange-flower water until frothy. Leave to stand for a few minutes.

2 With a small, soft brush, paint the flower petals evenly inside and out with the egg white. Generously sprinkle them with sugar, making sure that all the surfaces are evenly covered.

3 Fill a baking tray with a layer of sugar about 1cm (½in) deep. Gently lay the sugared flowers on top, and generously sprinkle with sugar. Leave to dry in a warm, well-ventilated place for 1–2 days or until the flowers are hard and dry to the touch. Store in an airtight container, between layers of waxed paper.

VARIATION

EGG-FREE VERSION
Instead of coating the flowers with egg white, you can use a cool gum arabic solution made by dissolving 2 teaspoons gum arabic and 1 tablespoon of sugar in 250ml (8fl oz) water in a bowl placed over a pan of hot water.

TIP
The most suitable flowers for crystallizing are strongly perfumed roses, violets, pansies, orange blossom, and the blossom of orchard fruit such as apples and pears.

Edible leaves can be crystallized using the same method. Vary the quantity of egg white and sugar to match the number of flowers being covered.

Pickled Garlic

☆ **DEGREE OF DIFFICULTY** EASY　🍲 **COOKING TIME** 4–5 MINUTES　🍴 **SPECIAL EQUIPMENT** STERILIZED JARS WITH VINEGAR-PROOF SEALANTS (SEE PAGES 12–13)　🫙 **YIELD** ABOUT 1KG (2LB)　🫙 **SHELF LIFE** 2 YEARS

🔪 **SERVING SUGGESTIONS** SERVE AS A PICKLE, OR USE INSTEAD OF FRESH GARLIC

INGREDIENTS

500ml (17fl oz) distilled malt vinegar or white wine vinegar

2 tbsp salt

1kg (2lb) fresh garlic

1 Put the vinegar and salt in a non-corrosive pan. Bring to the boil, and boil for 2–3 minutes, then remove from the heat and leave to cool.

2 Separate the garlic cloves and blanch to remove the skin (see page 21). If using fresh, "green" garlic, remove the outer skin and slice the bulbs crossways in half.

3 Blanch the garlic in boiling water for 1 minute, then drain and put in the sterilized jars. Pour in the vinegar, weight down the garlic (see page 166), then seal. The garlic will be ready in 1 month.

TIP
Although this recipe is great with white garlic, it is even better when made with fresh, "green" garlic.

Pickled garlic originates in Persia, where it is either served on its own or used in cooking instead of fresh garlic. Pickling mellows and changes the flavour of garlic, giving it a delicate, elusive perfume.

*The garlic cloves
are kept intact
by blanching to
remove the skin*

Herrings in Spiced Oil

☆ **DEGREE OF DIFFICULTY** EASY ⬛ **COOKING TIME** ABOUT 25 MINUTES ⬛ **SPECIAL EQUIPMENT** THERMOMETER; WIDE-NECKED, STERILIZED JAR WITH SEALANT (SEE PAGES 12–13)  **YIELD** ABOUT 500G (1LB) **SHELF LIFE** 6 MONTHS

⬛ **SERVING SUGGESTIONS** SERVE WITH CHILLED VODKA; USE TO MAKE OPEN SANDWICHES OR AS AN APPETIZER

INGREDIENTS

1kg (2lb) salted herrings, or about 500g (1lb) prepared herring fillets

500ml (17fl oz) light olive, groundnut, or refined sesame oil

5cm (2in) cinnamon stick, crushed

1 lemongrass stalk, chopped

3–4 dried red chillies, split open

4–5 cloves

4–5 cardamom pods

1 Soak the salted herrings in several changes of cold water for 24 hours, then drain well. Cut in half lengthways and remove all the bones. Rinse, dry well on paper towels, and cut into bite-sized pieces. If using prepared herring fillets, omit the soaking.

2 Put all the remaining ingredients in a pan and bring slowly to the boil. Keep at just below boiling point for about 20 minutes, then remove from the heat and leave until the mixture has cooled to 50°C (122°F).

3 Arrange the herring pieces in the warm sterilized jar. Pour the warm oil into the jar, making sure the fish are covered. Shake it gently to ensure there are no air pockets and that the spices are evenly distributed, then seal. The fish will be ready in 3–4 weeks.

TIP
Use firm-fleshed herrings such as *maatjes* or home-salted herrings (see Salt-Cured Sprats, page 212). Salted mackerel can be prepared in the same way.

This robust, spicy preserve is my own invention and is fast becoming a favourite among chilli-loving friends.

Rollmops

 DEGREE OF DIFFICULTY EASY **COOKING TIME** ABOUT 12 MINUTES **SPECIAL EQUIPMENT** 2 LITRE (3½ PINT) STERILIZED WIDE-NECKED JAR WITH VINEGAR-PROOF SEALANT (SEE PAGES 12–13) **YIELD** ABOUT 1.5KG (3LB) **SHELF LIFE** 6 MONTHS, REFRIGERATED **SERVING SUGGESTIONS** SERVE AS AN APPETIZER WITH CHILLED SCHNAPPS OR VODKA, AS PART OF A BUFFET, OR WITH A WARM POTATO SALAD AS A LIGHT MAIN COURSE

INGREDIENTS

8 whole salted herrings
or 8 filleted butterflied herrings
6 tbsp strong mustard
4 large dill-pickled gherkins, sliced into thick batons as long as the width of the herrings
1 large onion, thinly sliced into rings, blanched for a few seconds (see page 21)
2 tbsp capers

FOR THE MARINADE

500ml (17fl oz) white wine vinegar or cider vinegar
500ml (17fl oz) water or dry white wine
2 tsp juniper berries, crushed
1 tsp allspice berries, crushed
2–3 cloves, crushed

1 To prepare the whole herrings, pour over water to cover, and refrigerate for at least 12 hours, changing the water once or twice.

2 Put all the ingredients for the marinade in a non-corrosive pan. Bring to the boil, then simmer for 10 minutes. Leave to cool completely.

3 Drain and dry the herrings, then fillet. First cut off the head and tail. Lay the fish, skin side up, on a work surface and spread the belly flaps out to the side. Press down firmly along the length of the backbone with a thumb, to loosen it. Turn the fish over and pull the bone out in one piece. (If using prepared fillets, rinse and dry them.)

4 Lay the fillets skin side down on a board, and spread with the mustard. Place a piece of gherkin at the wide end of each, and scatter with a few onion rings and capers. Roll up like a Swiss roll, securing with 2 wooden skewers.

5 Layer the fish rolls with the remaining onion in the sterilized jar, finishing with a layer of onion. Pour in the marinade, making sure the onion is totally covered (topping up with cold vinegar if necessary), then seal and refrigerate. The fish will be ready in 1 week.

The best kind of fish to use for this pickle are maatjes *or* schmaltz *herrings, though other salted herrings will do. Butterflied herrings are boned with the fillets still joined together.*

Herrings in Mustard Sauce

☆☆ **DEGREE OF DIFFICULTY** MODERATE　**COOKING TIME** 35–40 MINUTES　**SPECIAL EQUIPMENT** DOUBLE BOILER; 2 x 500ML (17FL OZ) STERILIZED JARS WITH VINEGAR-PROOF SEALANTS (SEE PAGES 12–13)　**YIELD** ABOUT 1KG (2LB)　**SHELF LIFE** 1–2 WEEKS, REFRIGERATED　**SERVING SUGGESTION** SERVE WITH BUTTERED RYE BREAD, ACCOMPANIED BY CHILLED VODKA OR AQUAVIT

INGREDIENTS

6 whole salted herrings or
12 prepared fillets
250ml (8fl oz) white wine vinegar
or distilled malt vinegar
¼ tsp cloves
2 bay leaves
1 tsp black peppercorns
3 onions, thinly sliced
4 eggs (size 2)
1½ tbsp sugar
2 tbsp mustard powder
large pinch ground turmeric

1 To prepare the whole herrings, pour over water to cover and refrigerate for at least 12 hours, changing the water once or twice.

2 Put the vinegar, cloves, bay leaves, and peppercorns in a non-corrosive pan. Bring to the boil, reduce the heat, and simmer for a few minutes. Leave to cool.

3 Blanch the onion for 2 minutes (see page 21). Drain and dry the whole herrings, then fillet (see Rollmops, page 65). Rinse and dry the prepared fillets, if using. Cut into bite-sized pieces.

4 Beat the eggs with the sugar, mustard, and turmeric, and add to the vinegar mixture. Transfer to the double boiler or a bowl placed over a pan of hot water. Cook gently, stirring, until the mixture is thick enough to coat the back of a spoon. Pour over the onions and leave to cool.

5 Add the herring and mix well. Pack into the sterilized jars, then seal and refrigerate. The fish will be ready to eat in 3 days.

TIPS
• Do not allow the egg mixture to boil or it will curdle.
• Before sealing the jar, tap it on a work surface to ensure there are no air pockets.

Although the origins of this recipe are unknown, it probably comes from somewhere in northern or central Europe. Select large, salted herrings, which should be soaked overnight to remove the excess salt.

Herrings in Cream Sauce

☆ **DEGREE OF DIFFICULTY** EASY **SPECIAL EQUIPMENT** 2 x 500ML (17FL OZ) STERILIZED JARS WITH VINEGAR-PROOF SEALANTS (SEE PAGES 12–13) **YIELD** ABOUT 1KG (2LB) **SHELF LIFE** 1 WEEK, REFRIGERATED

🍴 **SERVING SUGGESTION** SERVE WITH RYE BREAD AS A FIRST COURSE

INGREDIENTS

6 whole salted herrings

or 12 prepared fillets

2 large onions, sliced into thin rings

6–8 allspice berries, crushed

2–3 dried bay leaves, crumbled

350ml (12fl oz) double cream

250ml (8fl oz) white wine vinegar

1 tbsp sugar

1 To prepare the whole herrings, pour over water to cover and refrigerate for at least 12 hours, changing the water once or twice.

2 Drain and dry the whole salted herrings, then fillet (see Rollmops, page 65). Rinse and dry the prepared fillets, if using. Cut the fish into bite-sized pieces.

3 Blanch the sliced onions for 2 minutes (see page 21). Mix the onion with the crushed allspice berries and bay leaves. Layer with the herring in the sterilized jar, finishing with a layer of onion.

4 Stir together the cream, wine vinegar, and sugar. Pour into the jars, making sure there are no air pockets, then seal and refrigerate. The fish will be ready to eat in 2–3 days.

This recipe was given to me by Penny Stonfield, one of the best traditional Jewish cooks I know. She makes large quantities of this delicious salad for special occasions.

TIP
If the whole herrings are still too salty after being soaked for 12 hours, rinse, cover with fresh water, and soak for a further 12 hours.

Smoked Chicken

DEGREE OF DIFFICULTY ADVANCED **COOKING TIME** ABOUT 15 MINUTES, SIMMERING; 3–3½ HOURS, SMOKING **SPECIAL EQUIPMENT** STRING; SMOKER; MEAT HOOK **YIELD** ABOUT 1.5KG (3LB) **SHELF LIFE** 1 MONTH, REFRIGERATED; 3 MONTHS, FROZEN **SERVING SUGGESTIONS** SERVE THINLY SLICED WITH A MIXED LEAF SALAD, WITH FRESH MANGO AS A CANAPÉ, OR SKEWERED WITH STRIPED SPICED PEARS (SEE PAGE 202)

INGREDIENTS

1.5–2kg (3–4lb) chicken

1 tbsp olive or groundnut oil

4–5 sprigs thyme

4–5 sprigs tarragon

1 bay leaf

FOR THE BRINE

2 litres (3½ pints) water

600g (1¼lb) salt

5–6 sprigs tarragon

4–5 strips lemon rind

IMPORTANT NOTE

Before starting this recipe, please read the information on pages 12 and 184.

1 To make the brine, put all the ingredients in a non-corrosive pan. Bring to the boil, stirring until the salt has dissolved, then reduce the heat and simmer for about 10 minutes. Strain and leave to cool completely.

2 Wash and dry the chicken, then trim off any loose skin or cavity fat. Tie the bird's legs together with string, then prick all over with a sharp wooden skewer.

3 Put the chicken in a deep glass dish and cover with the brine. Weight down (see page 166), then refrigerate for 6–8 hours.

4 Drain the chicken well. Insert a wooden skewer through the trussed wings, and tie a loop of string to it. Hang up to dry in a cool, dry, dark, airy place (6–8°C/42–46°F) for 24 hours.

5 Brush the chicken with the oil and hang, legs down, in the smoker or place on a smoker tray. Hot-smoke for 3–3½ hours at 110–125°C (225–240°F). Halfway through smoking, add the herbs to the smoking tray.

6 To check if cooked, insert a skewer into the thickest part of the thigh; the juices should run clear without any pinkness. The chicken can be served hot but is best left until cold, then wrapped in waxed paper and refrigerated until needed.

Other poultry and game birds can be prepared the same way, but vary the curing time according to the size of the bird: add or subtract 1 hour from the curing time for every 500g (1lb) over or under the given weight.

Dried Lamb Sausages

☆☆ **DEGREE OF DIFFICULTY** MODERATE **SPECIAL EQUIPMENT** MINCER; SAUSAGE MAKER OR
SAUSAGE FILLER; MEAT HOOKS **YIELD** ABOUT 1KG (2LB) **SHELF LIFE** 6 MONTHS, REFRIGERATED
SERVING SUGGESTIONS EITHER BARBECUE THE SAUSAGES OR ADD TO STEWS, COUSCOUS, OR TAGINES
WARNING THIS RECIPE CONTAINS SALTPETRE; SEE PAGE 12

INGREDIENTS

*1.5kg (3lb) boned shoulder or leg
of lamb, cut into large cubes*

*300g (10oz) lamb or beef fat,
cut into large cubes*

6 garlic cloves, crushed

4 tbsp olive oil

1 ½ tbsp salt

1 tbsp fennel seeds

2 tbsp sweet paprika

1 tsp dried mint

1–2 tsp chilli powder

½ tsp freshly ground black pepper

½ tsp saltpetre

*3.5 metres (3 ¾ yards) beef
runners (casing)*

IMPORTANT NOTE

Before starting this recipe, please read the information on pages 12 and 184.

1 Put the lamb and fat through the coarse disc of the mincer. Add all the remaining ingredients except the runners, and mix well. Pack into a glass bowl, making sure there are no air pockets. Cover and refrigerate for 12 hours.

2 Prepare the beef runners (see page 190, steps 3 and 4). Stuff with the meat, and divide into 15cm (6in) links (see page 191, step 5). Hang in a cool, dry, dark, airy place (6–8°C/42–46°F) for 4–5 weeks or until they have lost about 50 per cent of their original weight. Wrap in greaseproof paper and refrigerate.

TIP
The sausages may be consumed after 4 weeks, when they are still very aromatic, or hung until they are hard and dry for use in cooking.

Different versions of this recipe are made all over the Muslim world, where pork is not eaten.

High Summer

Seasonal Ingredients

At no other time of the year is there such a huge variety of produce from which to choose than at the peak of the summer. Furthermore, the array of colours is mind-blowing! Whatever you choose to do with the seasonal fruit and vegetable offerings, the end result will look amazing and taste delicious. Here are some of my favourite ingredients for preserving in high summer.

RASPBERRIES
Although they are a classic jelly ingredient, raspberries are also wonderful in jams, fruit cheeses, and curds, to name but a few preserving options.

CHERRIES
Delicious on their own, straight from the tree, cherries are also incredibly versatile. They do, however, have a low pectin content.

BLUEBERRIES
Their medium pectin and acidity levels mean they need a boost in that department for jams, but blueberries also make a lovely syrup.

STRAWBERRIES
Summer just wouldn't be the same without strawberries, which can be used in a wide variety of preserves.

PEACHES
With the exception of preserving in oil, there is almost nothing you can't do with peaches, despite their low pectin and acidity levels.

MELON
Low in pectin and acidity, melon is nonetheless suitable for jams and jellies, as long as it is given a boost with apples or lemons, for example.

APRICOTS
This versatile stone fruit is creamy and perfumed. It is ideal for poaching in syrup, as well as good for jellies, fruit butters, and much more besides.

PLUMS
There are hundreds of types of plum, ranging in taste from tart to very sweet. Their pectin and acidity levels vary depending on variety and ripeness.

GOOSEBERRIES
This is another fruit that is high in pectin and acidity, therefore ideal for jams and jellies. They can be quite sharp, though.

RED- AND BLACKCURRANTS
High in pectin and acidity, these currants are perfect for use as the main ingredient in jams and jellies.

Seasonal Ingredients continued

CUCUMBER
Commonly used in chutneys and relishes, cucumbers add a welcome crunch. The small varieties are also good for pickling.

TOMATOES
Red or yellow, this is the classic sauce vegetable (though technically a fruit). It is great for use in chutneys, relishes, and even jams, too.

CELERY
Use this salad-plate staple for pickling and spicing, or for adding to chutneys, relishes, and sauces.

PEPPERS
Regardless of the colour, peppers are often used in pickles and chutneys. Red and yellow varieties are sweeter than the green.

HERBS
There are hundreds of different herbs that each bring their own flavour sensations to a range of preserves. Find the ones that work best for you.

RUNNER BEANS
These are often used in chutneys and relishes, adding both crunch and colour. They can also be pickled or preserved in oil.

GINGER
This warm, spicy, aromatic root is an invaluable ingredient for many sweet and savoury preserves.

AUBERGINES
Regularly used as a key ingredient in chutneys and relishes, aubergines may also be preserved in oil and even used in jams.

CAULIFLOWER
Pickled cauliflower is a firm favourite, but this vegetable can also add texture to chutneys and relishes.

Peaches in Brandy

 DEGREE OF DIFFICULTY MODERATE **COOKING TIME** ABOUT 15 MINUTES **SPECIAL EQUIPMENT** SUGAR THERMOMETER; STERILIZED, WIDE-NECKED JAR AND SEALANT (SEE PAGES 12–13) **YIELD** ABOUT 1KG (2LB) **SHELF LIFE** 2 YEARS **SERVING SUGGESTIONS** USE TO MAKE A SUPERB OPEN FLAN, OR SERVE WITH CREAM OR ICE CREAM, WITH PLENTY OF THE BRANDIED SYRUP

INGREDIENTS

1.5kg (3lb) firm peaches

1 litre (1¾ pints) water

1.5kg (3lb) preserving
or granulated sugar

300ml (½ pint) good-quality brandy

100g (3½oz) glacé cherries, halved
(optional)

FOR THE SPICE BAG (SEE PAGE 31)

1 vanilla pod

small piece of cinnamon stick

3–4 cardamom pods

4 cloves

1 Blanch the peaches (see page 21), then run a sharp knife around each peach. Twist the top half loose to access the stone, and take it out with a knife.

2 Put the water and 500g (1lb) sugar in a large pan. Bring to the boil, skim any froth off the top, then reduce the heat. Simmer for 5 minutes to make a syrup.

3 Slide the peach halves into the syrup. Return to the boil, then reduce the heat and simmer gently for 4–5 minutes. Lift out the peaches with a slotted spoon, and leave to cool. Make a spice bag with the vanilla pod, cinnamon stick, cardamom pods, and cloves.

5 Set a cherry half in the cavity of each peach, if desired, and secure with a wooden cocktail stick. Pack the peaches loosely into the hot sterilized jar.

4 Put 600ml (1 pint) of the syrup in a pan with the remaining sugar and spice bag. Bring to the boil, skim, then boil rapidly until it reaches 104°C (219°F) on a sugar thermometer. Cool slightly, remove the spice bag, then stir in the brandy.

6 Pour the syrup over the peaches, shaking the bottle gently to dispel any air pockets, then seal. The peaches will be ready to eat in 2 weeks but improve with longer keeping.

Vanilla-Flavoured Peach Marmalade

☆ **DEGREE OF DIFFICULTY** EASY **COOKING TIME** 50–55 MINUTES **SPECIAL EQUIPMENT** PRESERVING PAN; SUGAR THERMOMETER; STERILIZED JARS AND SEALANTS (SEE PAGES 12–13) **YIELD** ABOUT 1KG (2LB) **SHELF LIFE** 1 YEAR **SERVING SUGGESTIONS** HEAVENLY WITH SCONES AND CREAM OR WITH CROISSANTS FOR BREAKFAST

INGREDIENTS

1.25kg (2½lb) firm, just ripe white or yellow peaches

1kg (2lb) preserving or granulated sugar

juice of 2 lemons

4 tbsp good-quality cognac

1–2 vanilla pods, cut into 7cm (3in) lengths

1 Skin the peaches by blanching in boiling water (see page 21). Halve them, remove the stones, and cut the flesh into thick slices.

2 Place the peach slices in the preserving pan with the sugar and lemon juice. Cover and leave to stand for a few hours.

3 Bring the mixture to the boil, then reduce the heat and simmer gently for 20 minutes or until the peaches are just soft.

4 Return to the boil, and boil rapidly, stirring frequently, for 20–25 minutes or until the setting point is reached (see page 16). The peaches produce a soft set marmalade.

5 Remove the pan from the heat, skim well, and leave to cool for about 10 minutes. Stir in the cognac.

6 Ladle the preserve into the hot sterilized jars, inserting a piece of vanilla pod into each, then seal. The marmalade will be ready to eat in about 1 month but improves with longer keeping.

TIP
Skim the marmalade thoroughly at all stages of cooking, because peaches tend to produce a large amount of froth.

Peach Chutney

☆ **DEGREE OF DIFFICULTY** EASY **COOKING TIME** ABOUT 1¼ HOURS **SPECIAL EQUIPMENT** NON-CORROSIVE PRESERVING PAN; SPICE MILL OR COFFEE GRINDER; STERILIZED JARS WITH VINEGAR-PROOF SEALANTS (SEE PAGES 12–13)

 YIELD ABOUT 1.75KG (3½LB) **SHELF LIFE** 6 MONTHS

SERVING SUGGESTIONS SUPERB WITH HOT CURRIES OR GAME

INGREDIENTS

1kg (2lb) peaches, skinned, stoned, and sliced 2.5cm (1in) thick

300g (10oz) cooking apples, peeled, cored, and chopped

250g (8oz) seedless grapes

2 lemons, finely sliced into semi-circles

275g (9oz) shallots, coarsely chopped

3 garlic cloves, finely shredded

75g (2½oz) fresh ginger root, finely shredded

500ml (17fl oz) cider vinegar or white wine vinegar

250g (8oz) sugar

1 tsp cloves

1 tsp cardamom pods

5cm (2in) piece cinnamon stick

2 tsp caraway seeds

1 Put all the fruit and the shallots, garlic, ginger, and vinegar in the preserving pan. Bring to the boil, then reduce the heat and simmer for about 25 minutes, until the apples are just soft and the shallots translucent.

2 Add the sugar, stirring until it has dissolved. Simmer for 35–40 minutes, until most of the liquid has evaporated and the mixture is thick. Remove the pan from the heat.

3 Grind the cloves, cardamom pods, and cinnamon stick to a powder in the spice mill or coffee grinder.

4 Add the ground spices to the chutney through a sieve (this will remove any fibres from the cardamom pods), then add the caraway seeds and mix well.

5 Ladle the mixture into the hot sterilized jars, then seal. The chutney will be ready to eat in 1 month.

Peaches sometimes make a pale chutney; to correct this, add 2 tablespoons of sweet paprika for a pinkish hue, or 2 teaspoons of ground turmeric for a golden yellow tint. Add them with the other ground spices.

Oven-Dried Peaches

 DEGREE OF DIFFICULTY EASY **COOKING TIME** UP TO 36 HOURS

SPECIAL EQUIPMENT STERILIZED JARS AND SEALANTS (SEE PAGES 12–13) **SHELF LIFE** 2 YEARS, FULLY DRIED;

2 MONTHS, SEMI-DRIED **SERVING SUGGESTIONS** USE FOR DESSERTS AND BAKING, OR EAT AS A SNACK

INGREDIENTS

peaches – as many as desired

1 Blanch some peaches in boiling water for a few seconds (see page 21). Refresh in cold water, then peel off the skin.

2 Halve the peaches, remove the stones, and either leave as they are, or slice into quarters or even smaller pieces.

3 As the fruit are prepared, put them in a bowl of acidulated water, then lift out and drain well.

4 Arrange the peaches flat side down on a wire rack set over a foil-lined baking tray. Put in an oven preheated to 110°C/ 225°F/gas ¼, leaving the door slightly ajar.

5 Peach halves will take 24–36 hours to dry; quarters, about 12–16 hours; and smaller pieces, 8–12 hours. Turn the peaches over when they are halfway through drying.

6 To store the peaches, arrange them in layers, between pieces of waxed paper, in an airtight container. Store in a cool place and keep in the dark if the container is transparent.

TIP
Make sure the dried peaches are completely cold before storing them.

If you intend to dry a large amount of produce on a regular basis, invest in a dehydrator.

Red Plum Jelly

 DEGREE OF DIFFICULTY EASY **COOKING TIME** 40–50 MINUTES **SPECIAL EQUIPMENT** PRESERVING PAN; STERILIZED JELLY BAG; SUGAR THERMOMETER; STERILIZED JARS AND SEALANTS (SEE PAGES 12–13) **YIELD** ABOUT 1.25KG (2½LB) **SHELF LIFE** 2 YEARS **SERVING SUGGESTIONS** SERVE WITH ROAST LAMB, VENISON, OR COLD CHICKEN

INGREDIENTS

1kg (2lb) red plums

15 bitter almonds, coarsely pounded,
or 1 tsp bitter almond extract

preserving or granulated sugar

4 tbsp slivovitz (or other plum brandy)

a few blanched bitter almonds
for each jar (optional)

1 Put the whole plums in the preserving pan with the bitter almonds or almond extract, and add enough cold water to cover. Bring to the boil, then reduce the heat and simmer for 20–25 minutes or until pulpy.

2 Pour the fruit and liquid into the sterilized jelly bag (see page 17). Leave to drain for 2–3 hours, until it stops dripping. Measure the juice, and allow 500g (1lb) sugar for every 500ml (17fl oz) juice.

3 Put the juice and sugar in the cleaned pan. Bring to the boil, stirring until the sugar has dissolved. Boil for a few minutes, then reduce the heat and skim well. Boil rapidly for 10 minutes or until the setting point is reached (see page 16).

4 Leave to cool for 5 minutes. Skim well and stir in the slivovitz. Pour into the jars, then seal if not adding the almonds.

5 If adding almonds, allow the jelly to semi-set, then insert a few into each jar. Cover each jar with a waxed paper disc dipped in a little slivovitz, then seal.

This jelly has an interesting hint of bitter almonds. Use a dark red variety of plums, such as River's Czar, Monarch, or Early River.

Plum Jam

 DEGREE OF DIFFICULTY EASY **COOKING TIME** ABOUT I HOUR **SPECIAL EQUIPMENT** PRESERVING PAN; SUGAR THERMOMETER; STERILIZED JARS AND SEALANTS (SEE PAGES 12–13) **YIELD** ABOUT 1.75KG (3½LB)

SHELF LIFE 2 YEARS **SERVING SUGGESTIONS** SUBSTITUTE FOR RASPBERRY JAM IN LINZER TORTE, OR USE TO MAKE A QUICK AND EASY PLUM CRUMBLE

INGREDIENTS

1.25kg (2½lb) plums, stoned and halved, or quartered if large

350ml (12fl oz) water

1kg (2lb) preserving or granulated sugar

TIP
Red plum jam can be enlivened by the addition of 75g (2½oz) finely shredded fresh ginger root, which should be stirred in with the sugar.

1 Put the plums and water in the preserving pan. Bring to the boil, then reduce the heat and simmer for about 25 minutes, stirring occasionally, or until the plums are soft.

2 Add the sugar, stirring until it has dissolved. Return to the boil, and boil for 25–30 minutes or until the setting point is reached (see page 16).

3 Remove the pan from the heat and leave the jam to settle for a few minutes. Ladle the jam into the hot sterilized jars, then seal.

VARIATIONS

DAMSON JAM
Replace the plums with whole damsons. Simmer with 750ml (1¼ pints) water until mushy, then sieve out the stones. Measure the pulp and add 625g (1¼lb) sugar for every 500ml (17fl oz) pulp. Boil for 10–15 minutes or until the setting point is reached.

GREENGAGE JAM
Replace the plums with greengages. Crack open 10 stones and tie the kernels in muslin. Place the fruit and kernels in the pan with the juice of 1 lemon and 250ml (8fl oz) water. Complete as for the main recipe.

Choose mirabelle plums for a golden jam, Victoria or River's Czar for a red jam, or greengage for a greenish-yellow one.

Greengage jam is a traditional French country preserve.

Povidle

☆ **DEGREE OF DIFFICULTY** EASY **COOKING TIME** 1½–2 HOURS **SPECIAL EQUIPMENT** PRESERVING PAN; STERILIZED JARS AND SEALANTS (SEE PAGES 12–13) **YIELD** ABOUT 1.5KG (3LB) **SHELF LIFE** 2 YEARS

SERVING SUGGESTIONS USE TO FILL ZWETSCHKENKNÖDLEN (LITTLE SWEET DUMPLINGS), OR SPOON OVER DUMPLINGS AND SERVE WITH SOURED CREAM

INGREDIENTS

2kg (4lb) purple plums, preferably Switzen

1kg (2lb) preserving or granulated sugar

1 Remove the stones from the plums, then chop them coarsely. Layer the plums and sugar in the preserving pan, cover with a clean cloth, and leave to stand for a few hours, until the juices start to run.

2 Bring the mixture to the boil, stirring until the sugar has dissolved. Reduce the heat and simmer for 1½–2 hours, stirring occasionally, until the mixture is dark red and thick. (There is no need to test for the setting point.)

3 Ladle the jam into the hot sterilized jars, then seal. The jam is ready to eat immediately but improves with keeping.

Strictly speaking, Povidle is a soft fruit cheese rather than a jam. The amount of sugar seems small, but it results in a sharp sweet-and-sour preserve sometimes known as Eastern European plum jam.

Pickled Plums

☆ **DEGREE OF DIFFICULTY** EASY 🍲 **COOKING TIME** 3–4 MINUTES 🍴 **SPECIAL EQUIPMENT** STERILIZED JARS
WITH VINEGAR-PROOF SEALANTS (SEE PAGES 12–13) 🫙 **YIELD** ABOUT 1KG (2LB) 🫙 **SHELF LIFE** 2 YEARS
🔪 **SERVING SUGGESTIONS** SERVE WITH COLD MEATS OR CHEESE

INGREDIENTS

500ml (17fl oz) cider vinegar

*150ml (¼ pint) apple or
pear concentrate*

1 tbsp salt

1kg (2lb) plums, preferably Switzen

8 cloves

8 allspice berries

*6–8 strands of finely shredded
fresh ginger root*

2 bay leaves

1 Put the cider vinegar, fruit concentrate, and salt in a non-corrosive pan. Bring to the boil, and boil for 1–2 minutes.

2 Prick the plums all over with a wooden cocktail stick and arrange in the hot sterilized jars with the spices and bay leaves. Add the boiling vinegar to cover, then seal. The plums will be ready to eat in 1 month.

*This Central European recipe
makes an unusual accompaniment
to bread and cheese.*

PLUMS

Delightfully versatile, plums are especially good for freezing, so they can even be enjoyed out of season. If you are using them for jams or chutneys, freeze them whole; otherwise, halve them first. Plums also work well in syrups and with any combination of spices.

Plum Chutney

☆ **DEGREE OF DIFFICULTY** EASY **COOKING TIME** ABOUT 1¼ HOURS **SPECIAL EQUIPMENT** HAMMER OR NUTCRACKER; MUSLIN; NON-CORROSIVE PRESERVING PAN; SPICE MILL OR COFFEE GRINDER; STERILIZED JARS WITH VINEGAR-PROOF SEALANTS (SEE PAGES 12–13) **YIELD** ABOUT 1KG (2LB) **SHELF LIFE** 2 YEARS **SERVING SUGGESTIONS** SERVE WITH COLD MEAT AND CHEESE, OR SIMPLY SPREAD ON BREAD

INGREDIENTS

500g (1lb) dark red plums

500g (1lb) light plums

6 large garlic cloves, coarsely chopped

6 fresh red chillies, coarsely chopped

75ml (3fl oz) water

125g (4oz) tamarind block
or 2 tbsp tamarind paste

750ml (1¼ pints) malt vinegar

400g (13oz) light soft brown
or white sugar

2 tsp salt

1 tsp cloves

1 tsp allspice berries

1 cinnamon stick, broken

½ tsp black cumin seeds (kalajeera)

1 Cut the plums in half and remove the stones. Crack the stones with a hammer or nutcracker, and tie them in a piece of muslin.

2 Put the plums, muslin bag, garlic, chillies, and water in the preserving pan. Bring to the boil, then simmer gently, stirring frequently, for 15–20 minutes or until the plums are soft.

3 If using a tamarind block, soak it in 125ml (4fl oz) hot water for 20 minutes, then sieve out and discard the large seeds.

4 Add the vinegar, sieved tamarind or tamarind paste, sugar, and salt to the pan. Bring to the boil, stirring until they have dissolved. Simmer for 25–30 minutes, stirring frequently, until most of the liquid has evaporated and the mixture is thick. Remove from the heat and take out the muslin bag.

5 Grind the cloves, allspice, and cinnamon to a powder in the spice mill or coffee grinder. Stir into the chutney with the cumin seeds. Ladle into the hot sterilized jars, then seal. The chutney will be ready to eat in 1 month.

This is a dark red, superbly flavoured chutney. The original recipe, which comes from Assam, includes 15 chillies and several spoons of chilli powder. I tried it, and it was wonderfully hot – a real treat for chilli lovers.

TIP
Select firm, fleshy plums with a good colour. I use a mixture of Victoria and dark red plums, but you can use just red plums if you are unable to obtain Victorias.

Chinese-Style Plum Sauce

☆ **DEGREE OF DIFFICULTY** EASY 🔥 **COOKING TIME** ABOUT 1¼ HOURS 🍴 **SPECIAL EQUIPMENT** NON-CORROSIVE PRESERVING PAN; STERILIZED BOTTLES WITH VINEGAR-PROOF SEALANTS OR CORKS (SEE PAGES 12–13)

🫙 **YIELD** ABOUT 1 LITRE (1¾ PINTS) 🫙 **SHELF LIFE** 2 YEARS, HEAT PROCESSED

🥄 **SERVING SUGGESTION** USE TO DRESS SALADS INSTEAD OF OIL AND VINEGAR

INGREDIENTS

2kg (4lb) red plums, or half plums and half damsons

1 litre (1¾ pints) red wine vinegar or rice vinegar

2 tsp salt

250ml (8fl oz) dark soy sauce

300g (10oz) honey or dark brown sugar

1 tbsp arrowroot or cornflour

FOR THE SPICE BAG (SEE PAGE 31)

1 tbsp star anise, crushed

2 tsp Sichuan pepper, crushed

1 tsp small dried red chillies, crushed

1 Put the plums, vinegar, salt, and spice bag into the preserving pan. Bring to the boil, then reduce the heat and simmer for about 25 minutes or until the plums are soft and mushy.

2 Discard the spice bag. Pass the plums through a sieve. Put the purée in the cleaned pan, and stir in the soy sauce and honey or sugar. Bring to the boil, then simmer for 45 minutes or until the purée has reduced by a quarter.

3 Mix the arrowroot to a paste with water. Stir into the pan and cook for 1–2 minutes, stirring. Pour into the hot sterilized bottles, then seal. Heat process, cool, check the seals, and dip corks in wax (see pages 13–15). The sauce is ready immediately but improves with keeping.

Sweet, sour, and hot, this Chinese sauce is a suitable accompaniment to roast duck, as well as a flavouring for soups and stews.

Apricot Jam

 DEGREE OF DIFFICULTY EASY **COOKING TIME** 45–55 MINUTES **SPECIAL EQUIPMENT** HAMMER OR NUTCRACKER; PRESERVING PAN; SUGAR THERMOMETER; STERILIZED JARS AND SEALANTS (SEE PAGES 12–13) **YIELD** ABOUT 1.5KG (3LB) **SHELF LIFE** 2 YEARS **SERVING SUGGESTIONS** USE TO GLAZE A LEG OF LAMB BEFORE ROASTING OR TO GLAZE FRUIT TARTS

INGREDIENTS

1.25kg (2 ½lb) apricots

juice of 1 lemon

1kg (2lb) preserving or granulated sugar

300ml (½ pint) water

1 Halve the apricots, then remove and reserve the stones. Put the apricots in a glass bowl and sprinkle with the lemon juice. Mix well and cover until needed.

2 Crack open 10 of the apricot stones with a hammer or nutcracker, and extract the kernels. Taste one – if it is very bitter, use only half of them. Blanch the kernels for 1 minute in boiling water and either split into two segments or chop finely.

3 Put the sugar and water in the preserving pan. Bring slowly to the boil, stirring until the sugar has dissolved, then boil rapidly for 3–4 minutes. Add the apricots, return to the boil, then simmer for 5 minutes.

4 Return to the boil, and boil rapidly, stirring frequently, for 20–25 minutes, or until the setting point is reached (see page 16). About 5 minutes before the jam is ready, stir in the split or chopped apricot kernels.

5 Remove the pan from the heat and leave the jam to settle for a few minutes. Skim well. Ladle the jam into the hot sterilized jars, then seal.

VARIATION

To make a smooth apricot jam, follow the recipe as far as step 3. Leave the jam to cool slightly, then pass through a sieve or a food mill. Return to the cleaned pan and proceed as above. Do not add the apricot kernels if the jam is to be used as a glaze.

TIP
For the best results, always choose ripe but firm apricots. Use the jam to fill pastries and cakes; or warm and sieve it to make a wonderful yellow glaze.

Fragrant and mellow, with a beautiful golden hue, this apricot jam is a very versatile preserve that perfectly captures the essence of summer.

Apricot kernels are found inside the apricot's stone

Candied Apricots

☆☆ **DEGREE OF DIFFICULTY** MODERATE 🍲 **COOKING TIME** DAY 1, ABOUT 10 MINUTES; DAY 2, ABOUT 5 MINUTES;

DAY 3, ABOUT 15 MINUTES; DAY 4, 3¼–4¼ HOURS 🥄 **SPECIAL EQUIPMENT** PRESERVING PAN; SUGAR THERMOMETER;

1.5 LITRE (2½ PINT) STERILIZED, WIDE-NECKED JAR AND SEALANT (SEE PAGES 12–13) OR AIRTIGHT CONTAINER

🫙 **YIELD** ABOUT 1.5KG (3LB) 🫙 **SHELF LIFE** 2 YEARS IN SYRUP; 3–4 MONTHS WITH CRYSTALLIZED FINISH

🍽 **SERVING SUGGESTIONS** USE TO DECORATE CAKES, SWEETS, AND DESSERTS, OR SERVE AS A SWEETMEAT

INGREDIENTS

1kg (2lb) apricots

1.5kg (3lb) sugar

250ml (8fl oz) water

juice of 1 lemon or 1 tsp citric acid

TIP
To hasten the sugar absorption process, first steep the pricked fruit in a strong salt solution (75g/2½oz salt per 500ml/17fl oz water) for 24–48 hours.

1 Prick each apricot a few times with a sharp wooden skewer.

2 Put 1kg (2lb) of the sugar in the preserving pan with the water and lemon juice or citric acid. Bring to the boil, stirring until the sugar has dissolved, then skim well and boil until it reaches 110°C (230°F) on the sugar thermometer.

3 Slide the apricots into the pan and simmer for 3 minutes. Remove with a slotted spoon and place in a large glass bowl. Return the syrup to the boil, and boil for 5 minutes. Pour over the apricots, weight down with a plate (see page 166), and leave for 24 hours.

4 Drain the apricots. Return the syrup to the pan, adding 250g (8oz) of the sugar. Bring slowly to the boil, stirring until the sugar

has dissolved. Skim well, and boil for about 5 minutes.

5 Add the apricots to the pan. Return to the boil, then reduce the heat and simmer gently for about 5 minutes. Remove the apricots with a slotted spoon and place in the bowl. Bring the syrup back to the boil, and boil for 5 minutes. Pour over the apricots, weight down, and leave for 24 hours.

6 Drain the apricots. Return the syrup to the pan and add the rest of the sugar. Bring to the boil, stirring until it has dissolved. Skim, then boil for 2–3 minutes.

7 Add the apricots to the pan. Return to the boil, then reduce the heat to minimum and simmer very gently (so it bubbles only occasionally) for 3–4 hours or until the fruit is clear and candied.

8 Arrange the fruit in the hot sterilized jar, top up with the hot syrup, then seal. Alternatively, lift the fruit out of the syrup on to wire racks. Leave for 24 hours or until dry to the touch. Sprinkle with caster sugar, then dry in the oven for 12–24 hours (see Candied Pineapple Rings, page 228).

The fruit keeps only a few months. To prevent deterioration, store it in the heavy syrup or crystallize just before use. Keep soft fruit like apricots whole, to maintain their shape. Firmer fruit can be halved or stoned.

Rumtopf

☆ **DEGREE OF DIFFICULTY** EASY 🍴 **SPECIAL EQUIPMENT** RUMTOPF POT OR LARGE JAR OR CASSEROLE WITH LID

🍯 **YIELD** AS THE SIZE OF POT OR JAR 🍯 **SHELF LIFE** KEEPS INDEFINITELY 🚫 **SERVING SUGGESTIONS** SERVE AS A

TOPPING ON ICE CREAM AND OTHER DESSERTS, OR EAT THE FRUIT WITH A SPOON, WASHING IT DOWN WITH THE LIQUOR

INGREDIENTS

*selection of any fresh, ripe, juicy fruit
– for example, strawberries and other
berries, black-, red-, and white currants,
peaches, pears, plums, and cherries*

FOR EVERY 1KG (2LB) PREPARED FRUIT:

*250g (8oz) preserving or granulated
sugar for a slightly sharp end product;
for a sweeter version, use up to 400g
(13oz) per 1kg (2lb)*

about 1 litre (1¾ pints) light rum

To prepare the fruit, remove any stems and bruised parts. Quarter large fruit, such as pears. Peaches should be blanched (see page 21) and peeled.

1 Mix the prepared fruit with the sugar in a large bowl. Cover and leave to stand for about 30 minutes.

2 Spoon into the rumtopf pot and pour over the rum. Cover with clingfilm and the lid.

3 Every week or so, mix the contents by shaking the pot.

4 As more fruit come into season, prepare as above and add to the pot, together with the appropriate amount of sugar and rum. It will be ready 3 months after the last fruit has been added.

TIP
If using a glass pot or jar, keep it in a dark place, because light affects the colour of the fruit.

This ingenious dish is made by layering fresh fruit with alcohol and sugar in an earthenware pot. It is topped up with more fruit as different varieties come into season. And it's ready just in time for Christmas!

Orchard Fruit Butter

 DEGREE OF DIFFICULTY EASY **COOKING TIME** 2¾–3¼ HOURS **SPECIAL EQUIPMENT** PRESERVING PAN; SPICE MILL OR COFFEE GRINDER; STERILIZED JARS AND SEALANTS (SEE PAGES 12–13) **YIELD** ABOUT 1.5KG (3LB) **SHELF LIFE** 2 YEARS **SERVING SUGGESTIONS** USE AS A FILLING FOR CAKES OR TARTS; SERVE WITH COLD MEATS

INGREDIENTS

1.25kg (2½lb) apples, chopped (no need to peel and core)

625g (1¼lb) pears, chopped (no need to peel and core)

625g (1¼lb) peaches, halved and stoned

1 litre (1¾ pints) sweet cider or water

1kg (2lb) soft brown or white sugar

1 tsp allspice berries

½ tsp cloves

2 tsp ground cinnamon

1 Put the chopped apples, pears, and peaches in the preserving pan with the cider or water. Bring to the boil, skim, reduce the heat, and simmer for 1 hour, or until the fruit is very soft and mushy.

2 Either press the fruit through a sieve or pass it through a food mill. Return the purée to the cleaned pan. Add the sugar, stirring until it has dissolved. Bring to the boil, then simmer, stirring frequently, for 1½–2 hours or until the mixture has reduced and become very thick.

3 Grind the allspice and cloves in the spice mill or coffee grinder. Add to the pan with the cinnamon, and continue to cook for a minute or two. Pour into the warm sterilized jars, then seal.

Mango butter (see page 224) can be flavoured with orange, vanilla, or cinnamon

Orchard fruit butter is lightly spiced with a warming hint of allspice, cloves, and cinnamon

Kiwi fruit butter (see page 225) has a slightly sharp taste

This is a convenient way to preserve a glut of orchard fruit. Try using different combinations, but remember that at least half the quantity of fruit should be apples.

Blueberry Jam

☆ **DEGREE OF DIFFICULTY** EASY 🍲 **COOKING TIME** ABOUT 45 MINUTES

🍴 **SPECIAL EQUIPMENT** PRESERVING PAN; SUGAR THERMOMETER; STERILIZED JARS AND SEALANTS (SEE PAGES 12–13)

🫙 **YIELD** ABOUT 1.5KG (3LB) 🫙 **SHELF LIFE** 2 YEARS

INGREDIENTS

1kg (2lb) blueberries

1kg (2lb) preserving or granulated sugar

4 tbsp water

juice of 1 lemon

1 Put the blueberries, sugar, water, and lemon juice in the preserving pan. Bring slowly to the boil, stirring occasionally until the sugar has dissolved. Reduce the heat and simmer for about 10 minutes.

2 Increase the heat and boil rapidly for 15–20 minutes, or until the setting point is reached (see page 16).

3 Remove the pan from the heat and leave the jam to settle for a few minutes. Ladle into the hot sterilized jars, then seal.

TIP
The best time to remove surface scum from the jam is after you have removed it from the heat but before it has cooled too much.

Blueberries make a soft set jam. Use as a topping for cheesecakes, or fold into whipped cream as a filling for sponge cakes.

Raspberry Jam

 DEGREE OF DIFFICULTY EASY **COOKING TIME** ABOUT 45 MINUTES **SPECIAL EQUIPMENT** PRESERVING PAN; SUGAR THERMOMETER; STERILIZED JARS AND SEALANTS (SEE PAGES 12–13) **YIELD** ABOUT 1.5KG (3LB) **SHELF LIFE** 2 YEARS **SERVING SUGGESTION** USE TO FILL SWISS ROLLS, LINZER TORTE, OR FOR AN ESPECIALLY LUXURIOUS QUEEN OF PUDDINGS

INGREDIENTS

1kg (2lb) raspberries

1kg (2lb) preserving or granulated sugar

juice of 1 lemon

1 Layer the raspberries and sugar in the preserving pan. Cover with a cloth and leave overnight.

2 The next day, add the lemon juice to the pan. Bring slowly to the boil, stirring frequently until the sugar has dissolved.

3 Increase the heat and boil rapidly for 20–25 minutes or until the setting point is reached (see page 16). Stir constantly towards the end of cooking to prevent it from sticking. If wished, pass half the jam through a sieve to reduce the seed content, then return to the boil for 5 minutes.

4 Remove the pan from the heat and leave the jam to settle for a few minutes. Ladle into the hot sterilized jars, then seal.

Densely packed with juicy berries, this jam gives a year-round taste of summer

This is made without water to give an intensely flavoured, perfumed jam.

Raspberry Syrup

☆ **DEGREE OF DIFFICULTY** EASY **COOKING TIME** ABOUT 1¼ HOURS **SPECIAL EQUIPMENT** STERILIZED JELLY BAG AND MUSLIN; 750ML (1¼ PINT) STERILIZED BOTTLES AND CORKS (SEE PAGES 12–13) **YIELD** ABOUT 750ML (1¼ PINTS) **SHELF LIFE** 2 YEARS **SERVING SUGGESTIONS** POUR OVER DESSERTS AND ICE CREAM, OR DILUTE WITH WATER TO MAKE A DRINK; THE SYRUP MAKES A PLEASANT TREAT WHEN FROZEN

INGREDIENTS

1kg (2lb) raspberries

75ml (3fl oz) water

preserving or granulated sugar

This hot syrup-making method is easier than the cold method (see Blackcurrant Syrup, page 101) but does not produce the same intensity of flavour.

1 Put the raspberries and water in a bowl and mash well. Set over a pan of simmering water for 1 hour, mashing occasionally.

2 Pour into the sterilized jelly bag (see page 17). Leave for a few hours or until it stops dripping. Squeeze the bag to extract as much liquid as possible. Filter the juice through a double layer of muslin (see page 21).

3 Measure the juice and allow 400g (13oz) sugar for every 500ml (17fl oz) juice. Put in a pan and bring slowly to the boil, stirring occasionally until the sugar has dissolved. Skim off the froth, and boil for 4–5 minutes. Do not overcook or the mixture will start to set.

4 Pour into the hot sterilized bottle, and cork. Leave to cool, then seal with wax (see page 13).

Cassis

☆ **DEGREE OF DIFFICULTY** EASY 🍴 **SPECIAL EQUIPMENT** 1.5 LITRE (2½ PINT) STERILIZED, WIDE-NECKED JAR; STERILIZED JELLY BAG AND MUSLIN; STERILIZED BOTTLES AND SEALANTS (SEE PAGES 12–13) 🫙 **YIELD** ABOUT 1 LITRE (1¾ PINTS) 🫙 **SHELF LIFE** KEEPS INDEFINITELY; ONCE OPENED, CONSUME WITHIN 3 MONTHS

🥄 **SERVING SUGGESTION** ADD 1–2 TEASPOONS TO A GLASS OF DRY WHITE WINE OR CHAMPAGNE

INGREDIENTS

1kg (2lb) ripe blackcurrants, washed

500ml (17fl oz) brandy

350–500g (11½oz–1lb) preserving or granulated sugar

1 Place the blackcurrants in the sterilized jar and crush them well with a potato masher. (Do not use any damaged or mouldy berries.)

2 Pour over the brandy, then cover the jar tightly. Leave in a cool, dark place for about 2 months, shaking the jar from time to time.

3 Pour the fruit and liquid into the sterilized jelly bag (see page 17). Leave for a few hours or until it stops dripping. Squeeze the bag to extract as much liquid as possible. Filter the juice through a double layer of muslin (see page 21), then return it to the jar.

4 Add the sugar to taste (I prefer the smaller amount), then seal. Leave in a cool, dark place for 2 weeks, shaking the jar every few days, until all the sugar has dissolved and the liquid is clear.

5 Filter the liquid again if necessary. Pour into sterilized bottles, then seal. The liqueur can be used immediately but improves with keeping.

TIP
Other berries, such as strawberries, redcurrants, blueberries, and raspberries, can be treated in the same way.

This traditional French blackcurrant liqueur is extremely delicious and very easy to make.

Blackcurrant Jam

☆ **DEGREE OF DIFFICULTY** EASY **COOKING TIME** ABOUT 1 HOUR **SPECIAL EQUIPMENT** PRESERVING PAN;
SUGAR THERMOMETER; STERILIZED JARS AND SEALANTS (SEE PAGES 12–13) **YIELD** ABOUT 1.5KG (3LB)
 SHELF LIFE 2 YEARS **SERVING SUGGESTION** SERVE WITH THICK NATURAL YOGURT AS A SIMPLE DESSERT

INGREDIENTS

1kg (2lb) blackcurrants

750ml (1¼ pints) water

750g (1½lb) preserving
or granulated sugar

a little brandy, to seal

1 Put the blackcurrants and water in the preserving pan. Bring slowly to the boil, then reduce the heat and simmer gently for 20–25 minutes, stirring occasionally, until the mixture has reduced by a third.

2 Add the sugar to the pan. Slowly return to the boil, stirring until the sugar has dissolved, then boil rapidly for 15–20 minutes or until the setting point is reached (see page 16).

3 Remove the pan from the heat and leave to stand until the jam is completely cold.

4 Ladle the cold jam into the sterilized jars. Cover each jar with a waxed paper disc dipped in a little brandy, then seal.

VARIATION

If you prefer a smooth, seedless jam, press the fruit pulp through a sieve at the end of step 1. Return the mixture to the cleaned pan and proceed as for the main recipe.

Blackcurrants are high in pectin, which makes them ideal for jams and jellies.

Old-Fashioned Blackcurrant Jelly

☆☆ **DEGREE OF DIFFICULTY** MODERATE 🍲 **COOKING TIME** ABOUT 1¾ HOURS 🍴 **SPECIAL EQUIPMENT** CASSEROLE OR STONE JAR; STERILIZED JELLY BAG; PRESERVING PAN; SUGAR THERMOMETER; STERILIZED JARS AND SEALANTS (SEE PAGES 12–13) 🫙 **YIELD** ABOUT 1.5KG (3LB) 🫙 **SHELF LIFE** 2 YEARS 🍽 **SERVING SUGGESTIONS** FOLD INTO WHIPPED CREAM TO MAKE A SIMPLE FRUIT FOOL, OR USE TO GLAZE A JOINT OF LAMB BEFORE ROASTING

INGREDIENTS

1kg (2lb) blackcurrants

preserving or granulated sugar

1 Put the blackcurrants in the casserole. Cover and bake in the oven at 140°C/275°F/gas 1 for 1 hour or until they are mushy and juicy. Alternatively, put the stone jar in a pan of water and simmer for 1 hour.

2 Pour the fruit and liquid into the sterilized jelly bag (see page 17). Leave to drain until it stops dripping.

3 Remove the pulp from the jelly bag and put it into the preserving pan, adding enough cold water to cover. Bring to the boil, then reduce the heat and simmer for 20 minutes. Drain through the jelly bag as before.

4 Combine the two batches of juice and measure it. Allow 500g (1lb) sugar for every 500ml (17fl oz) juice.

5 Put the fruit juice and sugar in the preserving pan. Heat slowly, stirring until the sugar has dissolved, then increase the heat and bring to the boil.

6 Skim well and boil rapidly for 10 minutes or until the setting point is reached (see page 16). Pour the liquid into the hot sterilized jars, then seal.

Although it is fairly lengthy, this method produces an intensely flavoured and highly coloured jelly.

Blackcurrant Syrup

☆ **DEGREE OF DIFFICULTY** EASY   **COOKING TIME** ABOUT 20 MINUTES   **SPECIAL EQUIPMENT** FOOD PROCESSOR; STERILIZED JELLY BAG AND MUSLIN; STERILIZED BOTTLES AND CORKS (SEE PAGES 12–13)   **YIELD** ABOUT 750ML (1¼ PINTS)   **SHELF LIFE** 2 YEARS   **SERVING SUGGESTIONS** DILUTE TO MAKE A DRINK, OR POUR OVER DESSERTS AND ICE CREAMS

INGREDIENTS

1kg (2lb) ripe blackcurrants

preserving or granulated sugar

1 Purée the blackcurrants in the food processor. Transfer to a bowl, cover, and leave for 24 hours.

2 Pour the fruit purée into the sterilized jelly bag (see page 17). Leave for a few hours or until it stops dripping. Squeeze the bag to extract as much liquid as possible. Filter the juice through a double layer of muslin (see page 21).

3 Measure the juice and add 400g (13oz) sugar for every 500ml (17fl oz) juice. Stir well until the sugar has dissolved.

4 Pour the syrup into the sterilized bottles, filling them to within 5cm (2in) of the top. Cork, heat process, then seal with wax (see pages 13–15).

Blackcurrants make the best syrup – perfumed and refreshing. This recipe extracts the juice when cold, which produces a very fresh flavour. The slight fermentation period before draining the fruit destroys as much pectin as possible; otherwise, the syrup will start to set.

Green Tomato and Orange Jam

 DEGREE OF DIFFICULTY EASY **COOKING TIME** 1½–1¾ HOURS **SPECIAL EQUIPMENT** MINCER OR FOOD PROCESSOR; PRESERVING PAN; STERILIZED JARS AND SEALANTS (SEE PAGES 12–13) **YIELD** ABOUT 2KG (4LB) **SHELF LIFE** 1 YEAR **SERVING SUGGESTION** SUPERB ON HOT BUTTERED TOAST

INGREDIENTS

4 large sweet oranges

2 lemons

1kg (2lb) green tomatoes

750ml (1¼ pints) water

1kg (2lb) preserving
or granulated sugar

1½ tbsp coriander seeds,
roughly crushed

1 Cut the oranges into slices and remove the pips. Squeeze the juice from the lemons, and reserve the pips. Tie all the pips into a piece of muslin.

2 Put the tomatoes and oranges through the mincer or process them in the food processor until they are finely chopped.

3 Place the chopped tomato and orange in the preserving pan with the water and muslin bag. Bring to the boil, then reduce the heat and simmer for about 45 minutes or until the orange peel is soft.

4 Add the sugar and the lemon juice to the pan, stirring until the sugar has dissolved.

5 Bring to the boil, and boil over a medium heat, stirring occasionally, for 30–35 minutes or until it is thick enough for a wooden spoon drawn through the centre to leave a clear channel.

6 Remove the pan from the heat and leave the jam to settle for a few minutes. Skim if necessary, then remove the muslin bag and stir in the crushed coriander seeds. Ladle the jam into the hot sterilized jars, then seal.

Sweet oranges are available all year round, so this jam can be made in summer, when green tomatoes are in season.

Oven-Dried Tomatoes Preserved in Oil

☆ **DEGREE OF DIFFICULTY** EASY **COOKING TIME** 8–12 HOURS **SPECIAL EQUIPMENT** 600ML (1 PINT)

STERILIZED JAR WITH SEALANT (SEE PAGES 12–13) **YIELD** ABOUT 300G (10OZ) **SHELF LIFE** 2 YEARS

SERVING SUGGESTIONS USE TO FLAVOUR SALADS, PASTA SAUCES, STEWS, AND BREADS;

FRESH FROM THE OVEN, THE TOMATOES MAKE A DELICIOUS FIRST COURSE WITH A YOGURT DRESSING

INGREDIENTS

1kg (2lb) beef or plum tomatoes, halved

2 tbsp salt

1 tbsp sugar

1 tbsp dried basil or mint

4 tbsp extra-virgin olive oil

1 sprig rosemary

1–2 dried chillies (optional)

1–2 garlic cloves, cut into slivers (optional)

olive oil, to cover

1 Arrange the tomato halves, cut side up, on a wire rack placed over a foil-lined baking tray. Sprinkle the tomatoes with the salt, sugar, and dried basil or mint, then finely drizzle the extra-virgin olive oil over the top.

2 Put the tray in an oven set to the lowest possible temperature, and leave the door slightly ajar to allow the moisture to escape. Bake for 8–12 hours or until the tomatoes are dry but still pliable.

3 Pack the dried tomatoes into the sterilized jar along with the rosemary, dried chillies, and garlic (if using).

4 Pour olive oil into the jar, making sure the tomatoes are completely covered. Poke the contents of the jar with a wooden skewer to ensure there are no air pockets, then seal. The tomatoes will be ready to eat in 1–2 days but improve with keeping.

Tomatoes develop a strong, concentrated flavour when dried and can enhance many savoury dishes.

Spiced Cherry Tomatoes

☆ **DEGREE OF DIFFICULTY** EASY 🍴 **SPECIAL EQUIPMENT** I LITRE (1¾ PINT) STERILIZED JAR WITH VINEGAR-PROOF SEALANT (SEE PAGES 12–13) 🫙 **YIELD** ABOUT 1KG (2LB) 🫙 **SHELF LIFE** I YEAR
🍽 **SERVING SUGGESTIONS** USE AS A GARNISH, OR SERVE WITH DRINKS

INGREDIENTS

1kg (2lb) firm red or yellow cherry tomatoes, preferably with stalks attached

10–12 mint or basil leaves

sugar-free sweet vinegar, to cover

FOR THE SUGAR-FREE SWEET VINEGAR

4 litres (7 pints) cider vinegar or distilled malt vinegar

300ml (½ pint) concentrated apple or pear juice

2 tbsp black peppercorns

1 tbsp allspice berries

2 tsp cloves

2 tbsp coriander seeds

3 cinnamon sticks

a few fresh or dried chillies (optional)

1 Put the vinegar and fruit juice in a non-corrosive pan. Bring to the boil and skim well. Make a spice bag with the remaining ingredients (see page 31). Add to the boiling vinegar and boil for 10 minutes.

2 Remove the spice bag, pour the vinegar into the hot sterilized bottles, then seal. (The vinegar is ready to use immediately but improves with keeping.)

3 Lightly prick each tomato in several places with a wooden cocktail stick. Arrange in the sterilized jar with the mint or basil.

4 Pour in the sugar-free sweet vinegar, making sure that it covers the tomatoes by at least 2.5cm (1in). Poke the tomatoes with a wooden skewer to ensure there are no air pockets.

5 Weight down the tomatoes (see page 166), then seal. The tomatoes will be ready to eat in 4–6 weeks but improve with longer keeping.

In this decorative pickle, the tomato flesh softens and bursts in the mouth on biting. Small green or yellow tomatoes work equally well.

Mint leaves
add a cleansing,
summery taste

The peppercorns in
the vinegar add a
little zing to the
tomatoes

Red Tomato Marmalade

 DEGREE OF DIFFICULTY EASY **COOKING TIME** ABOUT 50 MINUTES

SPECIAL EQUIPMENT PRESERVING PAN; SUGAR THERMOMETER; STERILIZED JARS AND SEALANTS (SEE PAGES 12–13)

 YIELD ABOUT 1.5KG (3LB) **SHELF LIFE** 2 YEARS

INGREDIENTS

1kg (2lb) firm, ripe tomatoes, skinned, deseeded, and coarsely chopped

1kg (2lb) preserving or granulated sugar

finely sliced rind and juice of 2 lemons

1½ tbsp coriander seeds, coarsely crushed (optional)

1 Put the tomatoes in the preserving pan with the sugar and lemon rind and juice. Bring slowly to the boil, then simmer for 5 minutes. Skim and add the coriander seeds, if using.

2 Return the mixture to the boil, and boil, stirring frequently, for 30 minutes, until the setting point is reached (see page 16). Remove the pan from the heat and leave the fruit to settle for a few minutes. Ladle the marmalade into the hot sterilized jars, then seal.

Coriander seeds and lemon add a tangy taste to the marmalade

Tomatoes make an extraordinarily tasty marmalade, with an elusive flavour that will intrigue and surprise you.

Yellow Tomato Preserve

 DEGREE OF DIFFICULTY EASY **COOKING TIME** ABOUT 1 HOUR

 SPECIAL EQUIPMENT PRESERVING PAN; SUGAR THERMOMETER; STERILIZED JARS AND SEALANTS (SEE PAGES 12–13)

YIELD ABOUT 1.5KG (3LB) **SHELF LIFE** 2 YEARS

INGREDIENTS

1kg (2lb) yellow tomatoes

2 lemons, thinly sliced into semi-circles

1 lemongrass stalk, finely chopped (optional)

75ml (3fl oz) water

750g (1 ½lb) preserving or granulated sugar

250g (8oz) soft light brown sugar

1 Put all the ingredients in the preserving pan. (There is no need to chop the tomatoes.) Bring slowly to the boil, then simmer gently for 15 minutes.

2 Return to the boil, and boil steadily, stirring frequently, for 25 minutes or until the setting point is reached (see page 16).

3 Remove the pan from the heat, and leave the tomatoes to settle for a few minutes. Ladle the preserve into the hot sterilized jars, then seal.

Yellow tomatoes make a wonderfully golden jam. Select sound, slightly underripe tomatoes with a good yellow colour. Soft, overripe fruit will make a watery preserve.

Red Tomato Chutney

 DEGREE OF DIFFICULTY EASY **COOKING TIME** 45–50 MINUTES **SPECIAL EQUIPMENT** NON-CORROSIVE PRESERVING PAN; SPICE MILL OR COFFEE GRINDER; STERILIZED JARS WITH VINEGAR-PROOF SEALANTS (SEE PAGES 12–13) **YIELD** ABOUT 1KG (2LB) **SHELF LIFE** 1 YEAR  **SERVING SUGGESTION** SPREAD A FEW TABLESPOONS OVER THE BOTTOM OF A FLAN CASE BEFORE ADDING A SAVOURY FILLING

INGREDIENTS

3 tbsp groundnut or sesame oil

300g (10oz) onions, coarsely chopped

1 head garlic, peeled and coarsely chopped

90g (3oz) fresh ginger root, finely shredded

2–3 fresh red chillies, deseeded and cut into thick strips (optional)

1kg (2lb) firm red plum or beef tomatoes, skinned, deseeded, and chopped

125g (4oz) jaggery or soft brown sugar

250ml (8fl oz) red wine vinegar

6 cardamom pods

90g (3oz) basil or mint, coarsely chopped

1 Heat the oil in the preserving pan and add the onions, garlic, ginger, and chillies (if using). Fry gently for 5 minutes, or until the onions just start to colour. Add the tomatoes, and cook for about 15 minutes or until they are soft.

2 Add the sugar and vinegar, stirring until the sugar has dissolved. Bring to the boil, then simmer for 25–30 minutes, stirring frequently, until most of the liquid has evaporated and the mixture is thick. Remove the pan from the heat.

3 Grind the cardamom pods in the spice mill or coffee grinder. Add to the chutney through a sieve and stir in the basil or mint. Ladle into the hot sterilized jars, then seal. The chutney will be ready to eat in 1 month but improves with keeping.

This is a mild and fragrant chutney. Originally, jaggery (unrefined Indian sugar) was used, but it is hard to obtain, so brown sugar can be substituted.

Spicy Tomato Ketchup

☆☆ **DEGREE OF DIFFICULTY** MODERATE 🍲 **COOKING TIME** 2¼–2½ HOURS 🍴 **SPECIAL EQUIPMENT** FOOD PROCESSOR; NON-CORROSIVE PRESERVING PAN; STERILIZED BOTTLES AND VINEGAR-PROOF SEALANTS OR CORKS (SEE PAGES 12–13) 🍶 **YIELD** ABOUT 1 LITRE (1¾ PINTS) 🍯 **SHELF LIFE** 2 YEARS, HEAT PROCESSED
🍳 **SERVING SUGGESTIONS** USE TO FLAVOUR SOUPS, STEWS, AND SAUCES, OR SERVE WITH PASTA

INGREDIENTS

2kg (4lb) tomatoes

500g (1lb) shallots or onions, peeled

75g (2½oz) fresh ginger root, peeled

6 garlic cloves, peeled

3–4 chillies, deseeded (optional)

6 celery stalks with leaves

FOR THE SPICE BAG (SEE PAGE 31)

2 tbsp coriander seeds

1 tsp cloves

1 tsp crumbled mace blades

FOR EVERY 1 LITRE (1¾ PINTS) PULP:

250ml (8fl oz) cider vinegar

75g (2½oz) soft brown
or white sugar

2 tsp salt

1 tbsp sweet paprika

1 Coarsely chop the tomatoes, shallots or onions, ginger, garlic, and chillies (if using) in the food processor.

2 Put the mixture in the preserving pan. Tie the celery stalks together with string, and add to the pan with the spice bag. Bring to the boil, then simmer for 25 minutes or until the shallots or onions are translucent.

3 Remove the celery and spice bag. Press the mixture through a sieve or food mill, then return to the cleaned pan. Bring to the boil,

and cook for ¾–1 hour or until the purée has reduced by half.

4 Measure the purée and add the vinegar, sugar, salt, and paprika. Boil for 1 hour, stirring frequently, until reduced and thick. Pour into the hot sterilized bottles, then seal. Heat process, cool, check the seals, and dip corks in wax (see pages 13–15). The ketchup is ready immediately but improves with keeping.

VARIATION

DAMSON KETCHUP
Replace the tomatoes with 2kg (4lb) damsons, pitted.

This recipe produces a thick, wonderfully rich, not-too-sweet ketchup. If you prefer a sweeter taste, increase the amount of sugar to 100g (3½oz) per 1 litre (1¾ pints) of pulp, and omit the chillies.

TIP
The best celery to use is the leafy "cutting" celery. If it is not available, use a head of celery instead.

Tomato Sauce

☆ **DEGREE OF DIFFICULTY** EASY **COOKING TIME** 45–50 MINUTES **SPECIAL EQUIPMENT** STERILIZED BOTTLES OR JARS WITH CORKS OR SEALANTS (SEE PAGES 12–13) **YIELD** ABOUT 1.25 LITRES (2 PINTS) **SHELF LIFE** 1 YEAR, HEAT PROCESSED **SERVING SUGGESTIONS** USE AS A BASE FOR STEWS, PASTA SAUCES, AND PIZZAS

INGREDIENTS

4 tbsp olive oil

300g (10oz) onions, chopped

6 garlic cloves, chopped

6 celery stalks with leaves, chopped

2kg (4lb) beef or plum tomatoes, skinned, deseeded, and coarsely chopped

250ml (8fl oz) water or dry white wine

2 tsp salt

2 tsp honey or sugar (optional)

FOR THE HERB BUNDLE (SEE PAGE 31)

3–4 sprigs thyme

4 sage leaves

2 bay leaves

2 strips orange or lemon rind (optional)

1 Heat the olive oil in a large heavy-based pan. Add the onions, garlic, and celery, and fry gently for about 10 minutes or until the onion is translucent.

2 Add the remaining ingredients to the pan. Bring to the boil, then simmer, uncovered, for 30–45 minutes, until most of the liquid has evaporated.

3 Remove the herbs. Pour the sauce into the hot sterilized bottles or jars; seal. Heat process, cool, check the seals, and dip corks in wax (see pages 13–15). The sauce is ready immediately.

Tomato sauce is one of the most popular standbys of the modern kitchen. There are plenty of ready-made sauces to choose from, but none compares with the fresh, full flavour of a homemade one.

Pickled Green Tomatoes

☆ **DEGREE OF DIFFICULTY** EASY   **COOKING TIME** ABOUT 5 MINUTES   **SPECIAL EQUIPMENT** 1.5 LITRE (2½ PINT) STERILIZED JAR WITH VINEGAR-PROOF SEALANT (SEE PAGES 12–13)   **YIELD** ABOUT 1KG (2LB)   **SHELF LIFE** I YEAR

SERVING SUGGESTIONS SERVE WITH MEAT OR CHEESE, OR WITH DRINKS

INGREDIENTS

1kg (2lb) green tomatoes

a few sprigs of dill

2–3 bay leaves

2–3 fresh or dried red chillies

1½ tbsp mustard seeds

1 tbsp black peppercorns

4–5 cloves

1 litre (1¾ pints) cider vinegar

125ml (4fl oz) water

4 tbsp honey or sugar

1 tbsp salt

1 Lightly prick each tomato in several places with a wooden cocktail stick. Put in the sterilized jar with the herbs and spices.

2 Put the vinegar, water, honey or sugar, and salt in a non-corrosive pan. Bring to the boil, and boil rapidly for 5 minutes, then remove from the heat and leave until warm.

3 Pour the warm vinegar into the jar. If there is not enough liquid to cover the tomatoes, top up with cold vinegar. Weight down the tomatoes (see page 166), then seal. The tomatoes will be ready to eat in 1 month but improve with 2–3 months' keeping.

> **TIP**
> Try cucumbers and courgettes or fruit such as gooseberries and plums. Always blanch green vegetables before pickling (see page 21).

This is an ideal way to use a glut of green tomatoes. This crunchy, sour pickle comes from Eastern Europe and is popular in North America, where it is an essential item in any good delicatessen.

TOMATOES

There are many types of tomato to choose from, varying in colour, size, and sweetness. In preserving, tomatoes can be used at all stages of maturity. Choose firm, vine-ripened specimens with a fine flavour, rather than "forced" tomatoes, which contain too much moisture.

Cooked Tomato and Pepper Salsa

☆ **DEGREE OF DIFFICULTY** EASY **COOKING TIME** ABOUT 5 MINUTES **SPECIAL EQUIPMENT** FOOD PROCESSOR; NON-CORROSIVE PRESERVING PAN; STERILIZED JARS WITH VINEGAR-PROOF SEALANTS (SEE PAGES 12–13)
 **YIELD** ABOUT 1KG (2LB) **SHELF LIFE** 6 MONTHS, HEAT PROCESSED

INGREDIENTS

750g (1½lb) mixed coloured peppers

2–3 fresh red or green chillies, deseeded

1 large red onion

2 garlic cloves, peeled

3 tbsp olive, corn, or groundnut oil

3 tbsp red wine vinegar or lemon juice

2 tsp salt

500g (1lb) firm red tomatoes, skinned, deseeded, and finely chopped

3 tbsp chopped coriander or parsley

1 Coarsely chop the vegetables, then finely chop in the food processor with the garlic, oil, vinegar or lemon juice, and salt.

2 Put in the preserving pan with the tomatoes and herbs. Bring to the boil, then simmer for 5 minutes. Pour into the hot sterilized jars, then seal. Heat process, cool, and check the seals (see pages 14–15). The salsa is ready immediately.

Salsa, meaning sauce, is Mexican in origin. This salsa can also be eaten uncooked: add the tomatoes and herbs to the chopped ingredients, and marinate for 2–3 hours before using. Refrigerate, and eat within 2 weeks.

Red Pepper and Kiwi Fruit Pickle

☆☆ **DEGREE OF DIFFICULTY** MODERATE 🍲 **COOKING TIME** ABOUT 40 MINUTES

🍴 **SPECIAL EQUIPMENT** NON-CORROSIVE PRESERVING PAN; STERILIZED JARS WITH VINEGAR-PROOF SEALANTS

(SEE PAGES 12–13) 🍯 **YIELD** ABOUT 1.5KG (3LB) 🍯 **SHELF LIFE** 1 YEAR 🚫 **SERVING SUGGESTIONS** DRESS WITH OLIVE OIL AND SERVE AS A SALAD, OR USE TO DECORATE A COLD MEAT PLATTER

INGREDIENTS

3 red peppers, cut into wide strips

1 tbsp salt

1kg (2lb) hard, unripe kiwi fruit, peeled and cut into large chunks

juice of 1 lemon

1 litre (1 ¾ pints) cider vinegar or white wine vinegar

150g (5oz) honey, preferably single blossom

250g (8oz) light soft brown sugar or white sugar

1 tbsp black peppercorns

2 tsp juniper berries

1 tsp allspice berries

1 Sprinkle the red pepper strips with the salt and leave for 15 minutes. Put the kiwi fruit chunks in a glass bowl and sprinkle with the lemon juice. Mix gently and leave to marinate for 15 minutes.

2 Put the vinegar, honey, sugar, and spices in the preserving pan. Bring to the boil, and boil rapidly for 10 minutes, until the syrup is slightly reduced.

3 Rinse the peppers under cold water and drain well. Add them to the boiling syrup. Return to the boil, then reduce the heat and simmer for 5 minutes. Add the kiwi fruit to the pan, and simmer for a further 5 minutes.

4 Using a slotted spoon, lift the peppers and kiwi fruit out of the pan and carefully pack them into the hot sterilized jars. Boil the syrup rapidly for 10 minutes or until slightly reduced again. Pour the boiling syrup into the jars to cover, then seal. The pickle will be ready to eat in 1 week but improves with keeping.

This is an exotic, colourful, and mild pickle. Be careful not to overcook the kiwi fruit – it softens very quickly.

TIP
For extra colour, use a combination of red, yellow, and orange peppers.

Red Pepper Ketchup

☆☆ **DEGREE OF DIFFICULTY** MODERATE **COOKING TIME** 1½–2 HOURS **SPECIAL EQUIPMENT** FOOD PROCESSOR;
NON-CORROSIVE PRESERVING PAN; STERILIZED BOTTLES WITH VINEGAR-PROOF SEALANTS OR CORKS (SEE PAGES 12–13)
YIELD ABOUT 1 LITRE (1¾ PINTS) **SHELF LIFE** 2 YEARS, HEAT PROCESSED
SERVING SUGGESTIONS SERVE WITH GRILLED OR FRIED FISH OR AS A SAUCE FOR PASTA

INGREDIENTS

2kg (4lb) red peppers

500g (1lb) shallots or onions, peeled

*250g (8oz) cooking apples, cored
and coarsely chopped*

*2–3 fresh red chillies, deseeded and
coarsely chopped (optional)*

1.5 litres (2½ pints) water

*750ml (1¼ pints) red wine vinegar
or cider vinegar*

*150g (5oz) white or light soft
brown sugar*

1 tbsp salt

1 tbsp arrowroot or cornflour

FOR THE HERB BUNDLE (SEE PAGE 31)

1 sprig tarragon

*2 sprigs each mint, thyme, sage,
and parsley*

2 strips lemon rind

FOR THE SPICE BAG (SEE PAGE 31)

1 tbsp coriander seeds

1 tbsp black peppercorns

1 tsp cloves

1 Either roast the peppers over an open flame or grill them for 5–7 minutes, until evenly charred. Put in a plastic bag for 5 minutes (to make peeling easier).

2 Remove the peppers from the bag and rub off the skin with your fingers under cold running water. Remove the core and seeds, and wash the peppers well.

3 Finely chop the pepper flesh, using a knife or a food processor, along with the shallots or onions, apples, and chillies (if using). Next, make a herb bundle and spice bag (see page 31).

4 Put the herb bundle and spice bag in a non-corrosive preserving pan with the vegetables and enough water to cover. Bring to the boil, then simmer for 25 minutes or until soft.

5 Leave to cool, then discard the herbs and spice bag. Pass the mixture through a food mill or sieve.

Bottles with corks need to be sealed with wax to keep them airtight

6 Place the resulting purée in the cleaned preserving pan, and add the vinegar, sugar, and salt. Bring to the boil, stirring until the sugar has dissolved, then simmer for 1–1½ hours, until it is reduced by half.

7 Mix the arrowroot or cornflour to a paste with a little vinegar, and stir into the sauce. Boil for 1–2 minutes, until slightly thickened.

A funnel is the easiest way to fill bottles

8 Pour the ketchup into hot sterilized bottles, and seal. Heat process (see pages 14–15), then leave to cool. Check the seals, and dip corks in wax (see page 13).

Onion and Pepper Pickle

 **DEGREE OF DIFFICULTY** EASY **COOKING TIME** ABOUT 8 MINUTES **SPECIAL EQUIPMENT** 2 LITRE (3½ PINT) STERILIZED JAR WITH VINEGAR-PROOF SEALANT (SEE PAGES 12–13) **YIELD** ABOUT 2KG (4LB) **SHELF LIFE** 6 MONTHS **SERVING SUGGESTION** DRAIN THE VEGETABLES, DRESS WITH A LITTLE OIL, AND SERVE AS A REFRESHING SALAD

INGREDIENTS

1.25kg (2½lb) onions, sliced into thin rings

2 red peppers, sliced into thin rings

2 yellow peppers, sliced into thin rings

4 tbsp salt

1 litre (1¾ pints) white wine vinegar or cider vinegar

100g (3½oz) sugar

2 tbsp dried mint

2 tbsp paprika

1 tbsp dill seeds

2 tsp salt

1 Put the sliced onions and red and yellow peppers in a large glass bowl, and sprinkle with the 4 tablespoons of salt. Mix well, cover with a clean cloth, and leave to stand for 2 hours.

2 Drain off the liquid that has accumulated in the bottom of the bowl, then rinse the vegetables under cold running water and drain again.

3 Put the vinegar, sugar, mint, paprika, dill seeds, and the 2 teaspoons of salt in a non-corrosive pan. Bring to the boil, then reduce the heat and simmer for 5 minutes.

4 Pack the vegetables into the hot sterilized jar. Pour in the boiling vinegar mixture, making sure that all the vegetables are completely covered. Poke the contents of the jar with a wooden skewer to ensure there are no air pockets, then seal. The pickle will be ready to eat in about 1 week but improves with keeping.

A colourful pickled salad. Use as many different colours of pepper as you can find, though green peppers lose their colour very quickly. I sometimes add other vegetables, such as sliced carrots or celeriac.

Peppers in Oil

☆☆ **DEGREE OF DIFFICULTY** MODERATE   **COOKING TIME** ABOUT 12 MINUTES   **SPECIAL EQUIPMENT** 1 LITRE (1¾ PINT) WIDE-NECKED, STERILIZED JAR WITH SEALANT (SEE PAGES 12–13); THERMOMETER   **YIELD** ABOUT 1KG (2LB)   **SHELF LIFE** 1 YEAR   **SERVING SUGGESTION** SERVE AS PART OF AN ANTIPASTI SELECTION

INGREDIENTS

1.5kg (3lb) red or yellow peppers

4 lemons

1 tbsp salt

3 or 4 garlic cloves, peeled and crushed

3 tbsp capers

2–3 sprigs rosemary

2–3 sprigs thyme

1–2 bay leaves

525ml (17.5fl oz) olive oil

1 Roast and skin the peppers (see page 116). Grate the rind from 1 of the lemons, then squeeze the juice from all of them. Put the rind and juice in a large glass bowl with the salt, and stir until the salt has dissolved.

2 Put the warm peppers and the crushed garlic cloves in the bowl with the lemon juice. Mix well, cover the bowl with a clean cloth, and refrigerate for 24 hours.

3 Bring the marinade back to room temperature and drain, reserving the juice. Pack the peppers in the hot sterilized jar with the capers and herbs.

4 Whisk the olive oil with the lemon juice left over from marinating the vegetables. Put in a pan and heat until it reaches 80°C (176°F).

5 Pour the hot liquid carefully into the jar, filling it to the top, making sure that all the peppers are completely covered, then seal. The peppers will be ready to eat in 4–6 weeks.

TIP
Many other vegetables – such as aubergines, courgettes, and shallots – can be prepared in a similar way after being grilled or barbecued.

Hungarian Pickled Peppers

 DEGREE OF DIFFICULTY EASY **COOKING TIME** ABOUT 15 MINUTES ❙❙ **SPECIAL EQUIPMENT** 2 LITRE (3½ PINT) STERILIZED WIDE-NECKED JAR WITH VINEGAR-PROOF SEALANT (SEE PAGES 12–13) **YIELD** ABOUT 1KG (2LB) **SHELF LIFE** 1 YEAR **SERVING SUGGESTION** SERVE AS AN ACCOMPANIMENT TO COLD MEATS AND CHEESE

INGREDIENTS

1kg (2lb) red peppers

2 small dried chillies

2 bay leaves

white wine vinegar

water

sugar

salt

FOR THE SPICE BAG (SEE PAGE 31)

2 tsp black peppercorns

1 tsp allspice berries

2 bay leaves

1 Wash the peppers thoroughly, leaving the stalks attached, then arrange them in the hot sterilized jar with the dried chillies and the bay leaves. Fill the jar with water.

2 Drain the water off into a measuring jug. Pour half of it away and replace it with vinegar. For every 1 litre (1¾ pints) liquid, add 2 tablespoons each of sugar and salt.

3 Put the vinegar/water/sugar/salt mixture in a non-corrosive pan with the spice bag. Bring to

the boil, reduce the heat, and simmer for 10 minutes. Leave to cool slightly.

4 Pour the warm liquid into the jar, making sure that the peppers are completely covered, then seal. After a few days, check that there is still enough liquid to cover the peppers – their cavities tend to absorb the vinegar. They will be ready to eat in 2 weeks.

"Tomato" peppers – so named for their shape – are red or pale yellow and have a dense flesh that makes them ideal for pickling. If you cannot find them, use small, colourful sweet peppers, but do not use green ones – they lose their colour.

Chillies add a little
piquancy to the
pickled peppers

Bay leaves provide a
cool counterpoint to
the chillies

Harrief

 DEGREE OF DIFFICULTY MODERATE **COOKING TIME** 1–1½ HOURS **SPECIAL EQUIPMENT** FOOD PROCESSOR; NON-CORROSIVE PRESERVING PAN; STERILIZED JARS WITH VINEGAR-PROOF SEALANTS (SEE PAGES 12–13) **YIELD** ABOUT 1KG (2LB)  **SHELF LIFE** 1 YEAR **SERVING SUGGESTION** USE AS A CONDIMENT

INGREDIENTS

2kg (4lb) red peppers

250g (8oz) fresh red chillies, deseeded

250g (8oz) garlic cloves, peeled

150ml (¼ pint) fruity olive oil

250ml (8fl oz) cider vinegar

3 tbsp salt

1–2 tbsp chilli powder (optional)

2 tbsp cumin seeds, freshly ground

2 tsp arrowroot

1 Roast and skin the peppers (see steps 1 and 2, page 116). Rinse well, then core and deseed. Put in the food processor with the chillies, garlic, and oil.

2 Process until the vegetables are finely chopped. Transfer to the preserving pan and add the vinegar, salt, and spices. Bring to the boil, then reduce the heat and simmer for 1–1½ hours, until the mixture is reduced by a third.

Mix the arrowroot to a paste with a little vinegar, and stir into the sauce. Raise the heat, and boil the sauce rapidly for 1 minute, stirring constantly. (If you would like a smoother sauce, pass it through a sieve or food mill at this point.)

3 Pour the sauce into the hot sterilized jars, then seal. The sauce is ready immediately but improves with keeping.

TIP
It is hard to give an exact quantity of chillies, since different varieties vary greatly in heat. For this recipe, I use the large red Westland for a hot but not scorching result.

This Moroccan speciality is my favourite hot sauce. I make it in large quantities and use it to add instant piquancy to sauces, soups, stews, salads, and pasta.

Air-Dried Chillies

☆ **DEGREE OF DIFFICULTY** EASY **SHELF LIFE** 2 YEARS, FULLY DRIED; 2 MONTHS, SEMI-DRIED

 SERVING SUGGESTION CHOP OR CRUMBLE AND ADD TO SAUCES FOR A SPICY KICK

INGREDIENTS

red chillies – as many as desired

1 Wrap strong cotton thread around the cut stem of each chilli, and tie it with a knot. Repeat the process for each chilli, at intervals of about 2.5cm (1in).

2 Hang in the sun or in an airy room for 2 weeks or until shrivelled and dry.

3 Store in a cloth or paper bag to reduce the likelihood of moisture getting into them.

TIP
If you use one of the hotter varieties of chilli pepper, wear gloves to handle them.

This is an incredibly simple way to preserve chillies. It is best to use firm, glossy chillies that are just turning red.

Ginger Chutney

☆ **DEGREE OF DIFFICULTY** EASY 🥘 **COOKING TIME** 1–1¼ HOURS 🍴 **SPECIAL EQUIPMENT** NON-CORROSIVE PRESERVING PAN; STERILIZED JARS WITH VINEGAR-PROOF SEALANTS (SEE PAGES 12–13) 🫙 **YIELD** ABOUT 1.5KG (3LB) 🫙 **SHELF LIFE** 2 YEARS 🔪 **SERVING SUGGESTIONS** SERVE WITH GAME, CHEESE, OR GRILLED FISH

INGREDIENTS

300g (10oz) fresh ginger root, shredded

300g (10oz) red peppers, diced

250g (8oz) cucumber, quartered lengthways and thickly sliced

250g (8oz) raisins

250g (8oz) onions, coarsely chopped

4 lemons, halved lengthways, pips removed, thinly sliced

1 litre (1¾ pints) cider vinegar or white wine vinegar

500g (1lb) preserving or granulated sugar

2 tsp salt

1 Put all the ingredients, except the sugar and salt, into the preserving pan. Bring the mixture to the boil, then reduce the heat and simmer gently for about 30 minutes, until the fruit and vegetables have softened.

2 Add the sugar and salt to the pan, stirring until they have dissolved. Simmer for a further 30–45 minutes, until most of the liquid has evaporated and the chutney is thick.

3 Ladle the mixture into the hot sterilized jars, then seal. The chutney will be ready to eat in 1 month but improves with keeping.

TIP
Do not throw ginger peel away; wash it well, cover with vinegar, and steep for 3 months. Filter and use the vinegar to flavour salads and rice dishes.

This is adapted from a recipe for Indian chutney that I found in an undated pickling book, by Marion Harris Neil, probably published over 100 years ago.

Toby's Pickled Cucumbers

☆ **DEGREE OF DIFFICULTY** EASY　**COOKING TIME** ABOUT 5 MINUTES　**SPECIAL EQUIPMENT** 1.5 LITRE (2½ PINT) STERILIZED JAR WITH VINEGAR-PROOF SEALANT (SEE PAGES 12–13)　**YIELD** ABOUT 1KG (2LB)　**SHELF LIFE** 3 MONTHS, REFRIGERATED　**SERVING SUGGESTIONS** SERVE AS A SALAD OR SAVOURY SNACK WITH DRINKS

INGREDIENTS

500g (1lb) large cucumbers, sliced
1cm (½in) thick
2 tbsp salt
375g (12oz) onions, sliced into
thin rings
275g (9oz) carrots, coarsely grated
or sliced into fine julienne
4 garlic cloves, sliced
1 tsp black peppercorns
3–4 bay leaves
750ml (1¼ pints) water
350ml (12fl oz) white wine vinegar
or distilled malt vinegar
4 tbsp sugar
1–2 dried red chillies

1 Put the sliced cucumbers in a colander and sprinkle with half the salt. Mix well and leave to stand for about 20 minutes. Rinse the vegetables under cold running water and drain well.

2 Mix the onion rings and carrots together in a bowl, pour over boiling water to cover, then drain well.

3 Arrange a layer of sliced cucumbers in the bottom of the hot sterilized jar. Place a few slices of garlic, a few peppercorns, and a bay leaf on top, and cover with a layer of the onion and carrot mixture.

4 Repeat the layers until all the vegetables are used up. The jar should be almost full but loosely packed.

5 Put the water, white wine vinegar, sugar, dried red chillies, and remaining salt in a non-corrosive pan. Bring to the boil, and boil steadily for a few minutes. Skim well and remove the chillies.

6 Pour the hot vinegar mixture into the jar, filling it right to the top to make sure the cucumbers are covered. Poke the vegetables with a wooden skewer to ensure there are no air pockets, then seal the jar and keep refrigerated. The pickle will be ready to eat in 2 days.

This is adapted from a recipe given to me by Toby Kay of Johannesburg, but its origins are probably Central European. Drained and dressed with a little oil and chopped herbs, it makes a colourful salad.

Olive Oil Pickle

 ☆ **DEGREE OF DIFFICULTY** EASY **COOKING TIME** ABOUT 8 MINUTES **SPECIAL EQUIPMENT** STERILIZED JARS WITH VINEGAR-PROOF SEALANTS (SEE PAGES 12–13) **YIELD** ABOUT 1.5KG (3LB) **SHELF LIFE** 1 YEAR **SERVING SUGGESTION** DELICIOUS WITH MATURE HARD CHEESE, SUCH AS CHEDDAR, RED LEICESTER, OR WHITE STILTON

INGREDIENTS

750g (1½lb) pickling cucumbers, sliced 5mm (¼in) thick

625g (1¼lb) onions, finely sliced

75g (2½oz) salt

500ml (17fl oz) cider vinegar

75ml (2½fl oz) water

1 tbsp dill seeds

1 tbsp celery seeds

1 tbsp yellow mustard seeds

75ml (2½fl oz) good fruity virgin olive oil

1 Put the sliced cucumbers and onions in a large glass bowl, cover with cold water, and add the salt. Mix well until the salt has dissolved, then weight down (see page 166). Cover the bowl with a clean cloth and leave to stand overnight.

2 The next day, drain the vegetables. Rinse well under cold running water, then drain again, squeezing out as much liquid as possible. Pack into the hot sterilized jars.

3 Put the vinegar, water, herbs, and spice in a non-corrosive pan. Bring to the boil, and boil for 5 minutes. Remove the pan from the heat and allow the mixture to cool slightly, then whisk in the oil.

4 Pour the vinegar into the jars. Poke the vegetables with a wooden skewer to ensure there are no air pockets. Check that the oil and spices are evenly distributed and the vegetables are covered, then seal. The pickle will be ready to eat in 2 weeks but improves with keeping.

TIPS
• **You can replace the cucumbers with thinly sliced, colourful peppers or carrots.**
• **The easiest way to slice the vegetables is with a mandolin.**

A classic from the colonial American kitchen, this pickle is easy to make and is a great standby. It is mildly sour, refreshing, and keeps extremely well.

Bread and Butter Pickle

☆ **DEGREE OF DIFFICULTY** EASY   **COOKING TIME** ABOUT 15 MINUTES   **SPECIAL EQUIPMENT** NON-CORROSIVE PRESERVING PAN; STERILIZED JARS WITH VINEGAR-PROOF SEALANTS (SEE PAGES 12–13)   **YIELD** ABOUT 2KG (4LB)   **SHELF LIFE** 1 YEAR   **SERVING SUGGESTIONS** SERVE WITH COLD MEATS OR SPREAD ON BREAD AND BUTTER WITH CHEESE

INGREDIENTS

750g (1 ½lb) pickling cucumbers

625g (1 ¼lb) onions, sliced 5mm (¼in) thick

375g (12oz) red or yellow peppers, sliced 5mm (¼in) thick

3 tbsp salt

1 litre (1 ¾ pints) cider vinegar, white wine vinegar, or malt vinegar

500g (1lb) light soft brown or white sugar

2 tsp ground turmeric

1 tbsp mustard seeds

2 tsp dill seeds

1 Put the cucumbers in a bowl and pour boiling water over them. Drain, refresh under cold running water, and drain again. Slice the cucumbers into 1cm (½in) thick pieces.

2 Put the cucumbers, sliced onions, and peppers in a large glass bowl and sprinkle with the salt. Mix well, then cover the bowl with a clean cloth and leave to stand overnight.

3 The next day, drain off the liquid in the bowl. Rinse the vegetables under cold running water and drain well. Taste a slice of cucumber; if it is too salty, cover the vegetables with more cold water and leave to stand for about 10 minutes, then drain, rinse, and drain again.

4 Put the vinegar, sugar, ground turmeric, mustard seeds, and dill seeds in the preserving pan. Bring to the boil, and boil rapidly for 10 minutes. Add the drained vegetables, return to the boil, then remove from the heat.

5 Pack the pickle into the hot sterilized jars, then seal. The pickle is ready to eat immediately.

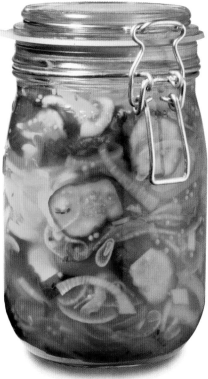

This delicious old-fashioned pickle was made to be spread on bread and butter – hence its name. However, some maintain that the name came about because the pickle was as common as bread and butter.

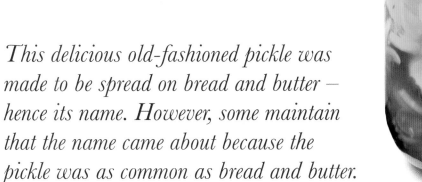

Brined Cucumbers

☆ **DEGREE OF DIFFICULTY** EASY ⬚ **COOKING TIME** I MINUTE ⫿ **SPECIAL EQUIPMENT** 1.5 LITRE (2½ PINT) WIDE-NECKED, STERILIZED JAR WITH VINEGAR-PROOF SEALANT (SEE PAGES 12–13) ⬚ **YIELD** ABOUT IKG (2LB) ⬚ **SHELF LIFE** 6 MONTHS; 3 MONTHS FOR BEETROOT ⬚ **SERVING SUGGESTIONS** CHOP THE CUCUMBERS AND ADD TO SAUCES OR POTATO SALADS; USE TO DECORATE CANAPÉS

INGREDIENTS

1kg (2lb) small, firm, pickling cucumbers

5–6 fat garlic cloves, bruised but not peeled

2–3 dill flower heads and stalks

3–4 fresh or dried red chillies

2–3 bay leaves

salt

a few vine leaves (optional)

TIP
Don't throw away the brine from this pickle after the gherkins have been eaten. You can use it as a base for soups, to flavour savoury dishes, or to make a salad dressing.

1 Put the cucumbers into a pan, and blanch in boiling water for 1 minute (see page 21).

2 Arrange the cucumbers, garlic, dill, chillies, and bay leaves in the sterilized jar. Fill the jar with water, then drain into a measuring jug. Add 1½ tablespoons salt for every 500ml (17fl oz) water, stirring until dissolved.

3 Pour the brine into the jar, place the vine leaves on top, if using, then weight down (see page 166). Cover with a clean cloth and leave in a warm, well-ventilated place to ferment for 1–2 weeks. When fermentation starts, the brine will turn cloudy.

4 When the liquid starts to clear, indicating that fermentation is over, seal the jar tightly and store. The cucumbers are ready to eat immediately.

VARIATIONS

FERMENTED TOMATOES

Use 1kg (2lb) small, firm, red tomatoes, and prick in several places with a wooden cocktail stick. Arrange in a 2 litre (3½ pint) wide-necked, sterilized jar with 3–4 fresh chillies (slit), 8 garlic cloves, 6–8 celery leaves, and 1 tablespoon black peppercorns. Cover with water and proceed as for the main recipe, adding 2 tablespoons salt for every 500ml (17fl oz) water, and 2 tablespoons cider vinegar. Complete as for main recipe.

FERMENTED BEETROOT

Use 1.5kg (3lb) small, peeled beetroot, kept whole or cut into large chunks. Arrange in the jar and cover with the brine, as for the main recipe. Weight down, cover, and ferment. After several days, froth will start to form. Remove it every few days and wipe the top of the jar clean. The beetroot will be ready in about 1 month, then seal the jar tightly. Use the liquid to make borscht; the beetroot can be added to borscht or eaten as a pickle.

My mother, a superb pickler, maintains that the crunchiness and vivid green colour of pickled cucumbers are achieved by blanching them briefly.

*Vine leaves help the
fermentation process
and add their
characteristic flavour
to the pickle*

*Dill adds a fragrant
aniseed aroma to
the brine*

Piccalilli

☆☆ **DEGREE OF DIFFICULTY** MODERATE **COOKING TIME** ABOUT 12 MINUTES **SPECIAL EQUIPMENT** SPICE MILL OR COFFEE GRINDER; STERILIZED JARS WITH VINEGAR-PROOF SEALANTS (SEE PAGES 12–13) **YIELD** ABOUT 3KG (6LB) **SHELF LIFE** 1 YEAR **SERVING SUGGESTION** DELICIOUS WITH CHEESE

INGREDIENTS

250g (8oz) runner beans, cut into bite-sized pieces

250g (8oz) cauliflower, divided into small florets

300g (10oz) carrots, cut into medium-thick slices

250g (8oz) gooseberries, topped and tailed

250g (8oz) honeydew melon, cut into cubes

200g (7oz) seedless grapes

125g (4oz) salt

400g (13oz) yellow mustard seeds

1 litre (1¾ pints) spiced vinegar (see page 243)

1 tbsp ground turmeric

1 Put all the vegetables and fruit in a large glass bowl. Cover with cold water and add 100g (3½oz) of the salt. Mix well until the salt has dissolved, then weight down (see page 166) and leave to stand for 24 hours.

2 The next day, coarsely grind the mustard seeds in the spice mill or coffee grinder; if necessary, do this in batches.

3 Drain the vegetables and fruit, rinse under cold running water, and drain well. Taste; if too salty, cover with cold water and leave to soak for 10 minutes, then drain, rinse, and drain again. Add the ground mustard seeds and mix well.

4 Put the spiced vinegar, turmeric, and remaining salt in a non-corrosive pan. Bring to the boil, skim well, and boil rapidly for 10 minutes.

5 Pour the boiling vinegar over the vegetables and fruit in the bowl, and mix well. Pack into the hot sterilized jars, then seal. The pickle is ready to eat immediately but improves with keeping.

TIPS
• Any combination of crunchy vegetables and fruit can be pickled in the same way.
• For a milder flavour, add the mustard seeds to the vinegar and boil for 3–4 minutes.

At the end of the 1600s, this very British pickle was known as "pickle lila", an Indian pickle. My crunchy version is the exotic forefather of the unpleasantly harsh, bright yellow product found in supermarkets.

Chow-Chow

☆☆ **DEGREE OF DIFFICULTY** MODERATE **COOKING TIME** ABOUT 2 MINUTES ❚❙ **SPECIAL EQUIPMENT** NON-CORROSIVE PRESERVING PAN; STERILIZED JARS WITH VINEGAR-PROOF SEALANTS (SEE PAGES 12–13) **YIELD** ABOUT 3KG (6LB) 🍯 **SHELF LIFE** 1 YEAR 🔪 **SERVING SUGGESTION** SERVE AS A RELISH WITH COLD MEATS OR CHEESE

INGREDIENTS

250g (8oz) cornichons
or mini cucumbers

1 small cauliflower, divided into florets

250g (8oz) green tomatoes, diced

300g (10oz) carrots, cut
into thick matchsticks

250g (8oz) French beans, trimmed

300g (10oz) small pickling
onions, peeled

4 red peppers, sliced

1 small head of celery, sliced

100g (3½oz) salt

FOR THE PICKLING MIXTURE

100g (3½oz) plain or
wholemeal flour

75g (2½oz) mustard powder

1½ tbsp celery seeds

1½ tbsp ground turmeric

1 tbsp salt

1.25 litres (2 pints) cider vinegar
or malt vinegar

300g (10oz) light soft brown
or white sugar

1 If using cornichons, leave them whole; otherwise, slice the mini cucumbers into thick rings.

2 Put all the vegetables in a large glass bowl. Cover with cold water and add the salt. Mix well until the salt has dissolved, then weight down (see page 166) and leave to stand overnight.

3 The next day, drain the vegetables well and blanch for 2 minutes (see page 21).

4 To make the pickling mixture, combine the flour, mustard powder, celery seeds, turmeric, and salt in a small bowl. Gradually add 250ml (8fl oz) of the vinegar, mixing well to make a smooth, thin paste.

5 Put the remaining vinegar and the sugar in the preserving pan and bring to the boil. Gradually add the mustard paste, stirring all the time. Add the drained vegetables, return to the boil, then remove from the heat.

6 Pack the pickle into the hot sterilized jars, then seal. It will be ready to eat in 2 weeks but improves with keeping.

This flavoursome mustard pickle is traditionally made in summer, when vegetables are in abundance. Any fresh colourful veggies can be used.

Two-Colour Pickled Vegetables

☆ **DEGREE OF DIFFICULTY** EASY 🍴 **SPECIAL EQUIPMENT** 3 LITRE (5 PINT) WIDE-NECKED, STERILIZED JAR WITH VINEGAR-PROOF SEALANT (SEE PAGES 12–13)  **YIELD** ABOUT 1.5KG (3LB) **SHELF LIFE** 1 YEAR

🔪 **SERVING SUGGESTIONS** SERVE AS A WINTER SALAD OR AS THE CENTREPIECE OF A COLD BUFFET

INGREDIENTS

300g (10oz) small onions, peeled

300g (10oz) shallots, peeled

300g (10oz) carrots, scraped and sliced

100g (3½oz) salt

1.5 litres (2½ pints) spiced vinegar of your choice, to cover (see page 243)

1 Put the onions, shallots, and carrots in a large glass bowl and sprinkle with the salt. Mix well, then cover the bowl with a clean cloth and leave to stand for 24–48 hours, stirring the vegetables from time to time.

2 Drain off the liquid from the bowl. Rinse the vegetables under cold running water and drain well. Cover with more cold water, leave to stand for 1 hour, then drain again.

3 Arrange the vegetables in layers in the sterilized jar, then weight down (see page 166).

4 Pour the chosen vinegar into the jar, making sure that the vegetables are completely covered, then seal. The pickle will be ready to eat in 4–6 weeks.

If available, you can also use baby vegetables for this recipe. Any mixture will work, such as baby sweetcorn, cauliflowers, and white cabbage.

Use a "crinkle cutter" to make the carrot slices more interesting

Shallots tend to have a milder flavour than regular onions

Stuffed Pickled Aubergines

☆☆ **DEGREE OF DIFFICULTY** MODERATE 🍲 **COOKING TIME** 5–8 MINUTES 🍴 **SPECIAL EQUIPMENT** 1.5 LITRE (2½ PINT) WIDE-NECKED, STERILIZED JAR WITH VINEGAR-PROOF SEALANT (SEE PAGES 12–13) 🏺 **YIELD** ABOUT 1KG (2LB) 🏺 **SHELF LIFE** 6 MONTHS, REFRIGERATED 🥄 **SERVING SUGGESTIONS** SERVE AS A SIMPLE ACCOMPANIMENT TO A PLATE OF COLD MEATS AND A LEAFY SALAD, OR AS PART OF A MEZE MEAL

INGREDIENTS

1kg (2lb) baby purple aubergines

FOR THE STUFFING

6 garlic cloves, coarsely chopped

3–4 celery stalks and leaves, coarsely chopped

2–3 large carrots, coarsely grated

1–2 fresh red chillies, thinly sliced

1 tsp salt

FOR THE JAR

4–5 garlic cloves, peeled

2–3 fresh red or green chillies

a few vine leaves (optional)

salt

2–3 tbsp cider vinegar

1 Cut a deep slit lengthways in each aubergine to make a pocket. Steam for 5–8 minutes or until just softened. Remove from the heat and weight down (see page 166) to press out any moisture. Leave to stand overnight.

2 The next day, put the stuffing ingredients in a bowl and mix well. Open up the pocket in each aubergine, add 1 teaspoon of stuffing and press together to hold it in place.

3 Pack the aubergines into the sterilized jar with the garlic, chillies, and vine leaves (if using). Fill the jar with cold water, then drain it off into a measuring jug. Add 1½ teaspoons salt for every 500ml (17fl oz) water, stirring until the salt has dissolved. Add the vinegar, then pour into the jar and weight down (see page 166).

4 Cover the jar with a clean cloth and leave in a warm, well-ventilated place for 1–3 weeks, until fermentation has finished (see Brined Cucumbers, page 128). Seal the jar and keep refrigerated. The aubergines are ready immediately.

VARIATION

PICKLED AUBERGINES AND BEETROOT
Pickle the aubergines without the stuffing and add 1 thinly sliced raw beetroot, 6 coarsely chopped cloves of garlic, and 2–3 chopped fresh red chillies to the jar.

TIPS
• **Choose firm aubergines with taut, shiny, unblemished skin.**
• **The cider vinegar and the vine leaves help speed up the fermentation process in the jar.**

This deliciously fragrant pickle probably originated in Syria. It is still made in one form or another all over the Middle East.

Aubergine and Garlic Chutney

☆ **DEGREE OF DIFFICULTY** EASY   **COOKING TIME** 1–1¼ HOURS   **SPECIAL EQUIPMENT** NON-CORROSIVE PRESERVING PAN; STERILIZED JARS WITH VINEGAR-PROOF SEALANTS (SEE PAGES 12–13)   **YIELD** ABOUT 1.5KG (3LB)   **SHELF LIFE** 1 YEAR   **SERVING SUGGESTIONS** IDEAL WITH CHICKEN CURRY AND CHEESE, OR IN SANDWICHES

INGREDIENTS

1kg (2lb) aubergines, cut into
2.5cm (1in) cubes
2 tbsp salt
3 tbsp groundnut, olive, or sesame oil
1 tbsp nigella seeds
3 tbsp sesame seeds
4 heads garlic, peeled
250g (8oz) shallots, quartered
2–3 red or green chillies, deseeded
and coarsely chopped
750ml (1¼ pints) cider vinegar
or white wine vinegar
150g (5oz) soft brown sugar
3 tsp sweet paprika
small bunch of mint, chopped
(optional)

1 Put the aubergine cubes in a colander and sprinkle with half the salt. Mix well and leave to drain for 1 hour. Rinse well and pat dry with paper towels.

2 Heat the oil in the preserving pan, add the nigella and sesame seeds, and cook for a minute or two, until the sesame seeds start to pop.

3 Add the aubergine, garlic, shallots, and chillies to the pan and cook, stirring frequently, for about 5 minutes.

4 Add the vinegar and bring to the boil, then reduce the heat and simmer for 15 minutes, until the aubergines are soft. Add the sugar, paprika, and remaining salt, stirring until they have dissolved.

5 Increase the heat slightly and cook, stirring frequently, for 45 minutes–1 hour, until most of the liquid has evaporated and the mixture is thick. Add the mint, if using, and remove the pan from the heat.

6 Ladle the mixture into the hot sterilized jars, then seal. The chutney is ready to eat in 1 month but improves with keeping.

This soft, melt-in-the-mouth chutney combines the mild taste of aubergine with the wonderful aroma of garlic. Use large, firm, light-purple aubergines if possible.

Aubergine Preserve

☆☆ **DEGREE OF DIFFICULTY** MODERATE **COOKING TIME** 1¾–2¼ HOURS **SPECIAL EQUIPMENT** PRESERVING PAN; STERILIZED JARS AND SEALANTS (SEE PAGES 12–13) **YIELD** ABOUT 1.5KG (3LB)

SHELF LIFE 2 YEARS (THE PRESERVE MAY CRYSTALLIZE IN THIS TIME, BUT IT WILL STILL BE FINE TO EAT)

SERVING SUGGESTION SERVE AS A SWEETMEAT, MOROCCAN-STYLE

INGREDIENTS

1kg (2lb) baby aubergines

4 tbsp salt

1kg (2lb) preserving or granulated sugar

juice of 3 large lemons

rind of 1 lemon, cut into fine matchsticks

75g (2½oz) fresh ginger root, finely shredded

12 cloves

2 cinnamon sticks

1 Remove the green crown from around the stalk of each aubergine but leave the stalk attached. Prick each aubergine in a few places with a wooden cocktail stick.

2 Put the aubergines in a large glass bowl and sprinkle with the salt. Mix well, then cover and leave to stand for a few hours. Rinse thoroughly under cold running water.

3 Bring a large pan of water to the boil and add the rinsed aubergines. Return to the boil, then reduce the heat and simmer for 5 minutes. Lift out the aubergines and drain well.

4 Put the sugar and lemon juice in the preserving pan. Bring to the boil, stirring until the sugar has dissolved, then skim well. Add the lemon rind, ginger, cloves, and cinnamon sticks, and boil for 5 minutes.

5 Gently slide the aubergines into the boiling syrup. Reduce the heat and simmer very gently, stirring occasionally, for 1½–2 hours or until the aubergines have absorbed about half the syrup and look translucent.

6 Gently lift the aubergines out one at a time with a slotted spoon. Transfer to the hot sterilized jars. Return the syrup to the boil, pour it into the jars, then seal. The preserve is ready to eat immediately but improves with keeping.

TIPS
• Select very small, unblemished aubergines.
• If you do not like whole spices in your preserve, tie them in a piece of muslin (see Spice Bags, page 31), which can be lifted out at the end of cooking.

This unusual recipe comes from Morocco and makes a surprisingly fragrant sweet preserve. Traditionally, it is eaten by the spoonful and served with steaming hot tea or coffee and a glass of water.

Aubergines Preserved in Oil

☆☆ **DEGREE OF DIFFICULTY** MODERATE 🍲 **COOKING TIME** ABOUT 10 MINUTES

🍴 **SPECIAL EQUIPMENT** STEAMER; 1.5 LITRE (2½ PINT) WIDE-NECKED, STERILIZED JAR WITH SEALANT

(SEE PAGES 12–13); THERMOMETER 🫙 **YIELD** ABOUT 1KG (2LB) 🫙 **SHELF LIFE** 6 MONTHS

🥄 **SERVING SUGGESTIONS** SERVE AS PART OF A MEZE OR JUST WITH DRINKS

INGREDIENTS

*1kg (2lb) baby aubergines,
stalks removed*

salt

75g (2½oz) pecan halves

2 lemons, finely sliced into semi-circles

6 garlic cloves, cut into tiny slivers

500ml (17fl oz) olive oil, to cover

1 Steam the aubergines for 5–7 minutes or until just soft. Leave to cool.

2 Make a pocket in each aubergine by cutting a deep slit lengthways. Sprinkle the inside of the pocket with a tiny pinch of salt, then place a pecan half, a slice of lemon, and a sliver of garlic in each. Secure with a wooden cocktail stick.

3 Pack the aubergines into the warm sterilized jar. If there are any slices of lemon and garlic left over, arrange them between the aubergines.

4 Heat the olive oil in a pan until it reaches 80°C (176°F). Pour it carefully into the jar, making sure the aubergines are completely covered, then seal. The aubergines will be ready to eat in 3–4 weeks.

An adaptation of a Lebanese recipe, this makes an unusual and very fragrant preserve. Aubergines acquire an amazingly soft, melt-in-the-mouth texture when preserved this way. The oil left in the jar is superb for dressing salads.

Basil Oil

☆ **DEGREE OF DIFFICULTY** EASY **COOKING TIME** 3–4 MINUTES 🍴 **SPECIAL EQUIPMENT** THERMOMETER;

1 LITRE (1¾ PINT) STERILIZED JAR OR BOTTLE WITH SEALANT (SEE PAGES 12–13) **YIELD** ABOUT 1 LITRE (1¾ PINTS)

🏺 **SHELF LIFE** 1 YEAR, FILTERED 🔪 **SERVING SUGGESTIONS** USE TO FLAVOUR SALADS, SAUCES, AND SOUPS

INGREDIENTS

1 litre (1 ¾ pints) light olive oil

150g (5oz) basil

1 Heat the oil gently in a pan until it reaches 40°C (104°F).

2 Lightly bruise the basil and put it in the warm sterilized jar or bottle. Pour the warm oil into the jar, then seal. The oil will be ready to use in 3–4 weeks.

Bruising the basil leaves encourages the release of their fragrant aroma

TIP
Basil leaves tend to become slimy after 3–4 months' maceration, so if you plan to keep the oil for longer than a few weeks, it is best to filter it (see page 21). Re-bottle the oil and seal before storing.

Use herb-flavoured oils to dress salads or give an extra lift to soups and stews just before serving. Basil oil is especially fragrant, but rosemary with coriander and thyme with lemon are equally good.

Gooseberry Vinegar

 DEGREE OF DIFFICULTY EASY **COOKING TIME** 3–4 MINUTES **SPECIAL EQUIPMENT** FOOD PROCESSOR; STERILIZED JELLY BAG; STERILIZED BOTTLES WITH VINEGAR-PROOF SEALANTS (SEE PAGES 12–13) **YIELD** ABOUT 2 LITRES (3½ PINTS) **SHELF LIFE** 2 YEARS **SERVING SUGGESTIONS** USE TO DRESS FISH DISHES AND SAUCES

INGREDIENTS

1.25 litres (2 pints) cider vinegar

1kg (2lb) tart gooseberries

150g (5oz) sorrel or spinach

a few strips of lemon rind

1 Bring the vinegar to the boil in a non-corrosive pan, and boil rapidly for 1–2 minutes. Remove from the heat and leave to cool.

2 Wash the gooseberries and sorrel or spinach, then drain well. Put them in the food processor and coarsely chop.

3 Transfer to a large jar and add the lemon rind. Pour in the vinegar, then cover with a clean cloth and leave in a warm place for 3–4 weeks, shaking the jar from time to time.

4 Strain through the jelly bag, then filter (see page 21). Pour into the sterilized bottles, then seal. The vinegar may be cloudy at first, but the sediment should settle after a few weeks.

Salad Vinegar

 DEGREE OF DIFFICULTY EASY **COOKING TIME** 3–4 MINUTES **SPECIAL EQUIPMENT** THERMOMETER; 2 × 500ML (17FL OZ) STERILIZED BOTTLES WITH VINEGAR-PROOF SEALANTS (SEE PAGES 12–13) **YIELD** ABOUT 1 LITRE (1¾ PINTS) **SHELF LIFE** 2 YEARS **SERVING SUGGESTION** USE TO MAKE SALAD DRESSINGS

INGREDIENTS

1 litre (1¾ pints) white wine vinegar or cider vinegar

2 sprigs tarragon

2 sprigs thyme

2 fresh or dried red chillies (optional)

2 garlic cloves, peeled and bruised

2 tsp black peppercorns

1 Put the vinegar in a non-corrosive pan. Bring to the boil, and boil rapidly for 1–2 minutes. Remove from the heat and leave to cool to 40°C (104°F).

2 Wash the herbs only if necessary, then dry well and bruise by crushing them lightly with the flat side of a wide-bladed knife. Make a long slit in each chilli, if using.

3 Divide the tarragon, thyme, chillies, garlic, and black peppercorns evenly between the sterilized bottles. Pour in the warm vinegar, then seal. Shake the bottles occasionally during storage to blend the ingredients. The vinegar will be ready to use in about 3 weeks.

VARIATION

PROVENÇAL HERB VINEGAR
Use 3–4 sprigs each of rosemary, lavender, and thyme, with flowering heads if possible, and prepare following the method for the main recipe. Use this vinegar to enhance the flavour of strawberries and other fruit.

TIP
You can greatly improve this vinegar with long maturation, about 2–3 years, after which it should be filtered (see page 21) and used sparingly.

Thyme gives off a warm, earthy, peppery perfume and adds a spicy cleanliness to this vinegar.

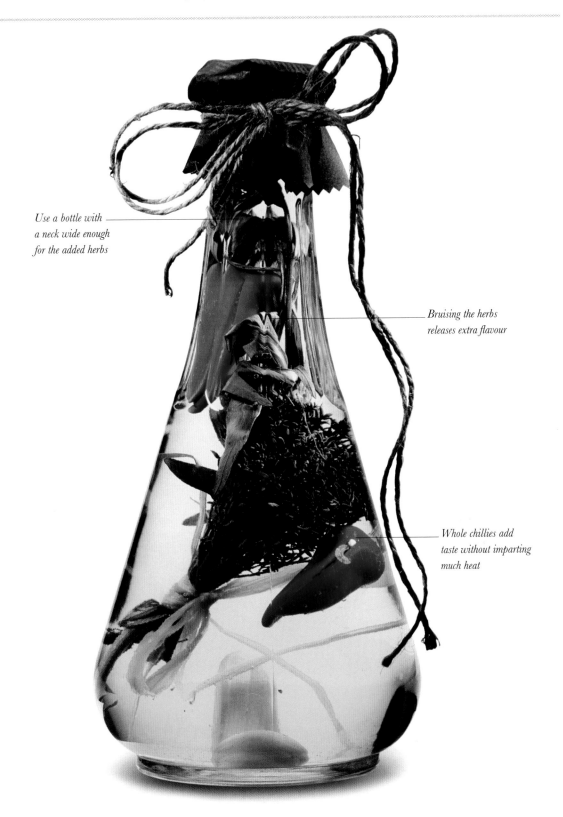

*Use a bottle with
a neck wide enough
for the added herbs*

*Bruising the herbs
releases extra flavour*

*Whole chillies add
taste without imparting
much heat*

Autumn

Seasonal Ingredients

For many of us, autumn brings back memories of harvest festivals at school and the abundance of new crops. Squashes and warming foods – onions and chillies, for example – come into season as we say goodbye to the last of the summer. Classic preserving produce such as raspberries and apples also make an appearance. Here are some of my favourite ingredients for preserving in autumn.

GREEN TOMATOES
Firmer and less sweet than red tomatoes, the green variety can still be used in much the same way, giving a different visual effect.

RASPBERRIES
The surprisingly long growing season of raspberries means they are still readily available for use well into the autumn.

GRAPES
Jellies made from grapes are real favourites, but grapes can also be used in pickles, chutneys, and syrups.

APPLES
Their high pectin level makes apples ideal for jellies and jams. They are essential in chutneys and relishes, too.

FIGS
There is always a touch of the exotic about figs, and this versatile fruit is a welcome ingredient in all manner of preserving techniques.

CHILLIES
The heat of a chilli is enough to perk up a dull autumn day – ideal in a jam or a chutney.

ONIONS
Warm yourself through the autumn with some heat-giving onions, whether in pickles, chutneys, or even jams.

MARROW
Commonly used as a key element in chutneys and pickles, marrow can also be employed in jams and jellies.

ARTICHOKES
Popular across the Mediterranean, artichokes are best when preserved in oil but can also be pickled.

SWEETCORN
Relishes just wouldn't be the same without sweetcorn, but this ingredient can add a little bite to a pickle, too.

PUMPKIN
This autumnal squash can be used for so much more than Halloween decoration. Pickles, chutneys, jams, and jellies are all viable pumpkin preserves.

Minted Apple Jelly

 DEGREE OF DIFFICULTY EASY **COOKING TIME** ABOUT 1¼ HOURS **SPECIAL EQUIPMENT** PRESERVING PAN; STERILIZED JELLY BAG; SUGAR THERMOMETER; STERILIZED JARS AND SEALANTS (SEE PAGES 12–13)

 YIELD ABOUT 1.25KG (2½LB) **SHELF LIFE** 2 YEARS **SERVING SUGGESTION** WONDERFUL WITH LAMB

INGREDIENTS

small bunch of mint

a few strips of lemon rind

1kg (2lb) apples, coarsely chopped

1.75 litres (3 pints) water or dry cider

preserving or granulated sugar

juice of 1 lemon

3–4 tbsp finely chopped mint

a little brandy, to seal

1 Tie the mint and lemon rind together with string. Put in the preserving pan with the apples and 1.25 litres (2 pints) of the water or cider.

2 Bring to the boil, then simmer, stirring occasionally, for about 25 minutes or until the apples are pulpy. Pour into the sterilized jelly bag (see page 17). Leave for 2–3 hours, until it stops dripping.

3 Remove the pulp from the jelly bag and return it to the cleaned pan. Add the remaining water or cider. Bring to the boil, then simmer for 20 minutes. Drain through the jelly bag as before.

4 Combine the two batches of juice and measure it. Allow 500g (1lb) sugar for every 500ml (17fl oz) juice. Pour the juice into the cleaned preserving pan, and add the lemon juice.

5 Bring to the boil, and boil for about 10 minutes. Add the sugar, stirring until it has dissolved, and boil rapidly for 8–10 minutes or until the setting point is reached (see page 16).

6 Remove the pan from the heat, and allow to cool for about 10 minutes. Stir in the chopped mint, then pour into the hot sterilized jars and leave to cool completely. Cover each jar with a waxed paper disc dipped in a little brandy, then seal.

TIP
Core the apples if you are using a food processor, since broken pips can impart a bitter flavour to the jelly. But put the cores in the pan with the apples, because they contain a lot of pectin.

Apples are nature's gift to jelly-makers, since they contain just the right balance of acidity and pectin to give a good set. Pure apple jelly can be insipid, so enliven the flavour with ingredients such as fragrant tea leaves or herbs.

Apple Chutney

☆ **DEGREE OF DIFFICULTY** EASY  **COOKING TIME** 45 MINUTES–1 HOUR 🍴 **SPECIAL EQUIPMENT** NON-CORROSIVE PRESERVING PAN; STERILIZED JARS WITH VINEGAR-PROOF SEALANTS (SEE PAGES 12–13) 🫙 **YIELD** ABOUT 2KG (4LB) 🫙 **SHELF LIFE** 1 YEAR 🔪 **SERVING SUGGESTIONS** SERVE WITH CHEESE, OR SPREAD ON BREAD AND BUTTER

INGREDIENTS

1.25kg (2½lb) underripe cooking apples (windfalls are good), peeled, cored, and coarsely chopped

625g (1¼lb) onions, coarsely chopped

2 lemons, finely sliced into semi-circles

300g (10oz) raisins

2 garlic cloves, finely chopped (optional)

500ml (17fl oz) cider vinegar

400g (13oz) dark molasses sugar

1 tbsp salt

1 tsp ground ginger

1 tsp ground cinnamon

1 tsp ground turmeric

1 Put the apples, onions, lemons, raisins, garlic (if using), and vinegar in the preserving pan. Bring to the boil, then simmer for 15–20 minutes, until the apples soften but still retain some texture.

2 Add the sugar, stirring until it has dissolved. Simmer for 30–45 minutes, until most of the liquid has evaporated and the mixture is thick. Remove from the heat. Add the salt and spices.

3 Ladle into the hot sterilized jars, then seal. The chutney will be ready to eat in 1 month.

This is a classic, mild, fruity British chutney. Try it with a combination of apples and pears, instead of just apples, too.

Apple and Pineapple Jelly

☆☆ **DEGREE OF DIFFICULTY** MODERATE 🍲 **COOKING TIME** ABOUT 1½ HOURS 🍴 **SPECIAL EQUIPMENT** PRESERVING PAN; STERILIZED JELLY BAG; SUGAR THERMOMETER; STERILIZED JARS AND SEALANTS (SEE PAGES 12–13) 🫙 **YIELD** ABOUT 1.25KG (2½ LB) 🫙 **SHELF LIFE** 2 YEARS 🚫 **SERVING SUGGESTION** USE AS A GLAZE FOR COOKED HAMS OR FRUIT TARTS

INGREDIENTS

1 small pineapple, about
500g (1lb), sliced

500g (1lb) apples, sliced

2 oranges, sliced

1.5 litres (2½ pints) water

preserving or granulated sugar

1 Put all the ingredients, except the sugar, in the preserving pan. Bring slowly to the boil, then reduce the heat and simmer for 30 minutes or until the fruit is soft and pulpy.

2 Pour the fruit and liquid into the sterilized jelly bag (see page 17). Drain for 2–3 hours or until it stops dripping.

3 Remove the fruit pulp from the jelly bag, return it to the pan, and add enough cold water to cover. Bring to the boil, then simmer for 30 minutes.

4 Drain through the jelly bag as before. Combine the two batches of juice and measure it. Allow 500g (1lb) sugar for every 500ml (17fl oz) juice.

5 Put the juice and sugar in the cleaned pan. Bring slowly to the

boil, stirring until the sugar has dissolved. Boil for a few minutes, then reduce the heat and skim well. Return to the boil, and boil rapidly for 10–12 minutes or until the setting point is reached (see page 16).

6 Remove the pan from the heat, leave the jelly to settle for a few minutes, and skim very well. Pour the liquid jelly into the hot sterilized jars, then seal.

VARIATION
QUINCE JELLY
Put 1kg (2lb) quinces and 1.25 litres (2 pints) water in the preserving pan. Bring to the boil, then simmer gently for 1–1½ hours. Top up with boiling water, if necessary, to keep the fruit covered. Strain through the jelly bag and return the pulp to the pan as for the main recipe. In step 5, add the juice of 2 lemons to the quince juice and sugar. Bring to the boil, and boil rapidly for 1–2 minutes, skim well, then return to a rapid boil for 10–15 minutes or until the setting point is reached. Pot as above. Serve with game and other dark meat.

There is no need to peel and core the fruit to make this clear, bright-yellow jelly. If you wish, you can add 1½ tablespoons of coriander seeds to the jelly in step 1.

Grape Jam

☆ **DEGREE OF DIFFICULTY** EASY **COOKING TIME** 1¼–1¾ HOURS **SPECIAL EQUIPMENT** PRESERVING PAN; STERILIZED JARS AND SEALANTS (SEE PAGES 12–13) **YIELD** ABOUT 1.25KG (2½ LB) **SHELF LIFE** 2 YEARS

 SERVING SUGGESTION USE AS A TOPPING FOR A STEAMED SPONGE PUDDING

INGREDIENTS

1kg (2lb) seedless green or red grapes

2 lemons, thinly sliced

750g (1½lb) preserving or granulated sugar

100g (3½oz) pecan nuts, lightly toasted

75ml (3fl oz) brandy

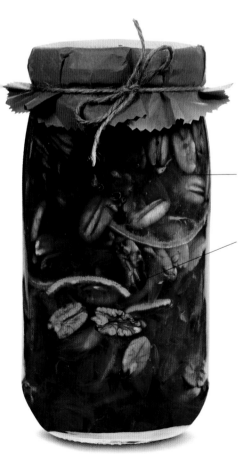

— *Toasted pecan nuts add a crunchy texture*

— *Thin slices of lemon give the jam a tangy note*

1 Put the grapes, lemon slices, and sugar in the preserving pan. Mix well, cover, and leave to stand for a few hours, until the juices start to run.

2 Bring to the boil, then cook over a moderate heat for 1–1½ hours, stirring frequently to prevent it from sticking to the bottom of the pan.

3 There is no need to test this jam for the setting point; it is ready when it is thick enough for a wooden spoon drawn through the centre of the mixture to leave a clear channel.

4 Remove the pan from the heat and leave the jam to settle for a few minutes. (This stops the fruit sinking to the bottom of the jar.) Stir in the pecan nuts and brandy. Ladle the jam into the hot sterilized jars, then seal.

VARIATIONS

- Other fruit – such as figs, fresh dates, plums, peaches, and apricots – can be prepared in the same way.
- Toasted walnuts or whole almonds can be used instead of pecan nuts.
- Use 3 oranges instead of the lemon, and add rum or an orange-flavoured liqueur in place of the brandy.
- For extra flavour, add 2–3 tablespoons orange-flower water.

This is a rich confection, crunchy with nuts. Jams like this are an essential part of the traditional Middle Eastern welcoming ceremony, when they are eaten with a spoon and accompanied by a glass of cold water.

Raspberry Jelly

 DEGREE OF DIFFICULTY MODERATE **COOKING TIME** 45–55 MINUTES

SPECIAL EQUIPMENT FOOD PROCESSOR; PRESERVING PAN; STERILIZED JELLY BAG; SUGAR THERMOMETER; STERILIZED

JARS AND SEALANTS (SEE PAGES 12–13) **YIELD** ABOUT 2KG (4LB) **SHELF LIFE** 2 YEARS

SERVING SUGGESTIONS GOOD WITH COLD LAMB AND CHICKEN

INGREDIENTS

1kg (2lb) raspberries

500g (1lb) cooking apples

500ml (17fl oz) water

preserving or granulated sugar

juice of 1 lemon

scented geranium leaves (optional)

a little brandy, to seal

1 Pick over the raspberries, washing them only if necessary. Remove the cores from the apples and set aside. Coarsely chop the apples.

2 Put the raspberries and apples in a food processor, and process until finely chopped. (You will probably need to do this in batches.)

3 Put the fruit and cores in a preserving pan, with water to cover. Bring to the boil, then simmer for 20–30 minutes, until the fruit is soft and pulpy.

TIP
Chopping the fruit in a food processor means that it requires less cooking, resulting in a jelly with a fresher, fruitier flavour.

4 Pour the fruit and liquid into a sterilized jelly bag suspended over a large bowl. Leave for 2–3 hours or until it stops dripping. Do not be tempted to squeeze the bag, or the jelly will be cloudy.

5 Measure the juice and allow 500g (1lb) sugar for every 500ml (17fl oz) juice. Return the juice to the cleaned pan, and add the sugar and lemon juice.

6 Heat gently, stirring from time to time with a wooden spoon, until the sugar has dissolved, then bring the liquid to a rapid boil.

Once the mixture has come to a rolling boil, froth will start to form on top as impurities rise to the surface

7 Skim well with a slotted spoon to remove the froth. Boil rapidly until the setting point is reached (see page 16), starting to check after about 10 minutes.

8 Ladle the jelly through a jam funnel into hot sterilized jars. Leave to cool until semi-set, then insert a geranium leaf into the centre of each jar. Cover each jar with a waxed paper disc dipped in a little brandy, then seal.

RASPBERRIES

Like all soft summer fruit, raspberries are full of flavour and make
excellent preserves. For use in jellies and jams, pick slightly underripe
fruit to ensure a high pectin content. To make raspberry vinegar, use
fully ripe fruit and follow the strawberry vinegar recipe on page 60.

Pumpkin Marmalade

☆ **DEGREE OF DIFFICULTY** EASY **COOKING TIME** ABOUT 1¼ HOURS **SPECIAL EQUIPMENT** PRESERVING PAN; STERILIZED JARS AND SEALANTS (SEE PAGES 12–13) **YIELD** ABOUT 1.75KG (3½ LB) **SHELF LIFE** 2 YEARS
 SERVING SUGGESTIONS SERVE FOR BREAKFAST OR WITH SCONES AND CREAM, OR USE AS A FLAN FILLING

INGREDIENTS

1.5kg (3lb) pumpkin

1 litre (1¾ pints) water

2 oranges, sliced into thin semi-circles

3 lemons, sliced into thin semi-circles

100g (3½oz) fresh ginger root, finely shredded

1kg (2lb) preserving or granulated sugar

1 Peel the pumpkin and remove all the seeds and fibres. Slice the flesh into pieces and grate coarsely lengthways, so the strands are as long as possible.

2 Put the grated pumpkin in the preserving pan with the water, oranges, lemons, and ginger. Bring to the boil, then simmer for 25–30 minutes or until the citrus peel is just soft.

3 Add the sugar, stirring until it has dissolved. Return to the boil, then cook over a medium heat for 25–30 minutes or until the mixture is thick enough for a wooden spoon drawn through the centre to leave a clear channel.

4 Remove the pan from the heat and leave the fruit to settle for a few minutes. Ladle the marmalade into the hot sterilized jars, then seal.

During autumn, pumpkins appear on the market in all sizes, shapes, and hues. Pumpkin is particularly good for making jams and marmalades because it absorbs sugar beautifully.

Orange and lemon slices impart a more traditional edge to this lesser-known marmalade

Fresh ginger adds a hot, tangy note that is rich and warming – perfect at the start of a cold day

Marrow and Ginger Preserve

☆ **DEGREE OF DIFFICULTY** EASY 🍲 **COOKING TIME** 2½–2¾ HOURS 🍴 **SPECIAL EQUIPMENT** PRESERVING PAN; STERILIZED JARS AND SEALANTS (SEE PAGES 12–13) 🫙 **YIELD** ABOUT 1.5KG (3LB) 🫙 **SHELF LIFE** 2 YEARS

🍽 **SERVING SUGGESTIONS** CHOP FINELY AND ADD TO FRUIT CAKES, OR SERVE AS A TOPPING FOR ICE CREAM

INGREDIENTS

1.5kg (3lb) marrow, peeled, cored, and cut into 4cm (1½in) cubes

1kg (2lb) preserving or granulated sugar

500ml (17fl oz) water

juice of 1 lemon

5cm (2in) piece fresh ginger root, finely shredded

3–4 strips of lemon rind

1 tbsp orange-flower water (optional)

1 Put the cubed marrow in a large pan and add enough cold water to cover. Bring to the boil, then reduce the heat and simmer for 10–15 minutes or until the marrow just starts to soften. Drain thoroughly.

2 Put all the remaining ingredients in the preserving pan. Bring to the boil, stirring until the sugar has dissolved. Boil for a few minutes, then add the marrow. Return to the boil, reduce the heat to minimum, and simmer very gently for 2–2½ hours or until the marrow is translucent.

3 Lift the marrow out of the pan with a slotted spoon. Transfer to the hot sterilized jars. Bring the syrup to a rapid boil, and boil for about 5 minutes.

4 Pour the syrup into the hot sterilized jars, then seal. The preserve is ready immediately but improves with keeping.

VARIATION

TURNIP PRESERVE
Replace the marrow with 1.5kg (3lb) peeled and cubed turnip. Cook following the main method.

This recipe is a perfect example of the magic of preserving: it transforms humble ingredients into a delicious and versatile product.

Marrow Chutney

 DEGREE OF DIFFICULTY EASY **COOKING TIME** 1½–2 HOURS ⚞ **SPECIAL EQUIPMENT** NON-CORROSIVE
PRESERVING PAN; STERILIZED JARS WITH VINEGAR-PROOF SEALANTS (SEE PAGES 12–13) 🝞 **YIELD** ABOUT 1.5KG (3LB)
🝞 **SHELF LIFE** 2 YEARS 🔪 **SERVING SUGGESTION** GOOD WITH CHEESE

INGREDIENTS

1kg (2lb) marrow, peeled, cored,
and cut into 2.5cm (1in) cubes

2 tbsp salt

2 large onions, coarsely chopped

300g (10oz) carrots, coarsely grated

100g (3½ oz) crystallized ginger,
coarsely chopped

1–2 fresh red chillies, finely chopped

2 tbsp black mustard seeds

1 tbsp ground turmeric

750ml (1¼ pints) cider vinegar

250g (8oz) sugar

1 Put the marrow in a colander and sprinkle with half the salt. Leave for 1 hour. Rinse and dry. Put in the preserving pan with the rest of the ingredients, except the sugar and remaining salt. Bring to the boil, then simmer for 25 minutes or until just soft.

2 Add the sugar and remaining salt, stirring until they have dissolved, then simmer for 1–1¼ hours, until most of the liquid has evaporated and the mixture is thick. Ladle into the hot sterilized jars, then seal. The chutney will be ready in 1 month.

TIP
If using a very large marrow, remember to remove the seeds and soft centre.

Green Tomato Chutney

 DEGREE OF DIFFICULTY EASY **COOKING TIME** ABOUT 1 HOUR ❚❙ **SPECIAL EQUIPMENT** NON-CORROSIVE
PRESERVING PAN; STERILIZED JARS WITH VINEGAR-PROOF SEALANTS (SEE PAGES 12–13) **YIELD** ABOUT 1.5KG (3LB)
SHELF LIFE 1 YEAR **SERVING SUGGESTIONS** AS AN ACCOMPANIMENT TO MATURE CHEESE OR ON SANDWICHES

INGREDIENTS

750g (1½lb) green tomatoes

500g (1lb) cooking apples

250g (8oz) onions, coarsely chopped

1 tbsp salt

125g (4oz) raisins

*500g (1lb) light soft brown
or white sugar*

250ml (8fl oz) cider vinegar

grated rind and juice of 2 large lemons

2 tbsp black or yellow mustard seeds

*2–3 fresh red chillies, deseeded and
chopped (optional)*

FOR THE SPICE BAG (SEE PAGE 31)

1 tbsp coriander seeds

2 tsp black peppercorns

2 tsp allspice berries

1 tsp cloves

2 cinnamon sticks, crushed

TIP
Green tomatoes are
notoriously difficult to
peel, so if you do not
mind skin in your
chutney, there is no
need to peel them.

1 Skin the tomatoes, if desired, then coarsely chop. Peel, core, and chop the apples. Add the peel and cores to the spice bag. Put the tomatoes, apples, onions, and salt in the preserving pan. Bring the mixture slowly to the boil, then simmer for 20 minutes.

2 Add the raisins, sugar, vinegar, lemon rind and juice, and spice bag. Return to the boil, stirring until the sugar has dissolved, then simmer for 30 minutes, until most of the liquid has evaporated and the mixture is thick.

3 Add the mustard seeds and chillies, if using. Ladle the mixture into the hot sterilized jars, then seal. The chutney will be ready to eat in 1 month.

Fig Chutney

 DEGREE OF DIFFICULTY EASY **COOKING TIME** ABOUT 1¼ HOURS **SPECIAL EQUIPMENT** NON-CORROSIVE PRESERVING PAN; STERILIZED JARS WITH VINEGAR-PROOF SEALANTS (SEE PAGES 12–13) **YIELD** ABOUT 2KG (4LB) **SHELF LIFE** 1 YEAR **SERVING SUGGESTIONS** SERVE WITH CHEESE AND COLD MEATS, OR ADD TO HOT CURRIES

INGREDIENTS

1.25 litres (2 pints) red wine vinegar

500g (1lb) light soft brown sugar

2 tbsp salt

1kg (2lb) firm, slightly underripe black figs, sliced into rounds 1cm (½in) thick

500g (1lb) onions, sliced into thin rings

250g (8oz) pitted dates, coarsely chopped

150g (5oz) fresh ginger root, finely shredded

2 tbsp sweet paprika

1 tbsp white mustard seeds

3 tbsp chopped fresh tarragon or 1 tbsp dried tarragon

1 Put the vinegar, sugar, and salt in the preserving pan, stirring until the sugar and salt have dissolved. Bring to the boil, then simmer for about 5 minutes.

2 Add the figs, onions, dates, and spices. Bring to the boil, then simmer for 1 hour, until most of the liquid has evaporated and the mixture is thick.

3 Remove from the heat, add the tarragon, and mix well. Ladle into the hot sterilized jars, then seal. The chutney will be ready to eat in 1 month.

I found this unusual recipe in an anonymous Victorian cookery book. It makes a dark and delicious chutney and is an ideal way to use up unripe figs.

Fig Konfyt

☆☆☆ **DEGREE OF DIFFICULTY** ADVANCED **COOKING TIME** DAY 2, 40–45 MINUTES; DAY 3, 2¼–2¾ HOURS

SPECIAL EQUIPMENT PRESERVING PAN; STERILIZED JARS AND SEALANTS (SEE PAGES 12–13)

YIELD ABOUT 1KG (2LB) **SHELF LIFE** 2 YEARS **SERVING SUGGESTIONS** SERVE AS A SWEETMEAT
OR WITH CREAM AS A DESSERT; USE INSTEAD OF GLACÉ FRUIT TO DECORATE CAKES

INGREDIENTS

1kg (2lb) green, unripe figs

4 tbsp salt

1 tbsp bicarbonate of soda (optional)

*1kg (2lb) preserving or
granulated sugar*

125ml (4fl oz) water

1 Trim the stalk end off each fig, then, with a small sharp knife, cut a deep cross into the top.

2 Place the figs in a large glass bowl. Cover with cold water and add the salt. Mix well until the salt has dissolved, then weight down with a plate (see page 166) and leave to stand overnight.

3 The next day, bring a large pan of water to the boil with the bicarbonate of soda, if using. (It helps preserve a good green colour.) Drain the figs and add to the pan.

4 Return to the boil, then reduce the heat and simmer gently for 25–30 minutes or until the figs are just tender. Have ready a large bowl of very cold water and immediately transfer the figs to it. Leave to cool, then drain the figs well. Place them in the preserving pan.

5 Put the sugar and water in a separate pan. Bring to the boil, stirring until the sugar has dissolved, then skim well. Boil for 5 minutes, then pour over the figs. Weight down and leave overnight.

6 The next day, bring slowly to the boil, then simmer very gently for 2–2½ hours or until the figs look translucent. Lift them out of the syrup with a slotted spoon and arrange in the hot sterilized jars.

7 Return the syrup to the boil, and boil for 10 minutes, until it has the consistency of runny honey. Pour into the jars, then seal.

VARIATION
Add a 5cm (2in) piece fresh ginger root, finely shredded, to the sugar syrup in step 5.

This is a recipe from South Africa, where making rich preserves is a fine art. The figs should be mature but not ripe, or they will not withstand the cooking process.

Rich Mincemeat

☆ **DEGREE OF DIFFICULTY** EASY 🍴 **SPECIAL EQUIPMENT** STERILIZED JARS AND SEALANTS (SEE PAGES 12–13)

🫙 **YIELD** ABOUT 2.5KG (5LB) 🫙 **SHELF LIFE** 2 YEARS 🥄 **SERVING SUGGESTIONS** USE TO MAKE MINCE PIES

OR TARTS, OR TO FILL BAKED APPLES; FOR SHEER INDULGENCE, SERVE TOPPED WITH THICK CREAM

INGREDIENTS

300g (10oz) cooking apples, coarsely grated

200g (7oz) carrots, finely grated

125g (4oz) dried apricots, coarsely chopped

125g (4oz) prunes, coarsely chopped

125g (4oz) glacé cherries, coarsely chopped

125g (4oz) fresh ginger root, finely grated

250g (8oz) raisins

250g (8oz) sultanas

250g (8oz) currants

175g (6oz) mixed peel

grated rind and juice of 2 lemons

grated rind and juice of 2 oranges

125g (4oz) honey or molasses sugar

2–3 tbsp sweet masala or your favourite sweet spice mix

250ml (8fl oz) brandy, plus extra for the jars

1 Put all the ingredients in a large bowl and mix very well. Cover with a clean cloth and leave to stand in a warm kitchen for 2–3 days.

2 Pack the mincemeat tightly into the sterilized jars and cover with waxed paper discs. Pour 1–2 tablespoons of brandy into each jar, then seal.

3 Every 6 months or so, open the jars, pour a little brandy over the top, and reseal.

VARIATION

For a milder mincemeat, add a quarter of its weight in grated apples or quince or ground almonds, or a mixture of these, before use.

TIP
If possible, use whole candied citrus peel rather than ready-chopped peel, and cut it yourself. Of course, you could always make your own candied peel (see page 39).

With this vegetarian mincemeat, add either grated chilled butter or vegetarian suet – about 125g (4oz) per 1kg (2lb) – just before use.

Pumpkin Chutney

☆ **DEGREE OF DIFFICULTY** EASY 🍲 **COOKING TIME** 1¼–1½ HOURS 🍴 **SPECIAL EQUIPMENT** NON-CORROSIVE
PRESERVING PAN; STERILIZED JARS WITH VINEGAR-PROOF SEALANTS (SEE PAGES 12–13) 🏺 **YIELD** ABOUT 2KG (4LB)
🏺 **SHELF LIFE** 2 YEARS 🔪 **SERVING SUGGESTIONS** MIX A FEW LARGE TABLESPOONS OF CHUTNEY
WITH PLAIN BOILED RICE; SERVE WITH LAMB CURRY AND BASMATI RICE; OR SERVE WITH COLD MEATS AND CHEESE

INGREDIENTS

*1.25kg (2½lb) pumpkin,
peeled, deseeded, and cut into
2.5cm (1in) chunks*

*750g (1½lb) apples, peeled,
cored, and coarsely chopped*

*75g (2½oz) fresh ginger
root, finely shredded*

*3–4 fresh red chillies, deseeded
and sliced*

2 tbsp white mustard seeds

2 tbsp black mustard seeds

*1 litre (1¾ pints) cider vinegar
or distilled malt vinegar*

1 tbsp salt

*500g (1lb) white or light soft
brown sugar*

1 Cut the pumpkin into
quarters, then peel and
remove the seeds and fibres.
Cut the flesh into 2.5cm (1in)
cubes. (Do not throw away
the seeds – they make a
delicious, healthy snack.
Wash them well to remove
any fibres, then dry them in
the sun or a cool oven.)

2 Put the pumpkin in a
non-corrosive preserving pan
with the chopped apples, fresh
ginger, chillies, mustard seeds,
vinegar, and salt, and mix well.
If you prefer a hotter chutney,
do not deseed the chillies.

3 Bring to the boil, then reduce the heat and simmer gently for 20–25 minutes or until the pumpkin is just soft but not mushy. Stir occasionally to prevent it sticking. If the mixture seems dry, add a little more vinegar or water. Add the soft brown sugar, stirring until it has dissolved.

4 Bring the mixture back to the boil. Cook for 50–60 minutes, until the mixture is thick and most of the liquid has evaporated. Stir frequently to prevent it sticking.

Red chilli peppers help give this chutney a lovely spicy kick

5 Ladle through a funnel into hot sterilized jars, then seal immediately. The chutney will be ready to eat in about 3 weeks but improves with longer keeping. Store in a cool, dark place.

Tomato and Pear Relish

☆ **DEGREE OF DIFFICULTY** EASY **COOKING TIME** 1½–2 HOURS **SPECIAL EQUIPMENT** NON-CORROSIVE PRESERVING PAN; STERILIZED JARS WITH VINEGAR-PROOF SEALANTS (SEE PAGES 12–13) **YIELD** ABOUT 1.5KG (3LB) **SHELF LIFE** 6 MONTHS; 2 YEARS, HEAT PROCESSED **SERVING SUGGESTIONS** SERVE WITH HAMBURGERS, IN SANDWICHES, OR WITH GRILLED FISH OR MEAT

INGREDIENTS

1kg (2lb) beef or plum tomatoes, skinned, deseeded, and coarsely chopped

625g (1¼lb) pears, peeled, cored, and coarsely chopped

300g (10oz) shallots or onions, finely chopped

6 celery stalks with leaves, finely chopped

2–3 fresh red chillies, deseeded and finely chopped (optional)

1 tbsp yellow mustard seeds

1 tbsp sweet paprika

1 tbsp dill seeds

250ml (8fl oz) water

1 litre (1¾ pints) cider vinegar or red wine vinegar

200g (7oz) light soft brown or white sugar

1 tbsp salt

1 Put the tomatoes, pears, shallots or onions, celery, chillies (if using), yellow mustard seeds, paprika, dill seeds, and water in the preserving pan.

2 Bring to the boil and skim well. Reduce the heat and simmer, stirring frequently, for about 20 minutes or until the pears are soft and mushy.

3 Add the vinegar, sugar, and salt. Simmer, stirring occasionally, for 1–1½ hours or until most of the liquid has evaporated and the relish is thick.

4 Remove the pan from the heat. Ladle the relish into the hot sterilized jars, then seal. If wished, heat process, cool, and check the seals (see pages 14–15).

VARIATIONS

TOMATO AND QUINCE RELISH
Replace the chopped pears with the same quantity of quince. Increase the cooking time in step 2 to 30–35 minutes or until the quince are soft but not mushy.

TOMATO AND APPLE RELISH
Replace the chopped pears with the same quantity of chopped apples, and flavour with crushed coriander seeds instead of the dill.

While the United States is the home of the relish, this particular recipe comes from the west coast of Canada, where pears are used instead of the customary apples.

Corn and Pepper Relish

☆ **DEGREE OF DIFFICULTY** EASY **COOKING TIME** 45–60 MINUTES ❘❘ **SPECIAL EQUIPMENT** FOOD PROCESSOR; NON-CORROSIVE PRESERVING PAN; STERILIZED JARS WITH VINEGAR-PROOF SEALANTS (SEE PAGES 12–13) **YIELD** ABOUT 2½ KG (5LB)  **SHELF LIFE** 1 YEAR ◯ **SERVING SUGGESTIONS** SERVE WITH HAMBURGERS OR AT BARBECUES

INGREDIENTS

300g (10oz) white cabbage, hard core removed, coarsely chopped

300g (10oz) onions, roughly sliced

6 celery stalks, coarsely chopped

2 green peppers, coarsely chopped

2 red peppers, coarsely chopped

10 fresh corn cobs, kernels sliced off

1.25 litres (2 pints) cider vinegar

500g (1lb) light soft brown sugar

2 tbsp yellow mustard seeds

1 tbsp salt

TIP
If you like your relish hotter, add some sliced chillies to the chopped vegetables.

1 Finely chop the cabbage, onions, celery, and peppers in a food processor. Put all the ingredients in the preserving pan. Bring to the boil, then simmer for 45–60 minutes, until the corn is tender and the sauce thick.

2 Pour into the hot sterilized jars, pushing the mixture down with a spoon, so that the vegetables are covered by the sauce. Make sure there are no air pockets, then seal. The relish is ready immediately but improves with keeping.

Even more American than apple pie, this relish is often served with a good hamburger. It tastes clean, sweet, and sharp.

Pickled Onions

 DEGREE OF DIFFICULTY EASY   **COOKING TIME** 3–4 MINUTES   **SPECIAL EQUIPMENT** 1.5 LITRE (2½ PINT)

STERILIZED JAR WITH VINEGAR-PROOF SEALANT (SEE PAGES 12–13)   **YIELD** ABOUT 1KG (2LB)

SHELF LIFE 2 YEARS   **SERVING SUGGESTIONS** SERVE WITH COLD MEAT, FISH, AND

CHEESE, OR USE TO DECORATE QUICHES AND SAVOURY FLANS

INGREDIENTS

1.25kg (2½lb) silverskin
or pickling onions
salt
2 bay leaves

4 tsp mustard seeds
2–4 dried red chillies (optional)
perfumed vinegar, to cover
(see page 243)

WEIGHTING DOWN

The process of weighting down keeps the ingredients immersed under liquid, protecting them from the deteriorating effects of oxidation.

Use non-porous objects that can be sterilized easily, such as a water-filled glass bottle or jar, or glazed plate. When using a wide-necked jar, a mesh made of wooden skewers can be added to the top of the container to keep the contents submerged. After weighting down, check that the liquid covers the ingredients by at least 1cm (½in), and add more if necessary.

1 For easy peeling, pour boiling water over the onions and leave until cool enough to handle. Peel off the skins, and place the onions in a glass bowl.

2 Make enough strong brine to cover the onions, using 75g (2½oz) salt for each litre (1¾ pints) water. Pour this over the onions, weight down (see box above), and leave in a cool place for 24 hours.

3 The next day, rinse the onions well to remove the salt, and arrange in hot sterilized jars with the mustard seeds, bay leaves, and chillies (if using).

Tie the spice bag to the side of the pan for easy removal

4 To make a flavoured vinegar, prepare a spice bag (see page 31) and place in a non-corrosive pan with the vinegar of your choice. Bring to the boil, and boil for about 5 minutes. For a fuller flavour, leave to cool, then discard the spice bag and bring the vinegar to the boil once more.

5 Pour the boiling vinegar over the onions, making sure they are completely submerged in the pickling liquid. Weight down (see opposite) and seal the jars with vinegar-proof lids (see page 13). Store in a cool, dark place. The onions will be ready to eat in 3–4 weeks.

Fresh Onion Chutney

 DEGREE OF DIFFICULTY EASY   **YIELD** ABOUT 250G (8OZ)   **SHELF LIFE** I WEEK, REFRIGERATED

SERVING SUGGESTIONS SERVE WITH CURRIES, AS AN APPETIZER, OR AS A REFRESHING SALAD

INGREDIENTS

500g (1lb) large, sweet purple or white onions, sliced into thin rings

1 tbsp salt

1–2 fresh green or red chillies, deseeded and finely chopped

3 tbsp white wine vinegar or cider vinegar

2 tbsp chopped mint or coriander

1 tsp nigella seeds (optional)

1 Put the onion rings in a colander and sprinkle with the salt. Mix well and leave to drain for about 1 hour.

2 Squeeze the onion to extract as much moisture as possible, then mix with the rest of the ingredients and leave to stand for 1 hour, to let the flavour develop. The chutney is ready immediately.

TIP
Grated apples, quince, carrots, and turnips can be used instead of the onions.

This recipe belongs to a large family of fresh, salad-like chutneys that are served to refresh the palate and revive the appetite.

Onion Marmalade

 DEGREE OF DIFFICULTY EASY **COOKING TIME** 2¼–2¾ HOURS **SPECIAL EQUIPMENT** NON-CORROSIVE PRESERVING PAN; STERILIZED JARS AND VINEGAR-PROOF SEALANTS (SEE PAGES 12–13) **YIELD** ABOUT 1.5KG (3LB) **SHELF LIFE** 2 YEARS **SERVING SUGGESTIONS** SERVE WITH LAMB, MUTTON, OR GAME

INGREDIENTS

1.25kg (2 ½lb) onions, sliced into thin rings

3 tbsp salt

1kg (2lb) preserving or granulated sugar

500ml (17fl oz) vinegar

1 ½ tsp cloves tied in a piece of muslin

2 tsp caraway seeds

1 Sprinkle the onions with the salt. Mix well and leave to stand for 1 hour. Rinse and dry.

2 Put the sugar, vinegar, and muslin bag in the preserving pan. Bring to the boil, then simmer for 5 minutes. Add the onions and caraway seeds. Return to the boil, skim, reduce the heat to minimum, and cook for 2–2 ½ hours, or until the syrup is thick and the onions are translucent and golden brown.

3 Remove the pan from the heat and leave the onions to settle for a few minutes. Ladle the mixture into the hot sterilized jars, then seal. The marmalade is ready to eat immediately but improves with keeping.

This unusual sweet preserve is exceptionally good. Remarkably, it does not taste of onions but has a sharp, refreshing flavour. I sometimes add dried mint to it.

ARTICHOKES

Popular all across the Mediterranean, globe artichokes are a great delicacy and are at their best when preserved in oil; see page 172 for the recipe. They can be served as an antipasto, with avocado or mozzarella cheese salads.

Preserved Artichokes

☆☆ **DEGREE OF DIFFICULTY** MODERATE **SPECIAL EQUIPMENT** 1 LITRE (1¾ PINT) WIDE-NECKED, STERILIZED JAR WITH SEALANT (SEE PAGES 12–13) **YIELD** ABOUT 750G (1½LB) **SHELF LIFE** 2 YEARS **SERVING SUGGESTIONS** SERVE AS PART OF AN ANTIPASTI SELECTION, OR SLICE AND SERVE WITH PASTA

INGREDIENTS

2 large lemons

1½ tbsp salt

1 tbsp finely chopped thyme

1.5kg (3lb) young globe artichokes

500ml (17fl oz) mild olive, groundnut, or refined sesame oil

TIP
If you are lucky enough to find baby artichokes for this recipe, just remove any tough outer leaves and cut them in half. The tender choke can be left in.

1 Grate the rind from 1 of the lemons and squeeze the juice from both of them. Keep the squeezed-out lemon halves.

2 Put the lemon juice and rind, salt, and thyme in a large glass bowl and mix well until the salt has dissolved.

3 Trim the artichoke stalks and peel off the leaves to expose the heart (see steps 1 and 2, below). Rub the flesh with the lemon halves. Scrape out the choke with a pointed spoon (see step 3, below).

4 If the artichoke hearts are large, cut them in half lengthways. As you finish preparing each artichoke, add it to the lemon mixture, turning to coat. Leave for 30 minutes.

5 Pack the artichokes into the sterilized jar. Whisk the oil with the lemon juice left over from marinating the artichokes and pour into the jar, making sure the vegetables are covered, then seal. They will be ready in 6–8 weeks. Occasionally shake the jar to mix the ingredients.

Globe artichokes are popular throughout the Mediterranean, where they are eaten raw in salads, cooked in casseroles, and preserved.

PREPARING THE ARTICHOKES

1 Cut off the stalk as close to the head as possible, then peel off the leaves, rubbing the exposed flesh with the reserved lemon half to prevent browning.

2 Trim the artichoke heart with a paring knife to remove any remaining tough areas. As before, rub any cut surfaces with the lemon half.

3 Spoon out and discard the fluffy choke from the centre using a grapefruit spoon, then place the hearts in the lemon mixture.

Pear and Tomato Cheese

☆ **DEGREE OF DIFFICULTY** EASY 🍲 **COOKING TIME** 2–2½ HOURS 🍴 **SPECIAL EQUIPMENT** PRESERVING PAN; STERILIZED JARS AND SEALANTS (SEE PAGES 12–13) OR INDIVIDUAL JELLY MOULDS, OILED **YIELD** ABOUT 1.25KG (2½LB)

🏺 **SHELF LIFE** 2 YEARS IN SEALED JARS 🥄 **SERVING SUGGESTIONS** GOOD WITH COLD ROAST MEATS, ESPECIALLY TURKEY, OR SPREAD ON BREAD

INGREDIENTS

1kg (2lb) plum tomatoes, coarsely chopped

750g (1½lb) ripe pears, cored and coarsely chopped

250g (8oz) apples, cored and coarsely chopped

1 lemon, coarsely chopped

500ml (17fl oz) water

preserving or granulated sugar

1 tsp freshly ground black pepper

1 tsp ground coriander

½ tsp ground cinnamon

¼ tsp ground cloves

1 Put the tomatoes, pears, apples, lemon, and water in the preserving pan. Bring to the boil, then reduce the heat and simmer for about 30 minutes, until the fruit is soft and mushy.

2 Press the mixture through a sieve or pass it through a food mill. Measure the resulting purée and allow 400g (13oz) sugar for every 500ml (17fl oz) purée.

3 Return the purée to the cleaned pan, and add the sugar and spices. Bring to the boil, then simmer, stirring frequently, for 1–1½ hours, until the mixture has reduced and become very thick.

4 Pour into the warm sterilized jars, then seal, or pack into the oiled moulds, leave to cool, then cover with clingfilm.

A curious combination of sweet and savoury, this cheese is traditionally made for the Christmas table. Instead of pears, either apples or quince can be used.

Mexican Chilli Sauce

☆☆ **DEGREE OF DIFFICULTY** MODERATE **COOKING TIME** ABOUT 1 HOUR **SPECIAL EQUIPMENT** FOOD PROCESSOR; NON-CORROSIVE PRESERVING PAN; STERILIZED BOTTLES WITH VINEGAR-PROOF SEALANTS OR CORKS (SEE PAGES 12–13) **YIELD** ABOUT 1 LITRE (1¾ PINTS) **SHELF LIFE** 1 YEAR, HEAT PROCESSED

 SERVING SUGGESTIONS USE TO ADD FLAVOUR TO STEWS, SOUPS, AND DIPS; ESPECIALLY GOOD WITH CHICKEN DISHES

INGREDIENTS

75–100g (2½–3½oz) chipotle chillies

1kg (2lb) plum tomatoes or other tomatoes, skinned and deseeded

300g (10oz) onions, sliced

4 garlic cloves, sliced

750ml (1¼ pints) cider vinegar or distilled malt vinegar

2 tbsp dark soft brown sugar

1 tbsp salt

1 tbsp ground coriander

1 tbsp arrowroot or cornflour

large bunch of coriander, chopped

1 Put the chillies in a bowl and pour over enough boiling water to cover them. Leave until the water is cold. Drain, reserving the water. Slit the chillies open lengthways, and remove the seeds with a knife.

2 Purée the chillies, tomatoes, onions, and garlic in the food processor. Place in the preserving pan, adding the water from soaking the chillies. Bring to the boil, then simmer for 30 minutes, or until slightly reduced.

3 Stir in the vinegar, sugar, salt, and ground coriander. Return to the boil, then simmer for 25–30 minutes, stirring, until the mixture has reduced by half.

4 Mix the arrowroot to a paste with a little water and stir into the pan. Add the coriander and cook for 1–2 minutes, stirring. Pour into the hot sterilized bottles, then seal. Heat process, cool, check the seals, and dip corks in wax (see pages 13–15). The sauce is ready immediately but improves after 3–4 weeks.

TIP
For an extra smooth sauce, pass the mixture through a fine sieve after step 3.

Chipotle chillies give this fiery sauce its characteristic smoky flavour. If they are not available, replace them with twice as many chargrilled fresh chillies.

Malay Chilli and Shallot Oil

☆ **DEGREE OF DIFFICULTY** EASY **COOKING TIME** ABOUT 23 MINUTES

SPECIAL EQUIPMENT FOOD PROCESSOR; STERILIZED BOTTLE WITH SEALANT (SEE PAGES 12–13)

YIELD ABOUT 1 LITRE (1¾ PINTS) **SHELF LIFE** 6 MONTHS

INGREDIENTS

100g (3½oz) dried chillies, stalks removed

325g (11oz) shallots, peeled

8–10 garlic cloves, peeled

1 litre (1¾ pints) groundnut or refined sesame oil

1 Put the dried chillies, whole shallots, and garlic in the food processor, and process until finely chopped.

2 Transfer the mixture to a pan and add the groundnut oil. Heat gently and cook for about 20 minutes or until the shallots are nicely browned.

3 Remove the pan from the heat and leave until the oil is cool. Filter the oil (see page 21), pour it into the sterilized bottle, then seal. The oil is ready to use immediately.

In Malaysia, this condiment appears on every table. With its wonderfully nutty, hot taste, it can be added to anything that needs extra flavour. Use in moderation to finish soups, stews, and rice dishes.

Chilli Oil

☆ **DEGREE OF DIFFICULTY** EASY 🍲 **COOKING TIME** ABOUT 18 MINUTES

🍴 **SPECIAL EQUIPMENT** FOOD PROCESSOR; THERMOMETER; STERILIZED BOTTLE WITH SEALANT (SEE PAGES 12–13)

🫙 **YIELD** ABOUT 1 LITRE (1¾ PINTS) 🫙 **SHELF LIFE** 1 YEAR

INGREDIENTS

100g (3½oz) red chillies

1 litre (1¾ pints) groundnut,
refined sesame, or corn oil

2 tbsp sweet or hot paprika

1 Remove the stalks from the chillies. Put them in the food processor, and process until chopped finely. Transfer the chillies to a pan and add the oil.

2 Heat the oil gently until it nearly reaches 120°C (248°F), then simmer for 15 minutes without letting the mixture get any hotter.

3 Remove from the heat, cool slightly and stir in the paprika. Leave to cool completely, then filter (see page 21). Pour into the sterilized bottle and seal. The oil is ready to use immediately.

Red hot and wonderfully versatile, a few drops of this oil will add fire to any dish.

TIP
Wear disposable household gloves when deseeding or chopping chillies. Alternatively, wash your hands well after handling them, and do not touch your eyes.

Schug

 DEGREE OF DIFFICULTY EASY **SPECIAL EQUIPMENT** MINCER OR FOOD PROCESSOR; SPICE MILL
OR COFFEE GRINDER; STERILIZED JARS AND SEALANTS (SEE PAGES 12–13) **YIELD** ABOUT 1KG (2LB)
SHELF LIFE 3 MONTHS, REFRIGERATED **SERVING SUGGESTION** USE AS A CONDIMENT

INGREDIENTS

1 large head garlic, peeled

750g (1 ½lb) fresh green chillies

150g (5oz) coriander
(about 2 bunches)

1 tbsp coriander seeds

2 tsp cumin seeds

2 tsp black peppercorns

1 tsp cardamom pods

1 tsp cloves

1 ½ tbsp salt

a little olive oil, to cover

1 Finely mince or chop the garlic, chillies, and fresh coriander in the mincer or food processor.

2 Grind all the spices to a fine powder in the spice mill or coffee grinder. Sieve into the chilli and garlic mixture, then stir in the salt and mix well.

3 Pack tightly into the sterilized jars. Cover with a thin layer of oil, then seal. Keep refrigerated. The schug is ready immediately.

TIP
If you prefer a milder version, replace half or more of the chillies with green peppers.

This is a fiercely hot chilli paste from Yemen, where it is used in a wide range of dishes. Extra chopped fresh coriander should be added just before serving.

Pâté de Campagne

☆☆ **DEGREE OF DIFFICULTY** MODERATE 🍲 **COOKING TIME** 1½–2 HOURS 🍴 **SPECIAL EQUIPMENT** MINCER; 2 x 1 LITRE (1½ PINT) TERRINES 🫙 **YIELD** ABOUT 2KG (4LB) 🫕 **SHELF LIFE** 1 MONTH, REFRIGERATED
🔪 **SERVING SUGGESTION** SERVE WITH CRUSTY BREAD, PICKLES, AND A GLASS OF WINE

INGREDIENTS

500g (1lb) skinless, boneless belly of pork, cut into large cubes

500g (1lb) lean pork such as shoulder, tenderloin, or leg, cut into large cubes

500g (1lb) pig's or calf's liver, sliced

150g (5oz) streaky bacon rashers

1–2 garlic cloves, finely chopped

1 tsp juniper berries, crushed

½ tsp freshly ground black pepper

1 tbsp finely chopped thyme

2 tsp salt

100g (3½oz) pitted prunes soaked in 5 tsp warm brandy for 2 hours

150ml (¼ pint) dry white wine

2 tbsp brandy

FOR THE TERRINES

2 pieces of caul fat or 500g (1lb) streaky bacon rashers, rind removed

6 thin slices of lemon or orange

4–6 bay leaves

500–750g (1–1½lb) lard, melted

juniper berries, bay leaves, and cranberries, to garnish (optional)

1 Mix together the meats and put through the fine plate of a mincer. Add the rest of the ingredients, and mix well. Cover and refrigerate for 3–4 hours to allow the flavours to develop.

2 Line the terrine with caul fat, leaving an overhang of at least 2.5cm (1in), so it can be folded over to cover the pâté. Alternatively, line it with bacon: remove the rinds then stretch the rashers with the back of a knife blade. Overlap the bacon in the dish and leave the ends to overhang.

3 Fill the dish with the meat, pushing it well into the corners, then rap it on a work surface to release any air pockets. Fold over the flaps of caul or bacon, and place the lemon or orange slices and bay leaves on top. Cover with the lid or foil.

4 Put the terrine in a roasting tin filled with enough warm water to come halfway up the sides of the dish. Cook in an oven preheated to 160°C/325°F/gas 3 for 1½–2 hours, until the pâté has shrunk from the sides of the dish and is surrounded by liquid fat.

5 Leave the pâté to cool, then cover with a piece of card wrapped in foil and weight down (see page 166) to make it easier to slice. Refrigerate overnight.

6 The next day, remove the lemon or orange slices and bay leaves, run a hot knife blade around the edge of the terrine and carefully unmould the pâté. Wipe off all traces of the jelly surrounding the meat with paper towels.

Garnish with juniper berries, bay leaves, and cranberries

7 Pour melted lard over the base of the terrine in a layer about 1cm (½in) thick. Leave to set, then place the pâté on top and pour over enough melted lard to cover the pâté by about 1cm (½in). Cover with the lid or foil and refrigerate. Leave to mature for 2–3 days before serving.

Smooth Liver Pâté

☆ **DEGREE OF DIFFICULTY** EASY **COOKING TIME** ABOUT 25 MINUTES

SPECIAL EQUIPMENT FOOD PROCESSOR; 500ML (¾ PINT) STERILIZED EARTHENWARE DISH OR 5 x 175ML (6FL OZ) RAMEKINS (SEE PAGES 12–13) **YIELD** ABOUT 500G (1LB) **SHELF LIFE** 2 WEEKS, REFRIGERATED

SERVING SUGGESTIONS SERVE ON TOAST OR BAKED EN CROÛTE IN PUFF PASTRY

INGREDIENTS

250g (8oz) chicken fat, goose fat, or clarified butter (see page 47)

250g (8oz) onions or shallots, chopped

500g (1lb) chicken, duck, or calf's liver, trimmed and washed

1 tsp salt

½ tsp freshly ground black pepper

2 tbsp brandy (optional)

2 tbsp finely chopped parsley (optional)

½ tsp finely grated orange or lemon rind (optional)

1 clove garlic, finely mashed (optional)

1 Heat 150g (5oz) of the fat in a heavy frying pan, add the onions or shallots, and fry gently for 15–20 minutes, until browned. Add the liver and fry for 2 minutes on each side or until cooked but still pink inside. Cool briefly.

2 Transfer the mixture to the food processor, and process until smooth. Add the remaining ingredients and mix well.

3 Press the mixture into the dish or individual ramekins. Leave to cool completely, then cover and refrigerate for a few hours. Melt the remaining fat and pour over the pâté to seal. Refrigerate for at least 12 hours before serving.

TIP
The onions and liver can be fried in good-quality olive oil instead of other fat. This results in a much softer mixture.

Rabbit Pâté

☆☆☆ **DEGREE OF DIFFICULTY** ADVANCED   **COOKING TIME** 1½–2 HOURS

SPECIAL EQUIPMENT MINCER; 1.5 LITRE (2½ PINT) TERRINE   **YIELD** ABOUT 1.25KG (3LB)

SHELF LIFE 3 WEEKS, REFRIGERATED   **SERVING SUGGESTIONS** SERVE WITH CARROT AND ALMOND CHUTNEY (SEE PAGE 206) OR STRIPED SPICED PEARS (SEE PAGE 202)

INGREDIENTS

1 large rabbit, boned, saddle fillets removed

400g (13oz) lean pork, cut into large cubes

150g (5oz) shallots, coarsely chopped

1 tbsp oil

200g (7oz) carrots, finely diced

3 eggs (size 2)

1 tbsp green peppercorns in brine, drained

2 tbsp salt

½ tsp freshly ground black pepper

2 tbsp finely chopped parsley

1 tbsp finely chopped thyme

1 tbsp finely chopped sage

a piece of caul fat or 250g (8oz) streaky bacon rashers, rind removed

about 500g (1lb) lard, melted

FOR THE MARINADE

75ml (3fl oz) slivovitz, kirsch, or brandy

3–4 sprigs thyme

3–4 sage leaves

1 tsp coarsely ground black pepper

2 bay leaves, lightly toasted in a small frying pan and crumbled

1 tsp finely grated lemon rind

1 Put the rabbit fillets, the rest of the rabbit and the pork in a bowl, and mix in all the ingredients for the marinade. Cover and refrigerate for 12 hours.

2 Fry the shallots in the oil for a few minutes until softened. Blanch the carrots for 1 minute, then drain, refresh, and drain again (see page 21).

3 Remove the rabbit fillets from the marinade and pat dry. Put the rest of the meat and the shallots through the fine disc of the mincer. Strain the marinade and add to the minced meat, together with the carrots, eggs, peppercorns, salt, and pepper. Mix very well, then cover and refrigerate for 2–3 hours.

4 Mix together the chopped herbs and spread them out on a baking tray. Roll the rabbit fillets in the herbs until they are evenly coated.

5 Line the terrine with the caul fat or bacon (see step 2, page 180). Spoon half the meat mixture into the terrine and smooth the surface with a palette knife.

6 Put the herb-coated rabbit fillets on top of the meat, in the centre. Spoon in the remaining meat mixture, making sure there are no air pockets, and smooth the top level with a palette knife. Fold over the ends of the caul fat or bacon and cover the pâté with the lid or a double layer of foil.

7 Place the terrine in a roasting tin filled with enough warm water to come about halfway up the sides of the dish. Bake in an oven preheated to 160°C/325°F/gas 3 for 1½–2 hours or until the pâté has shrunk from the sides of the dish and is surrounded by liquid.

8 Remove the dish from the roasting tin. Weight down the pâté (see page 166). Leave to cool, then refrigerate for 12 hours.

9 Turn out the pâté from the terrine and wipe off the jelly or any liquid with paper towels.

10 Pour a 1cm (½in) layer of the melted lard into the bottom of the cleaned terrine and refrigerate until set. Place the pâté on top of the set fat and pour over the remaining lard, making sure it fills the gaps down the sides and covers the pâté by about 1cm (½in). Cover and refrigerate. The pâté will be ready to eat in 2 days.

Cured Ham

 DEGREE OF DIFFICULTY ADVANCED **COOKING TIME** 25–30 MINUTES PER 500G (1LB) **SPECIAL EQUIPMENT**

LARGE CROCK; MEAT HOOKS; STERILIZED CALICO OR MUSLIN (SEE PAGE 12) **YIELD** 3.75–4.5KG (8¼–9¾LB)

SHELF LIFE 2 YEARS, UNCOOKED; 3 WEEKS, COOKED **SERVING SUGGESTIONS** SERVE THE HAM HOT

WITH A CHERRY SAUCE OR CUMBERLAND SAUCE, OR COLD AS THE CENTREPIECE OF A BUFFET

WARNING THIS RECIPE CONTAINS SALTPETRE; SEE PAGE 12

INGREDIENTS

1 leg of pork, weighing 5–6kg
(11–13lb)

500g (1lb) coarse salt

FOR THE BRINE

small bunch thyme

3 sprigs rosemary

3 bay leaves

2 tbsp juniper berries, crushed

2 tsp cloves

750g (1½lb) salt

250g (8oz) molasses sugar
or soft brown sugar

1 tbsp saltpetre

3 litres (5 pints) water or 2 litres
(3½ pints) water and 1 litre
(1¾ pints) strong ale

FOR THE PASTE

150g (5oz) plain flour

150g (5oz) salt

8–10 tsp water

IMPORTANT INFORMATION

- Do not try to cure meat in the summer or without proper facilities. All preparation and storage must be carried out below 8°C (46°F).
- Always follow the preparation and storage procedures in the recipes, and observe the proper hygiene rules (see page 12).
- The meat should have a pleasant smell at each stage of preparation; if it starts to smell off, do not eat it.
- If the brine starts to smell off, changes consistency, or becomes "ropy", discard it, rinse the ham well, and cover with a fresh, cold brine.

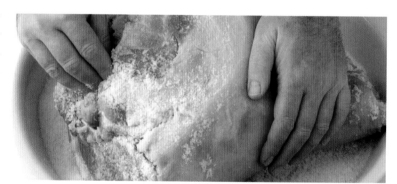

1 Rub the pork with salt, pushing it into all the crevices. Place on a thin layer of salt in a dish, and cover with the remaining salt. Refrigerate for 24 hours.

2 For the brine, put the spices in a muslin bag, then place all the ingredients in a large pan with the water. Bring slowly to the boil, stirring until the salt has dissolved. Skim well, then reduce the heat and simmer for 5 minutes. Remove the pan from the heat, and leave the brine until completely cold. Lift out the spices and herbs, then strain the brine through a muslin-lined sieve.

3 The next day, brush all the salt from the meat and put it in a large earthenware crock or other non-corrosive container. Strain the cold brine over it, covering the meat fully; if necessary, weight the meat down (see page 166). Cover with a lid or clingfilm, and leave in a cool place, at 6–8°C (42–46°F), for 2–2½ weeks. Check the meat daily to ensure the brine has not deteriorated (see Important Information, opposite).

Ensure the brine totally covers the meat

After hanging for 2–3 days, the surface of the ham will dry out

The colour of the skin will darken during drying

4 Remove the meat from the brine, rinse it well, then dry. Insert a meat hook into the knuckle end of the leg and hang it up in a cool, dry, dark, airy place (at 6–8°C/42–46°F) for 2–3 days. After the ham has hung for 2–3 days, it can be cooked. For a stronger flavour, continue the hanging process, as in step 5, below.

5 Mix the flour, salt, and water together to make a paste. Spread it over all the exposed meat, to seal, then hang the ham for a further 2–2½ weeks. If wished, the ham can be smoked before cooking.

Duck Pâté with Pistachio Nuts and Kumquats

☆☆☆ **DEGREE OF DIFFICULTY** ADVANCED **COOKING TIME** ABOUT 2 HOURS

SPECIAL EQUIPMENT MINCER; 2 x 1 LITRE (1¾ PINT) TERRINES **YIELD** ABOUT 2KG (4LB)

SHELF LIFE 3 WEEKS, REFRIGERATED **SERVING SUGGESTION** SERVE AS A FIRST COURSE WITH A SALAD AND SHALLOT CONFITURE (SEE PAGE 45) OR ONION MARMALADE (SEE PAGE 169)

INGREDIENTS

3kg (6lb) duck with its liver, skinned and boned

300g (10oz) pork tenderloin or lean pink veal, cut into large cubes

500g (1lb) boned and skinned belly of pork, cut into large cubes

2 eggs (size 2)

100g (3½oz) very green pistachio nuts, skinned (blanch them in boiling water, cool, and rub off skins)

1 tbsp salt

1 tsp freshly ground black pepper

1 tbsp finely chopped tarragon

2 pieces of caul fat or 300g (10oz) streaky bacon rashers, rind removed

about 16 kumquats

about 500–750g (1–1½lb) lard, melted

FOR THE MARINADE

100ml (3½fl oz) brandy

2 garlic cloves, crushed

rind and juice of 1 large orange

a few sprigs of thyme, bruised

1 Put the duck meat and liver and pork tenderloin (or veal) in a bowl. Add all the ingredients for the marinade and mix well. Cover and refrigerate for 12 hours.

2 Remove the duck breasts and liver from the marinade and cut into 1cm (½in) cubes. Put the remaining meat and the belly of pork through the fine disc of the mincer.

3 Add the cubed duck breast and liver to the minced meat, together with the marinating liquid and the eggs, nuts, salt, pepper, and tarragon. Mix well.

4 Line the terrines with the caul fat or the bacon (see step 2, page 180). Spoon a quarter of the meat mixture into each terrine and smooth the surface.

5 Arrange a row of whole kumquats down the centre of each dish. Divide the remaining meat mixture between the dishes,

making sure there are no air pockets, then smooth the surface. The mixture should be about 2.5cm (1in) from the rim of each terrine. Fold over the ends of the caul fat or bacon, and cover each dish with its lid or a double layer of foil.

6 Place the terrine in a roasting tin filled with enough warm water to come about halfway up the sides of the dishes. Bake in an oven preheated to 160°C/325°F/ gas 3, for 2 hours or until each pâté has shrunk from its dish and is surrounded by liquid.

7 Remove the dishes from the roasting tin and leave to cool. Weight down each pâté (see page 166), then refrigerate for about 12 hours. Turn out each pâté, and wipe off any jelly or liquid with paper towels.

8 Set each pâté in the melted lard (see step 7, page 181), then cover and refrigerate for at least 12 hours before serving.

Confit of Duck

☆ **DEGREE OF DIFFICULTY** EASY 🪣 **COOKING TIME** ABOUT 2 HOURS 🍴 **SPECIAL EQUIPMENT** STERILIZED MUSLIN;

STERILIZED EARTHENWARE CROCK OR LARGE JAR WITH AIRTIGHT SEALANT (SEE PAGES 12–13) 🫙 **YIELD** ABOUT 1.5–2KG (3–4LB)

🫙 **SHELF LIFE** 6 MONTHS, REFRIGERATED 🚫 **SERVING SUGGESTION** HEAT AND SERVE WITH SAUTÉ POTATOES

WARNING THIS RECIPE CONTAINS SALTPETRE; SEE PAGE 12

INGREDIENTS

2 tbsp pickling salt

¼ tsp saltpetre

6 duck legs, any loose skin removed

750g (1½lb) lard, or goose
or duck fat

4 garlic cloves

1 tsp black peppercorns

½ tsp cloves

1 Mix the salt and saltpetre together, and rub well all over the duck. Refrigerate for 24 hours.

2 Brush the salt off the duck, then dry well but do not wash. Gently heat the fat in a large, heavy pan. Add the duck, garlic, peppercorns, and cloves. Ensure that the fat completely covers the duck. If not, melt some more fat and add to the pan to cover.

3 Cook very gently for 2 hours or until no liquid comes out of the meat when pierced with a skewer. Lift out and allow to cool completely. Strain the fat through the muslin (see page 21).

4 Cover the bottom of the sterilized crock or jar with a little of the fat. Pack the duck into the jar and cover with the remaining fat. Allow to solidify, adding more fat if necessary to cover the meat by at least 1cm (½in). Seal the jar or cover the crock with waxed paper or a double layer of foil. The duck is ready to eat immediately.

This easy-to-make speciality is indispensable in southwest France. Traditionally, goose is used, but the rich flavour of duck lends itself perfectly to this technique. Turkey, chicken, and rabbit can be preserved in the same way.

Wind-Dried Duck Sausages

☆☆ **DEGREE OF DIFFICULTY** MODERATE 🍴 **SPECIAL EQUIPMENT** MINCER; SAUSAGE MAKER OR SAUSAGE FILLER;

MEAT HOOKS 🪝 **YIELD** ABOUT 1KG (2LB) 🏺 **SHELF LIFE** 6 MONTHS 🚫 **SERVING SUGGESTIONS** SERVE AS PART OF

A SAUSAGE PLATTER, OR ADD TO STIR-FRIES AND SLOW-COOKED CHINESE DISHES

WARNING THIS RECIPE CONTAINS SALTPETRE; SEE PAGE 12

INGREDIENTS

3kg (6lb) duck, boned, skin left on

300g (10oz) veal or pork tenderloin, cubed

3 tbsp sake or fortified rice wine

3–4 fresh Thai chillies, deseeded and chopped

1 tbsp salt

4–5 star anise, finely ground

1 tsp Sichuan pepper, finely ground

1 tsp fennel seeds, finely ground

about 3.8 metres (4 yards) sheep casing

a little groundnut oil

FOR THE CURE

250ml (8fl oz) soy sauce

4 tbsp honey or molasses sugar

3 garlic cloves, crushed

5cm (2in) piece fresh ginger root, shredded

½ tsp saltpetre

IMPORTANT NOTE

Before starting this recipe, please read the information on pages 12 and 184.

1 Put all the meat in a glass bowl. Mix together all the ingredients for the cure, and pour over the meat, rubbing it in well. Cover with clingfilm. Refrigerate for 24 hours, turning occasionally.

2 Put the duck breasts through the coarse disc of the mincer. Put the rest of the meat through the fine disc. Mix in the remaining ingredients except the casing and oil. Pack into a bowl, making sure there are no air pockets. Cover and refrigerate for 12 hours.

3 Prepare the casing (see steps 3 and 4, page 190). Stuff with the meat and divide into 10cm (4in) links (see step 5, page 191).

4 Hang up in a cool, dry, dark, airy place (at 6–8°C/42–46°F) for 4–5 weeks or until they have lost about 50 per cent of their original weight. After 10 days, or when the sausages reduce in size, rub with the oil.

In China, sausages like these are hung to dry in the cool, breezy mountain air, which is the ideal curing place. The same technique can be used to make sausages filled with pork or a mixture of pork fat and beef or venison.

Preserved Toulouse Sausages

 ☆☆ **DEGREE OF DIFFICULTY** MODERATE **COOKING TIME** ABOUT 20 MINUTES **SPECIAL EQUIPMENT** MINCER; SAUSAGE MAKER OR SAUSAGE FILLER; STERILIZED WIDE-NECKED JARS WITH SEALANTS (SEE PAGES 12–13); THERMOMETER **YIELD** ABOUT 3KG (6LB) **SHELF LIFE** 1 YEAR **SERVING SUGGESTION** ADD TO STEWS OR CASSEROLES **WARNING** THIS RECIPE CONTAINS SALTPETRE; SEE PAGE 12

INGREDIENTS

2.1kg (4¼lb) lean shoulder of pork, cubed

900g (1¾lb) pork back fat, cubed

60g (2oz) salt

1 tsp freshly ground white or black pepper

½ tsp saltpetre

3–4 metres (3¼–4¼ yards) hog casing

FOR EACH JAR

2 garlic cloves, blanched for 2 minutes (see page 21)

2 sprigs thyme

1 sprig rosemary

olive oil or lard, to cover

TIP
To eat the sausages fresh, omit the saltpetre and leave them in a coil or divide into 10cm (4in) links. Keep refrigerated, and cook within 2 days (see step 4).

IMPORTANT NOTE

Before starting this recipe, please read the information on pages 12 and 184.

1 Put the meat through the coarse disc of the mincer and the fat through the fine disc.

2 Put the minced meat and fat in a glass bowl with the salt, pepper, and saltpetre. Knead the mixture well with your hands to ensure the meat and fat are evenly distributed. Cover and refrigerate for at least 4 hours.

3 Prepare the casing (see steps 3 and 4, page 190). Stuff with the meat and divide into 5cm (2in) links (see step 5, page 191).

4 Fry, grill, or barbecue the sausages for 8–10 minutes per side or until they are completely cooked through but still slightly pink and moist inside. Immediately arrange the sausages in the hot sterilized jars, along with the garlic and herbs.

5 If using olive oil to cover, heat until it reaches 90°C (194°F), pour into the jars, making sure the sausages are covered, then seal.

6 If using lard to cover, melt it, then leave to cool slightly before pouring over the sausages in the jar. Refrigerate until the fat sets, and top up with more melted lard, so that it covers the sausages by at least 1cm (½in), then seal.

7 Store in a cool, dark place (at 6–8°C/42–46°F) or the bottom of the refrigerator. The sausages will be ready to eat in 1 month. The oil or lard from the jars can be used in cooking.

VARIATIONS

HERB SAUSAGES
Add 2 tablespoons chopped parsley or a mixture of parsley and thyme in step 2.

GARLIC SAUSAGES
Add 3 garlic cloves (crushed) and 2 tablespoons chopped herbs in step 2.

CUMBERLAND SAUSAGES
Add ¼ teaspoon grated nutmeg in step 2.

Garlic and Herb Salami

☆☆ **DEGREE OF DIFFICULTY** MODERATE **SPECIAL EQUIPMENT** MINCER; SAUSAGE MAKER OR
SAUSAGE FILLER; MEAT HOOKS **YIELD** ABOUT 750G (1½LB) **SHELF LIFE** 4–5 MONTHS, REFRIGERATED
 SERVING SUGGESTION REMOVE THE SKIN AND BAKE IN A BRIOCHE DOUGH
WARNING THIS RECIPE CONTAINS SALTPETRE; SEE PAGE 12

INGREDIENTS

*1kg (2lb) lean shoulder, hand, or
blade of pork, trimmed, all sinew
removed, and cut into large cubes*

1½ tbsp salt

½ tsp saltpetre

75ml (3fl oz) vodka

*350g (11½oz) pork back fat,
cut into large cubes*

5 garlic cloves, finely chopped

3 tbsp finely chopped thyme

2 tsp black peppercorns

½ tsp freshly ground black pepper

2 tsp coriander seeds, coarsely ground

¼ tsp allspice, freshly ground

*about 2 metres (2 yards) medium
hog casing*

475ml (1 pint) vinegar

1 Put the meat in a large bowl,
sprinkle with the salt, saltpetre,
and vodka, and mix well with your
hands. Cover and refrigerate for 12
hours. Put the meat through the fine
plate of a mincer, and the pork fat
through the coarse plate.

2 Mix together well, adding any
liquid left in the bowl. Add the
garlic, thyme, whole and ground
black peppercorns, coriander seeds,
and allspice. Mix thoroughly but
lightly, then chill for at least 2 hours.

3 Meanwhile, prepare the
casing. Rinse it to remove
the excess salt, then soak in cold
water for 30 minutes. Next, rinse
the inside of the casing by fitting
it over a slow-running cold tap
and allowing the water to run
through it for a few seconds.

4 Put the casing in a bowl of
water, add the vinegar, and
leave to soak until needed.

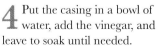

5 Fit one end of the casing to the sausage-maker or food mixer attachment. Stuff with the meat, packing it well. If there are any air pockets, prick with a skewer. Tie into individual sausages, or 20cm (8in) links.

6 Hang the sausages up to dry in a cool, dry, dark, airy place (at 6–8°C/42–46°F) for 5–6 weeks. Check them every few days. At all stages, they should have a savoury, appetizing smell and be dry to the touch.

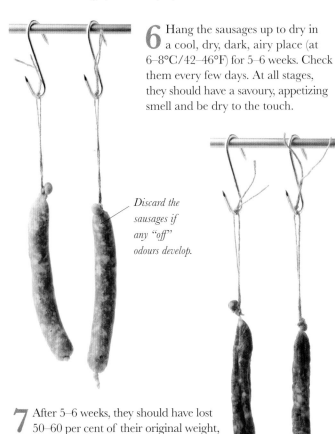

Discard the sausages if any "off" odours develop.

7 After 5–6 weeks, they should have lost 50–60 per cent of their original weight, and they are perfect for eating raw. To make well-flavoured cooking sausages, they can be hung for up to 3 months.

HOW TO STORE

- To store the sausages, individually wrap in sheets of greaseproof paper or waxed paper, and hang in a cool, dry, dark, airy place (6–8°C/42–46°F). Alternatively, fill a container with polystyrene granules and bury the sausages in the middle.
- The sausages can be frozen. Wrap each in greaseproof paper, then seal in freezer-proof plastic bags. Use within 3 months.

Rillettes

☆☆ **DEGREE OF DIFFICULTY** MODERATE  **COOKING TIME** ABOUT 4½ HOURS

SPECIAL EQUIPMENT 1 LITRE (1½ PINT) STERILIZED EARTHENWARE DISH OR TERRINE (SEE PAGES 12–13)

YIELD ABOUT 1KG (2LB) **SHELF LIFE** 6 WEEKS, REFRIGERATED

SERVING SUGGESTION A WONDERFUL PICNIC DISH SERVED WITH CRUSTY BREAD

INGREDIENTS

*1kg (2lb) boneless belly of pork, cut
into 1 x 5cm (½ x 2in) strips*

*500g (1lb) back fat, cut
into small pieces*

*125ml (4fl oz) water or
dry white wine*

2–3 sprigs thyme

2 garlic cloves, peeled

1½ tsp salt

*1 tsp freshly ground black
or white pepper*

1 blade mace

about 250g (8oz) lard, melted, to seal

1 Put all the ingredients except the melted lard in a heavy pan or a deep casserole, and bring slowly to the boil.

2 Cook, covered, over a very low heat for about 3 hours, stirring frequently to prevent it from sticking. Uncover the pan and continue to cook for about 1 hour or until the meat is very soft and falling apart.

3 Transfer the contents of the pan to a colander placed over a deep bowl. Remove the thyme, garlic, and mace, and lightly squeeze the meat to extract the fat. With the aid of two forks, shred the meat until it resembles a fine, fibrous mass.

4 Put the meat in a clean pan and add the strained-off fat and cooking juices. Heat gently for about 10 minutes, mixing well to achieve a homogeneous mass. Taste and adjust the seasoning, then pack into the dish or terrine. Leave to cool, then pour over the melted lard to seal. Cover and refrigerate. The rillettes is ready to eat immediately.

TIP
**Goose, duck, and rabbit
can all be prepared in
the same way.**

Rillettes is the French equivalent of British potted meat, except the meat is shredded. Each region of France has its own favourite, and most are only lightly flavoured, to allow the natural taste of the pork to come through.

Potted Meat

☆ **DEGREE OF DIFFICULTY** EASY **COOKING TIME** ABOUT 2 HOURS

 SPECIAL EQUIPMENT FOOD PROCESSOR; 6 x 175ML (6FL OZ) STERILIZED RAMEKINS OR A 1 LITRE (1¾ PINT)

EARTHENWARE DISH (SEE PAGES 12–13) **YIELD** ABOUT 750G (1½LB) **SHELF LIFE** 5 WEEKS, REFRIGERATED

SERVING SUGGESTION SERVE AS A FIRST COURSE WITH A WATERCRESS SALAD

INGREDIENTS

1kg (2lb) beef (rump or shoulder), all fat and sinew removed, cut into small pieces

250ml (8fl oz) good beef stock

3–4 anchovy fillets, chopped

150g (5oz) butter

2–3 sprigs of thyme

2 bay leaves

2 blades mace

1 tsp salt

½ tsp grated lemon rind

100g (3½oz) clarified butter (see page 47)

1 Put all the ingredients except the lemon rind and clarified butter in a casserole. Bring to the boil, cover tightly, then simmer on the lowest heat. Alternatively, bake in an oven preheated to 160°C/325°F/gas 3, for 2 hours or until the meat is tender.

2 Remove the herbs and mace, and drain the meat. Pour the cooking liquid into a pan, and boil until reduced to 250ml (8fl oz).

3 Process the meat and reduced liquid to a paste in the food processor. Mix in the lemon rind, and season. Pack into the ramekins or dish, and refrigerate for 2–3 hours. Seal the top with the melted clarified butter (see step 4, page 47). Cover and refrigerate. The meat will be ready in 2 days.

Potted meats were a useful standby in Victorian Britain and a prudent way to extend leftovers. Cooked and raw meat were simmered with gravy and seasoning, then mixed with butter and pounded to a fine paste.

TIP
This dish is made with raw meat, but any leftover cooked beef can also be used.

Early Winter

Seasonal Ingredients

As autumn turns to winter and the days get shorter and colder, it is the hardier root vegetables and late-ripening fruit that have their moment in the sun – what's left of it. These foodstuffs comfort us and keep us going through the long night ahead, but with a little alchemy we can eat them at other times of the year, too. Here are some of my favourite ingredients for preserving in winter.

CRAB APPLES
With their high pectin content, crab apples are perfect for jams and jellies, but they are also great for pickling and for use in chutneys and relishes.

BEETROOT
Jams and jellies made with beetroot have a glorious purple colour to them, but this vegetable is most commonly pickled.

CELERIAC
This root vegetable of the celery family is an ideal candidate for use in pickles. Not surprisingly, the flavour is reminiscent of celery.

TURNIPS
Pickles and chutneys sometimes include some turnip, but this slightly underappreciated vegetable with a "woody" texture can also be used in jams and jellies.

QUINCES
Astringent and virtually inedible raw, quinces are popular in jams for their high pectin content. They can also be used in place of apples.

CARROTS
The sweet, colourful carrot is a vegetable that can readily replace fruit in many recipes and even makes a great jam.

CRANBERRIES
Their high nutrient content and antioxidant properties have seen cranberries tagged with the "superfood" label in recent years.

PEARS
Delicious in syrup or preserved in alcohol, pears are also a very good ingredient for fruit butters and cheeses.

Hot Crab Apple Jelly

 DEGREE OF DIFFICULTY MODERATE **COOKING TIME** 50–55 MINUTES **SPECIAL EQUIPMENT** PRESERVING PAN; STERILIZED JELLY BAG; SUGAR THERMOMETER; STERILIZED JARS AND SEALANTS (SEE PAGES 12–13)

 YIELD ABOUT 1.25KG (2½LB) **SHELF LIFE** 2 YEARS  **SERVING SUGGESTIONS** SERVE WITH MEAT, ADD TO SANDWICHES, OR STIR A TABLESPOONFUL INTO GAME CASSEROLES JUST BEFORE SERVING

INGREDIENTS

1kg (2lb) crab apples, cut in half

4–5 fresh or dried red chillies, coarsely chopped, plus 1 fresh chilli for each jar

preserving or granulated sugar

a little brandy, to seal

1 Put the crab apples and the chopped chillies in the preserving pan and add enough cold water to cover. Bring to the boil, then simmer for 25 minutes or until the fruit is pulpy.

2 Pour the fruit and liquid into the sterilized jelly bag (see page 17). Drain for 2–3 hours or until it stops dripping.

3 Measure the juice and allow 500g (1lb) sugar for every 500ml (17fl oz) juice. Put the juice and sugar in the cleaned pan. Bring slowly to the boil, stirring until the sugar has dissolved. Reduce the heat and skim well. Return to the boil for 15 minutes or until the setting point is reached (see page 16).

4 Remove the pan from the heat and leave to settle for a few minutes. Skim well. Pour the liquid jelly into the hot sterilized jars.

5 Slit the chillies lengthways and trim off the stalks. When the jelly is semi-set, carefully insert a chilli into each jar. Pierce any air pockets that form by prodding with a long, thin wooden skewer. Cover each jar with a waxed paper disc dipped in brandy, then seal.

Crab apples make a firm jelly that can be flavoured in many ways.

Pears in Eau de Vie

 DEGREE OF DIFFICULTY EASY **SPECIAL EQUIPMENT** 2 LITRE (3½ PINT) STERILIZED, WIDE-NECKED JAR AND SEALANT (SEE PAGES 12–13) **YIELD** ABOUT 1KG (2LB) **SHELF LIFE** 2 YEARS

SERVING SUGGESTION SERVE AS A DESSERT TO CHEER UP A COLD WINTER NIGHT

INGREDIENTS

3–4 ripe pears

300–400g (10–13oz) preserving or granulated sugar

1 vanilla pod

about 1 litre (1¾ pints) eau de vie

1 Wash the pears, dry, and prick them in a few places with a silver needle or a sharp wooden skewer.

2 Arrange the pears in the sterilized jar. Add the sugar and vanilla pod and pour in enough eau de vie to cover the pears, then seal.

3 Keep in a cool, dark place for 3–4 months. For the first few weeks, shake the jar every few days to help dissolve the sugar.

TIPS
• Pear brandy or vodka can be substituted for eau de vie.
• For a sweeter result, add up to 500g (1lb) sugar.

In France, pear buds are inserted into slim-necked bottles to grow in their own hothouse. The bottles are then filled with alcohol and left to mature. This is my homage to that heady pear liqueur.

After fermentation, vanilla pods can give off a sweetly creamy flavour

Striped Spiced Pears

☆☆ **DEGREE OF DIFFICULTY** MODERATE **COOKING TIME** ABOUT 50 MINUTES

SPECIAL EQUIPMENT CANELLE KNIFE; NON-CORROSIVE PRESERVING PAN; 1 LITRE (1¾ PINT) WIDE-NECKED, STERILIZED JAR WITH VINEGAR-PROOF SEALANT (SEE PAGES 12–13)  **YIELD** ABOUT 1KG (2LB)  **SHELF LIFE** 2 YEARS

SERVING SUGGESTIONS SERVE WITH GAME OR TURKEY

INGREDIENTS

juice of 1 lemon

1kg (2lb) hard pears

1.25 litres (2 pints) red wine vinegar

500ml (17fl oz) red wine

500g (1lb) sugar

250g (8oz) honey

FOR THE SPICE BAG (SEE PAGE 31)

1 tbsp black peppercorns

2 tsp cloves

2 tsp allspice berries

1 tsp lavender flowers (optional)

2 bay leaves

1 large cinnamon stick

a few strips of lemon rind

1 Stir the lemon juice into a large bowl of cold water. Peel alternate strips of skin from the pears with the canelle knife or a vegetable peeler to give a striped effect. Put the pears in the lemon juice and water mixture.

2 Put the vinegar, wine, sugar, honey, and spice bag in the preserving pan. Bring to the boil, skim well, and boil for 5 minutes.

3 Add the pears, reduce the heat, and simmer gently for 35–40 minutes, until they have softened a little but still show some resistance when pierced with a knife. Lift the pears out of the pan with a slotted spoon and arrange them in the hot sterilized jar.

4 Boil the syrup rapidly until it is reduced by half and slightly thickened. Remove the spice bag. Pour the hot syrup into the jar, making sure the pears are totally covered, then seal. The pears will be ready to eat in 1 month.

This fragrant preserve is particularly attractive because of the striped appearance of the whole pears. It is especially good with game.

Fresh Cranberry and Orange Relish

☆ **DEGREE OF DIFFICULTY** EASY **SPECIAL EQUIPMENT** FOOD PROCESSOR; STERILIZED JARS AND SEALANTS (SEE PAGES 12–13) **YIELD** ABOUT 750G (1½ LB) **SHELF LIFE** 1 MONTH, REFRIGERATED **SERVING SUGGESTIONS** SERVE WITH TURKEY OR OTHER POULTRY, HAM, OR GRILLED FISH

INGREDIENTS

500g (1lb) fresh cranberries

2 oranges, coarsely chopped, pips removed

3–4 tbsp honey

2–3 tbsp orange-flavoured liqueur, such as Grand Marnier or triple sec

1 tsp coriander seeds, freshly ground

1 tsp salt

1 Put all the ingredients in the food processor, and process, using the pulse button, until the cranberries and oranges are coarsely chopped.

2 Pack into the sterilized jars, then seal and refrigerate. The relish is ready immediately, and if you are using it within 2–3 days, there is no need to bottle it.

Fresh cranberries have a refreshingly sour flavour. Use them to add colour and a sharp note to stuffings, salads, and fish. This recipe is the perfect accompaniment to Christmas turkey and ham.

Quince Cheese

☆☆ **DEGREE OF DIFFICULTY** MODERATE 🍲 **COOKING TIME** 3–3¾ HOURS

🍴 **SPECIAL EQUIPMENT** PRESERVING PAN; AIRTIGHT CONTAINER 🫙 **YIELD** ABOUT 2.25KG (4½LB)

🫙 **SHELF LIFE** 2 YEARS 🔪 **SERVING SUGGESTION** SERVE AS A SWEETMEAT

INGREDIENTS

1.5kg (3lb) ripe quinces

about 2 litres (3 ½ pints) water
or dry cider

2–3 strips of lemon rind

juice of ½ lemon

preserving or granulated sugar

mild oil, such as almond or
groundnut, for brushing

caster sugar for dusting

1 Wash the quinces well to remove any fluff, then chop them coarsely. There is no need to core them, since the mixture will be sieved.

2 Put the quinces in a preserving pan with enough water or dry cider to cover, and add the lemon rind and juice. Bring to the boil, then reduce the heat and simmer for 30–45 minutes, until the fruit is very soft and pulpy.

3 Pass the mixture through a sieve or a food mill to purée.

4 To calculate how much sugar to add, spoon the purée into a measuring jug. Allow 400g (13oz) sugar for every 500ml (17fl oz) purée.

5 Return the quince purée to the pan and add the sugar. Slowly bring to the boil, stirring until the sugar has dissolved. Simmer for 2½–3 hours, stirring frequently. Quinces will turn a deep red colour with long cooking. After a while, the mixture will become very thick and will start to "plop". It is ready when a wooden spoon drawn across the base of the pan leaves a clear channel. Remove from the heat and leave to cool slightly.

6 Brush a deep baking tray generously with oil. Pour the cheese into the tray and smooth to an even layer, 2.5–4cm (1–1½in) thick. Leave to cool completely, then cover with a cloth and keep in a warm, dry place for 24 hours.

7 Loosen the cheese with a palette knife and turn out on to a piece of baking parchment. Cut into squares or diamonds and dust with caster sugar. Arrange the shapes on baking trays, cover them, and leave to dry.

Carrot and Almond Chutney

 **DEGREE OF DIFFICULTY** EASY  **COOKING TIME** 30–35 MINUTES

SPECIAL EQUIPMENT NON-CORROSIVE PRESERVING PAN; SPICE MILL OR COFFEE GRINDER; STERILIZED JARS WITH VINEGAR-PROOF SEALANTS (SEE PAGES 12–13) **YIELD** ABOUT 1.5KG (3LB) **SHELF LIFE** 2 YEARS

SERVING SUGGESTIONS SERVE WITH COLD MEATS, OR JUST SPREAD ON BREAD

INGREDIENTS

1.25kg (2½lb) carrots,
grated lengthways

125g (4oz) fresh ginger root, shredded

250ml (8fl oz) white wine vinegar

grated rind and juice of 2 large lemons

150ml (¼ pint) water

400g (13oz) white
or light brown sugar

4 tbsp honey

2 tbsp coriander seeds, freshly ground

1 tbsp salt

3–4 dried bird's eye chillies

3 tbsp flaked almonds

1 Put all the ingredients except the chillies and almonds in a glass bowl. Mix well, cover, and leave to stand overnight.

2 The next day, transfer the mixture to the preserving pan. Bring to the boil, then simmer for 20 minutes. Raise the heat, and boil hard for 10–15 minutes, until most of the liquid has evaporated and the mixture is thick.

3 Grind the chillies to a powder in the spice mill or coffee grinder. Stir into the pan with the almonds. Ladle into the hot sterilized jars, then seal. The chutney will be ready in 1 month but improves with keeping.

This is my adaptation of angel hair jam, a Middle Eastern classic made with long, thin strands of carrot. Full-flavoured, sweet, and sour, this chutney goes well with mature cheese.

Pickled Turnips or Radishes

☆ **DEGREE OF DIFFICULTY** EASY 🍴 **SPECIAL EQUIPMENT** I LITRE (1¾ PINT) WIDE-NECKED, STERILIZED JAR WITH VINEGAR-PROOF SEALANT (SEE PAGES 12–13) **YIELD** ABOUT 1KG (2LB) **SHELF LIFE** 3–6 MONTHS
🔪 **SERVING SUGGESTIONS** USE IN SALADS, OR SERVE AS A SNACK WITH DRINKS

INGREDIENTS

750g (1 ½lb) white turnips or large radishes, sliced 1cm (½in) thick

250g (8oz) raw beetroot, sliced 1cm (½in) thick

4–5 garlic cloves, sliced

salt

3 tbsp white wine vinegar or distilled malt vinegar

1 Arrange the turnips or radishes in the sterilized jar with the beetroot and garlic.

2 Fill the jar with enough cold water to cover the vegetables, then drain it off into a measuring jug. Add 1 ½ tablespoons salt for every 500ml (17fl oz) water, stirring until the salt has dissolved. Add the wine vinegar or distilled malt vinegar, then pour into the jar.

3 Weight down the vegetables (see page 166), cover with a clean cloth, and leave in a warm, well-ventilated place for about 2 weeks, until fermentation is over (see Brined Cucumbers, page 128). Seal the jar. The pickle will be ready to eat in about 1 month.

TIP
Any of the turnip family, such as mooli radishes, or kohlrabi, can be used instead.

This vividly coloured pickle is popular all over the Middle East and in the southern part of Russia.

BEETROOTS

Root vegetables such as beetroot have long formed the basis of hearty winter fare. They are also perennial favourites for pickling. Adapt the pickled onion recipe on page 166, using cooked whole baby beetroot (or large cubed beetroot) and omitting the salt.

Pickled Celeriac and Carrot Salad

 DEGREE OF DIFFICULTY EASY **COOKING TIME** 2–3 MINUTES   **SPECIAL EQUIPMENT** 2 x 1 LITRE (1¾ PINT) STERILIZED JARS WITH VINEGAR-PROOF SEALANTS (SEE PAGES 12–13) **YIELD** ABOUT 2KG (4LB) **SHELF LIFE** 3–6 MONTHS **SERVING SUGGESTION** ESPECIALLY GOOD WITH HOT OR COLD CHICKEN

INGREDIENTS

1 large celeriac, about 1kg (2lb),
peeled and shredded
or coarsely grated

5 large carrots, coarsely grated

2 onions, sliced into thin rings

2½ tbsp salt

2 tbsp dill seeds

shredded rind and juice of 1 orange

500ml (17fl oz) white wine vinegar
or cider vinegar

150ml (¼ pint) water

1 tbsp sugar (optional)

1 Mix the celeriac, carrots, and onions together in a glass bowl, and sprinkle with 2 tablespoons of the salt. Mix well and leave to stand for about 2 hours.

2 Rinse the vegetables under cold running water, then drain well. Stir in the dill seeds and orange rind, then pack loosely into the hot sterilized jars.

3 Put the orange juice, vinegar, water, sugar (if using), and the remaining salt in a non-corrosive pan. Bring to the boil, and boil for 2–3 minutes, then skim well. Pour into the jars to cover the vegetables. Poke the vegetables with a wooden skewer to ensure there are no air pockets, then seal. The pickle will be ready to eat in 1 week.

TIP
If you are not keen on the full, slightly bitter flavour of the orange rind, blanch it in boiling water for 1–2 minutes, then drain and refresh in cold water before use.

Be careful when choosing celeriac: it can become hollow and stringy when too mature. Select solid roots that are heavy for their size, and avoid any with green patches.

Salt-Cured Sprats

☆ **DEGREE OF DIFFICULTY** EASY 🍴 **SPECIAL EQUIPMENT** STERILIZED EARTHENWARE OR GLASS CONTAINER
WITH NON-CORROSIVE SEALANT (SEE PAGES 12–13) 🧂 **YIELD** ABOUT 750G (1½LB) 🏺 **SHELF LIFE** 2 YEARS,
REFRIGERATED ✎ **SERVING SUGGESTION** SERVE WITH A FRUIT VINEGAR AND OLIVE OIL DRESSING,
ACCOMPANIED WITH THINLY SLICED RAW ONION AND CHILLED VODKA

INGREDIENTS

1kg (2lb) sprats

500g (1lb) fine sea salt

1–1.5kg (2–3lb) pickling salt

1 tbsp black peppercorns

3–4 bay leaves

1 Using a small, sharp pair of scissors, make a little cut in each fish, just below the gills (enough to get the scissors in).

2 Next, carefully snip right down the belly of each fish, from gills to tail, and open out the cut slightly.

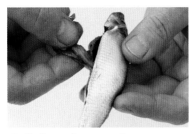

3 Pull out the stomach contents with your fingers and discard it, then rinse the fish under cold running water.

4 Sprinkle a little fine sea salt in the cavity of each fish and all over the outside, rubbing it well into the flesh.

5 Arrange the fish in layers in a shallow dish, adding a thin sprinkling of the fine salt between each layer. Cover and put in the refrigerator for 2–3 hours, until some of the moisture has been drawn off.

7 Sprinkle a layer of pickling salt over the base of a large container. Arrange some fish on top with few peppercorns and a bay leaf. Cover with a 5mm (¼in) layer of pickling salt. Repeat the layers, finishing with a layer of salt.

6 Lift out the fish and dry thoroughly on paper towels.

Over time, brine will start to develop in the container

Bay leaves release their fragrance slowly

Layering the various ingredients allows the flavours to intermingle

8 Have ready a plate that just fits the opening of the container. Place it over the fish and weight down (see page 166) – a bottle filled with water is ideal. Cover and refrigerate, or leave in a cool, dark place (6–8°C/42–46°F) for one week before eating.

TO KEEP THE FISH
- First, remove the oil that will have accumulated on top. If not enough brine has developed to cover the fish, top it up with a strong salt solution made with equal quantities of salt and water. Seal the container tightly and store in a cool, dark place.
- When you want to use the sprats, remove them from the brine and soak for a few hours in water or a mixture of milk and water.

All Year
& Exotic

Pomegranate Syrup

☆ **DEGREE OF DIFFICULTY** EASY 🍲 **COOKING TIME** ABOUT 15 MINUTES 🍴 **SPECIAL EQUIPMENT** STERILIZED
MUSLIN; STERILIZED BOTTLE AND SEALANT (SEE PAGES 12–13)  **YIELD** ABOUT 500ML (17FL OZ) 🫙 **SHELF LIFE** 2 YEARS
🚫 **SERVING SUGGESTIONS** DILUTE AND SERVE AS A DRINK, OR POUR OVER CUSTARDS, SWEETS
AND ICE CREAM; POUR OVER CRUSHED ICE TO MAKE A QUICK SORBET

INGREDIENTS

2kg (4lb) very red pomegranates

*400g (13oz) preserving
or granulated sugar*

1 tsp orange-flower water (optional)

TIP
**If you cannot find
sour pomegranates
(available from Indian
or Middle Eastern grocers),
use sweet ones instead,
and add the juice of
3 lemons or 1 teaspoon
of citric acid.**

1 Cut the pomegranates in half, horizontally, and use a lemon squeezer to extract all the juice; you should end up with about 500ml (17fl oz) juice.

2 Filter the juice through a double layer of muslin (see page 21) into a pan. Add the sugar and bring slowly to the boil, stirring until it has dissolved.

3 Boil for 10 minutes, then remove from the heat; skim well and stir in the orange-flower water, if using. Pour the syrup into the hot sterilized bottle, then seal.

Lemon Curd

☆☆ **DEGREE OF DIFFICULTY** MODERATE   **COOKING TIME** 30–45 MINUTES

SPECIAL EQUIPMENT DOUBLE BOILER; STERILIZED JARS AND SEALANTS (SEE PAGES 12–13)

YIELD ABOUT 750G (1½LB)   **SHELF LIFE** 3 MONTHS, REFRIGERATED

SERVING SUGGESTIONS SERVE WITH BREAD OR SCONES, OR USE TO FILL CAKES, TARTS, AND PASTRIES

INGREDIENTS

grated rind and juice of 6 lemons

*400g (13oz) preserving
or granulated sugar*

150g (5oz) butter, softened

5 eggs (size 3), beaten

1 Put the lemon rind and juice in a small pan with the sugar. Heat gently, stirring until the sugar has dissolved. Add the butter and stir until melted.

2 Transfer the mixture to the double boiler or a bowl placed over a pan of barely simmering water. Sieve in the eggs and cook very gently, stirring frequently, for 25–40 minutes, until the mixture coats the back of a spoon. Do not allow it to boil or it will curdle.

3 Pour the curd into the warm sterilized jars, and seal. Allow to cool, then keep refrigerated.

This recipe uses less sugar than most lemon curds; if you prefer a sweeter end result, increase the quantity by up to a third.

Passion Fruit Curd

 ☆☆ **DEGREE OF DIFFICULTY** MODERATE **COOKING TIME** 30–45 MINUTES

SPECIAL EQUIPMENT DOUBLE BOILER; STERILIZED JARS AND SEALANTS (SEE PAGES 12–13) **YIELD** ABOUT 1KG (2LB)

SHELF LIFE 3 MONTHS, REFRIGERATED **SERVING SUGGESTION** USE TO FILL TARTS

INGREDIENTS

750g (1½lb) passion fruit

juice of 1 lemon

300g (10oz) preserving
or granulated sugar

150g (5oz) butter, softened

4 eggs (size 2), beaten

1 Slice the passion fruit in half, and scoop out the seeds and pulp; there should be about 500ml (17fl oz).

2 Put in a small pan, add the lemon juice and sugar, and heat gently, stirring until the sugar has dissolved. Add the softened butter and stir until melted.

3 Transfer the mixture to the double boiler or a bowl placed over a pan of barely simmering water. Sieve in the eggs and cook very gently, stirring frequently, for 25–40 minutes, until the mixture coats the back of a spoon. Do not allow it to boil or it will curdle.

4 Pour the curd into the warm sterilized jars, and seal. Allow to cool, then keep refrigerated.

TIP
Choose wrinkled
passion fruit – they
are riper and contain
more juice.

The passion fruit seeds add a surprisingly crunchy texture to this curd. If you prefer a smooth curd, use 1kg (2lb) of fruit, and sieve it before adding the eggs.

Guava Jelly

☆ **DEGREE OF DIFFICULTY** EASY 🍲 **COOKING TIME** 45–55 MINUTES 🍴 **SPECIAL EQUIPMENT** PRESERVING PAN; STERILIZED JELLY BAG; SUGAR THERMOMETER; STERILIZED JARS AND SEALANTS (SEE PAGES 12–13) **YIELD** ABOUT 1KG (2LB) 🫙 **SHELF LIFE** 2 YEARS 🔪 **SERVING SUGGESTIONS** SPREAD ON BREAD, OR SERVE WITH COLD MEAT AND CHEESE

INGREDIENTS

1kg (2lb) firm guavas, coarsely chopped

1 lime, coarsely chopped

preserving or granulated sugar

1 Put the guavas and lime in the preserving pan, and add cold water to cover. Bring slowly to the boil, then reduce the heat and simmer for about 30 minutes or until the fruit is soft and pulpy.

2 Pour the fruit and liquid into the sterilized jelly bag (see page 17). Leave to drain for 2–3 hours or until it stops dripping. Measure the juice and allow 325g (11oz) sugar for every 500ml (17fl oz) juice.

3 Put the fruit juice and sugar in the cleaned pan. Bring slowly to the boil, stirring until the sugar has dissolved, then reduce the heat and skim well.

4 Return to the boil, and boil rapidly for 10–12 minutes or until the setting point is reached (see page 16).

5 Pour the liquid jelly into the hot sterilized jars, then seal.

TIP
Do not worry if the jelly seems too soft. Leave for a day or two, and then check again. If still too soft, reboil until the setting point is reached.

Guavas are a subtropical fruit with a haunting, exotic perfume. They are delicious eaten raw and also make a very elegant, rust-red jelly. Do not use white guavas – the colour is too insipid.

Exotic Fruit Jam

☆ **DEGREE OF DIFFICULTY** EASY 🍲 **COOKING TIME** ABOUT 1 HOUR 🍴 **SPECIAL EQUIPMENT** FOOD PROCESSOR; PRESERVING PAN; SUGAR THERMOMETER; STERILIZED JARS AND SEALANTS (SEE PAGES 12–13) 🫙 **YIELD** ABOUT 1.5KG (3LB) 🫙 **SHELF LIFE** 2 YEARS 🥄 **SERVING SUGGESTIONS** SERVE WITH SCONES AND CLOTTED CREAM, OR USE AS A FILLING FOR CREAM CAKES

INGREDIENTS

*1 medium pineapple, about
1.25kg (2½lb), peeled and cored*

*1 kg (2lb) cooking apples, peeled,
cored, and coarsely chopped*

*300g (10oz) fresh lychees, peeled,
pitted, and halved, or 425g (14oz)
can lychees, drained and halved*

250ml (8fl oz) water

rind of 1 lemon

juice of 2 lemons

*1.25kg (2½lb) preserving or
granulated sugar*

1 Finely chop the pineapple and apple in a food processor. Transfer to the preserving pan and add the fresh or canned lychee halves, water, and lemon rind and juice.

2 Bring the mixture to the boil, then reduce the heat and simmer for 20–25 minutes or until the apples have turned to a pulp and the pineapple is soft.

3 Add the preserving sugar to the pan and stir well over a medium heat until it has dissolved. Increase the heat and bring the mixture to a rapid, rolling boil.

4 Boil the fruit mixture rapidly for 20–25 minutes, stirring frequently, until the setting point is reached (see page 16). Skim off any froth as it rises to the surface of the jam.

5 Remove the pan from the heat and leave for a few minutes to allow the jam to settle. Skim again if necessary.

The jam will start to thicken as it reaches the setting point

6 Ladle the jam into hot sterilized jars, then seal immediately with waxed paper discs and cellophane seals.

Pineapple in Kirsch

☆ **DEGREE OF DIFFICULTY** EASY **SPECIAL EQUIPMENT** 2 LITRE (3 PINT) STERILIZED, WIDE-NECKED JAR WITH SEALANT (SEE PAGES 12–13) **YIELD** ABOUT 1KG (2LB) **SHELF LIFE** 2 YEARS
 SERVING SUGGESTION SERVE WITH CREAM AS THE ULTIMATE DESSERT

INGREDIENTS

4–5 baby pineapples (queens), peeled, cored, and cut into rings 1cm (½in) thick

3–4 cinnamon sticks

3–4 strips of orange peel

300–500g (10oz–1lb) preserving sugar

5–6 bitter almonds, blanched (optional)

about 1¾ pints (1 litre) kirsch

1 Arrange the pineapple with the cinnamon and orange peel in the sterilized jar. Add the sugar and almonds (if using). I find 300g (10oz) sugar is sufficient, but if you prefer the pineapple sweeter, add the larger amount.

2 Pour enough kirsch into the jar to cover the pineapple, then seal. Keep in a cool, dark place for 2–3 months. For the first few weeks, shake the jar every few days to help dissolve the sugar.

When this luscious fruit is stored in alcohol, its delicate fragrance is preserved – as is the enzyme it contains that aids digestion. Vodka, eau de vie, or white rum are also suitable.

Spicy Prickly Pear Jelly

☆☆ **DEGREE OF DIFFICULTY** MODERATE **COOKING TIME** ABOUT 1 HOUR

SPECIAL EQUIPMENT NON-CORROSIVE PRESERVING PAN; STERILIZED JELLY BAG; SUGAR THERMOMETER; STERILIZED JARS WITH VINEGAR-PROOF SEALANTS (SEE PAGES 12–13) **YIELD** ABOUT 1.5KG (3LB) **SHELF LIFE** 2 YEARS

 SERVING SUGGESTIONS DELICIOUS WITH COLD MEATS OR STIRRED INTO STEAMED VEGETABLES

INGREDIENTS

1kg (2lb) purple, red, or orange prickly pears

300g (10oz) cooking apples, chopped

750ml (1¼ pints) water

500ml (17fl oz) cider vinegar or white wine vinegar

125ml (4fl oz) lemon juice

preserving or granulated sugar

1 tbsp arrack, ouzo, or Pernod

FOR THE SPICE BAG (SEE PAGE 31)

1 tsp allspice berries, lightly crushed

4–6 dried bird's eye chillies, including the seeds, crushed

3 dried bay leaves, crumbled

1 Wearing protective gloves, top and tail the prickly pears. Run a sharp knife the length of the fruit, and cut through the thick skin. Remove the skin and wash the fruit thoroughly. Place the fruit in a bowl, and crush to a pulp with a potato masher.

2 Put the pulp in the preserving pan with the apples and water. Bring slowly to the boil, then simmer for 25 minutes or until the fruit is soft and pulpy.

3 Pour the fruit and liquid into the sterilized jelly bag (see page 17). Leave for 2–3 hours or until it stops dripping. Add the vinegar and lemon juice to the prickly pear juice and measure the liquid. Allow 500g (1lb) sugar for every 500ml (17fl oz) liquid.

4 Put the liquid, sugar, and spice bag in the cleaned pan. Bring slowly to the boil, stirring until the sugar has dissolved. Boil for 25 minutes or until the setting point is reached (see page 16).

5 Remove the pan from the heat and discard the spice bag. Stir in the arrack, ouzo, or Pernod. Pour the liquid jelly into the hot sterilized jars, then seal.

Prickly pears are available from many ethnic food shops and some large supermarkets. Purple ones are especially good for this recipe.

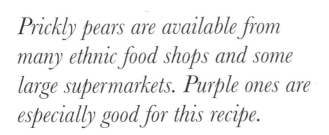

Mango Butter

☆ **DEGREE OF DIFFICULTY** EASY **COOKING TIME** ABOUT I HOUR **SPECIAL EQUIPMENT** PRESERVING PAN; STERILIZED JARS AND SEALANTS (SEE PAGES 12–13) **YIELD** ABOUT 1.5KG (3LB) **SHELF LIFE** 2 YEARS
 SERVING SUGGESTIONS USE AS A FILLING FOR CAKES AND FLANS, OR SPREAD ON BREAD

INGREDIENTS

2kg (4lb) ripe mangoes

300ml (½ pint) sweet cider or water

1kg (2lb) preserving or granulated sugar

grated rind and juice of 2 lemons

1 Prepare the mango flesh (see below) and cut into large chunks. Put the mango and cider or water in the preserving pan. Bring to the boil, then simmer for 15–20 minutes, until the fruit is soft and pulpy. Either press the mixture through a sieve or pass it through a food mill. Return the purée to the cleaned pan.

2 Add the sugar and lemon rind and juice, stirring until the sugar has dissolved. Bring to the boil, then simmer, stirring frequently, for 35–40 minutes or until reduced and thickened. Pour into warm sterilized jars, then seal.

HOW TO PREPARE MANGO FLESH

1 Cut the mango flesh from either side of the large central stone and score into squares.

2 Turn the mango halves inside out and cut off the cubes of flesh. Purée the flesh.

Wonderfully golden and fragrant, this simple butter is an ideal way to use up very ripe mangoes. Try adding different flavourings, such as grated orange rind, vanilla, or cinnamon.

Kiwi Fruit Butter

☆ **DEGREE OF DIFFICULTY** EASY   **COOKING TIME** ABOUT 1 HOUR   **SPECIAL EQUIPMENT** PRESERVING PAN;
STERILIZED JARS AND SEALANTS (SEE PAGES 12–13) **YIELD** ABOUT 1KG (2LB)   **SHELF LIFE** 2 YEARS
SERVING SUGGESTIONS USE AS A FILLING FOR FLANS, OR SPREAD ON BREAD

INGREDIENTS

*1kg (2lb) ripe kiwi fruit,
chopped (no need to peel)*

750ml (1 ¼ pints) dry cider or water

grated rind and juice of 1 lemon

*75g (2 ½oz) fresh ginger root,
finely shredded*

preserving or granulated sugar

*1 tsp freshly ground black
pepper (optional)*

1 Put the kiwi fruit, cider or water, and lemon juice in the preserving pan. Bring to the boil, skim, reduce the heat, and simmer for 15–20 minutes, until the fruit is soft and mushy.

2 Press the mixture through a sieve or pass it through a food mill. Measure the purée and allow 400g (13oz) sugar for every 500ml (17fl oz) purée. Return the purée to the cleaned pan.

3 Add the lemon rind, ginger, sugar, and pepper (if using), stirring until the sugar has dissolved. Bring to the boil, then simmer, stirring frequently, for 30–35 minutes or until the butter has reached the consistency of a soft-set jam. Pour into the warm sterilized jars, then seal.

Don't worry if this delightful butter doesn't thicken much in the pan; it will thicken considerably once it has cooled.

Melon Butter

☆ **DEGREE OF DIFFICULTY** EASY   **COOKING TIME** ABOUT 1¾ HOURS   **SPECIAL EQUIPMENT** PRESERVING PAN; STERILIZED JARS AND SEALANTS (SEE PAGES 12–13)   **YIELD** ABOUT 1KG (2LB)   **SHELF LIFE** 2 YEARS

 SERVING SUGGESTION USE AS A FILLING FOR CAKES

INGREDIENTS

2kg (4lb) ripe melons, peeled, deseeded, and chopped

500ml (17fl oz) sweet cider or water

1kg (2lb) preserving or granulated sugar

juice of 2 lemons

2 lemongrass stalks, finely chopped (optional)

1 tbsp orange-flower water

1 Put the melon in the preserving pan with the cider or water. Bring to the boil, skim, then simmer for 40 minutes or until the fruit is soft.

2 Either press the mixture through a sieve or pass it through a food mill. Return the purée to the cleaned pan.

3 Add the sugar, lemon juice, and lemongrass (if using), stirring until the sugar has dissolved. Bring to the boil, then simmer, stirring frequently, for 1 hour or until reduced and thickened.

4 Remove from the heat and stir in the flower water. Pour into the warm sterilized jars, then seal.

Melon makes a very pleasant butter with a subtle, fruity scent. Use fragrant varieties such as Ananas or Galia, or use ripe Charentais for a beautiful deep orange colour.

Carrot Jam

 DEGREE OF DIFFICULTY EASY **COOKING TIME** ABOUT 1¼ HOURS **SPECIAL EQUIPMENT** PRESERVING PAN; STERILIZED JARS AND SEALANTS (SEE PAGES 12–13) **YIELD** ABOUT 1.25 KG (2½LB) **SHELF LIFE** 2 YEARS

SERVING SUGGESTIONS USE TO FILL SPONGE CAKES, SWISS ROLLS, AND TARTS

INGREDIENTS

1kg (2lb) carrots, finely grated

250g (8oz) sultanas

500ml (17fl oz) water

750g (1½lb) preserving or granulated sugar

rind of 2 lemons

juice of 3 lemons

2 tsp ground ginger

1 Put the carrots, sultanas, and water in the preserving pan. Bring to the boil, reduce the heat, and simmer for 10–15 minutes, until the carrot is just soft.

2 Add the sugar, lemon rind, and juice, stirring until the sugar has dissolved. Bring to the boil, then simmer, stirring frequently, for 1 hour or until very thick. (There is no need to test for setting point.)

3 Add the ginger, and remove the pan from the heat. Ladle into the hot sterilized jars, then seal.

TIP
Almost any root vegetable can be used, but beetroot, parsnips, turnips, or kohlrabi need blanching several times first to mellow their strong flavour.

Root vegetable jams used to be made during the winter, when fresh fruit was not available.

Candied Pineapple Rings

☆☆ **DEGREE OF DIFFICULTY** MODERATE 🍲 **COOKING TIME** DAY 1, ABOUT 30 MINUTES; DAYS 2–6, 5 MINUTES EACH; DAY 7, NONE (REST DAY); DAY 8, 5 MINUTES, PLUS 12–24 HOURS DRYING 🍴 **SPECIAL EQUIPMENT** STERILIZED MUSLIN; PRESERVING PAN; AIRTIGHT CONTAINER 🫙 **YIELD** ABOUT 1KG (2LB) 🫙 **SHELF LIFE** 1 YEAR WITH A CRYSTALLIZED FINISH; 2 YEARS IN SYRUP 🔪 **SERVING SUGGESTION** DIP INTO, OR DRIZZLE OVER, MELTED CHOCOLATE

INGREDIENTS

1 large pineapple, peeled, cored, and cut into slices 1.5cm (⅝in) thick

1kg (2lb) preserving or granulated sugar

juice of 1 lemon

caster sugar for dusting

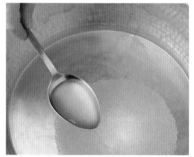

1 Put the pineapple rings in a pan and cover with water. Bring to the boil, then reduce the heat and simmer for 15–20 minutes, until softened slightly. Drain well, reserving the cooking liquid, and place in a glass bowl.

2 Strain 1 litre (1¾ pints) of the cooking liquid through a muslin-lined sieve into a preserving pan. Add 250g (8oz) sugar and the lemon juice. Bring to the boil, stirring until the sugar has dissolved. Boil for 2–3 minutes.

3 Ladle the hot sugar syrup over the pineapple rings, weight them down (see page 166) to ensure they are completely immersed, and leave to stand for 24 hours at room temperature.

4 The next day (Day 2), drain the pineapple rings well, keeping the sugar syrup. Return this to the preserving pan.

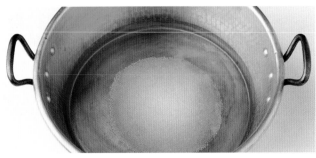

5 Add 100g (3½oz) sugar to the syrup and bring to the boil, stirring until the sugar dissolves. Boil for 1–2 minutes, then skim well and ladle over the pineapple rings. Weight down and leave for 24 hours.

6 On Day 3, repeat steps 4 and 5. On Day 4, drain the pineapple rings, place the syrup in the pan, and add another 150g (5oz) of sugar. Bring to the boil, stirring until the sugar has dissolved, and boil for 1–2 minutes, then skim and ladle over the pineapple. Weight down and leave for 24 hours. On Day 5, repeat the steps from Day 4. On Day 6, drain the pineapple rings, place the syrup in the pan, and add the remaining sugar. Bring to the boil, stirring until the sugar has dissolved, and boil for 1–2 minutes, then skim and ladle over the pineapple. Weight down and leave for 48 hours.

7 Put the fruit and syrup in a preserving pan and simmer for about 5 minutes. Lift out the pineapple rings with a slotted spoon. Arrange on a rack placed over a foil-lined baking tray. Allow to drain and cool. Put the rack and tray in the oven preheated to 120°C/250°F/gas ½, leaving the door slightly ajar. Leave for 12–24 hours, until the fruit is dry but just sticky to the touch. Leave to cool completely.

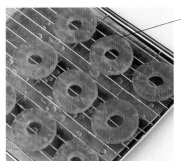

Pineapple rings are left to drain and cool on a wire rack

Layer the candied fruit and crystallized flowers (see page 61) between waxed paper

8 Dust the pineapple rings with caster sugar to coat. Store in an airtight container, between sheets of waxed paper.

Preserved Lemons

☆ **DEGREE OF DIFFICULTY** EASY 🍴 **SPECIAL EQUIPMENT** 1.5 LITRE (2½ PINT) STERILIZED JAR WITH VINEGAR-PROOF SEALANT (SEE PAGES 12–13) 🍯 **YIELD** ABOUT 1KG (2LB) 🍯 **SHELF LIFE** 2 YEARS 🔪 **SERVING SUGGESTIONS** USE TO FLAVOUR TAGINES AND COUSCOUS, OR TO ACCOMPANY GRILLED FISH

INGREDIENTS

1kg (2lb) small, thin-skinned lemons

salt

about 350ml (12fl oz) lemon or lime juice or acidulated water (see step 3)

1–2 tbsp olive oil

TIPS
• **Before using the lemons, wash them well under cold running water, then slice and prepare as directed in the recipe.**
• **Limes can be preserved the same way.**

1 Wash and scrub the lemons. Slice each one into quarters lengthways, from the pointed end, leaving the sections still attached at the stem end, so that they resemble flowers.

2 Gently open out each lemon and sprinkle with about a teaspoon of salt, then close up. Pack the lemons tightly into the sterilized jar and weight down (see page 166). Leave to stand in a warm place, preferably on a sunny windowsill, for 4–5 days. By then, some liquid should have accumulated in the jar.

3 Pour the citrus juice or acidulated water (1½ teaspoons citric acid dissolved in 500ml/17fl oz cold water) into the jar, making sure that the lemons are completely covered.

4 Pour the oil into the top of the jar in a thin layer – this will prevent mould from forming. Seal the jar immediately. The brine will look cloudy at first but should clear in 3–4 weeks, when the lemons will be ready to eat.

Preserved lemons are an essential ingredient in North African cooking. Salting softens the peel and gives the lemon a stronger flavour, so use with discretion.

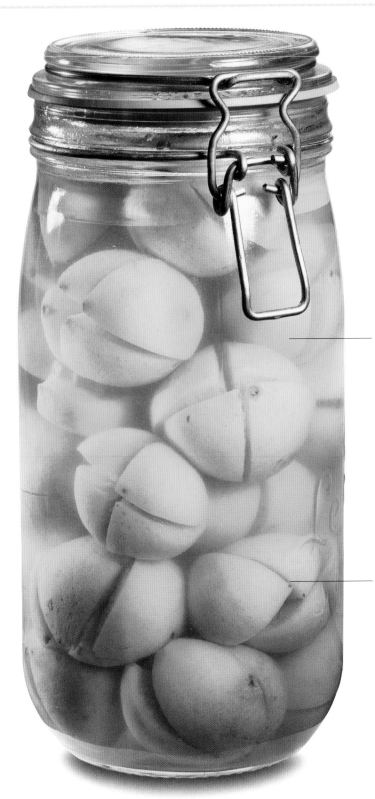

The peel of the preserved lemons is prized for its intense flavour

The deep cuts in the lemons allow the flavours to penetrate the fruit

Pickled Watermelon Rind

 DEGREE OF DIFFICULTY EASY **COOKING TIME** 1–1¼ HOURS **SPECIAL EQUIPMENT** NON-CORROSIVE PRESERVING PAN; STERILIZED JARS WITH VINEGAR-PROOF SEALANTS (SEE PAGES 12–13) **YIELD** ABOUT 1.5KG (3LB) **SHELF LIFE** 2 YEARS  **SERVING SUGGESTIONS** DELICIOUS WITH POULTRY AND COLD HAM

INGREDIENTS

500g (1lb) watermelon rind, green skin removed, with about 5mm (¼in) of the red flesh left on

4 tbsp salt

1kg (2lb) preserving sugar

750ml (1¼ pints) water

750ml (1¼ pints) white wine vinegar or cider vinegar

FOR THE SPICE BAG (SEE PAGE 31)

5cm (2in) piece fresh ginger root, chopped

1 cinnamon stick, broken

1 tbsp allspice berries

1 tbsp cloves

2–3 strips lemon or orange peel (optional)

1 Slice the watermelon rind into 2.5cm (1in) cubes and put in a large glass bowl with the salt. Add enough water to cover, then mix well until the salt has dissolved. Cover with a clean cloth and leave to stand overnight.

2 The next day, drain the watermelon rind. Put in the preserving pan and cover with fresh water. Bring to the boil, then reduce the heat and simmer for about 15 minutes. Drain well.

3 Put the sugar, water, vinegar, and spice bag in the cleaned preserving pan. Bring to the boil, and cook for about 5 minutes. Skim well, add the drained rind, and return to the boil, then reduce the heat and simmer gently for 45–60 minutes or until the rind is translucent.

4 Pack the mixture into the hot sterilized jars, then seal. The pickle will be ready to eat in about 1 month.

TIP
The green skin of the watermelon contains a laxative, so make sure you always remove all of it.

Watermelon rind is very versatile. It can be preserved in syrup, candied, or fermented in brine.

Exotic Fruit Chutney

 ☆ **DEGREE OF DIFFICULTY** EASY **COOKING TIME** 1–1¼ HOURS  **SPECIAL EQUIPMENT** NON-CORROSIVE PRESERVING PAN; STERILIZED JARS WITH VINEGAR-PROOF SEALANTS (SEE PAGES 12–13) **YIELD** ABOUT 3KG (6LB) **SHELF LIFE** 1 YEAR ✎ **SERVING SUGGESTIONS** SERVE WITH POULTRY, CHEESE, OR CURRIES

INGREDIENTS

250g (8oz) kumquats or oranges

1 small pineapple, peeled, cored, and cut into 2.5cm (1in) chunks

500g (1lb) cooking or dessert apples, peeled, cored, and coarsely chopped

300g (10oz) dried apricots, soaked if necessary and coarsely chopped

250g (8oz) baby sweetcorn, cut into 2.5cm (1in) lengths

1 litre (1¾ pints) cider vinegar or white wine vinegar

500g (1lb) sugar

3–4 fresh red chillies, deseeded and chopped

2 tbsp black mustard seeds

2 tbsp salt

1 tbsp green peppercorns

100g (3½oz) mint, coarsely chopped

1 If using kumquats, leave them whole; slice oranges in half, then cut into medium-thick slices. Put all the fruit in the preserving pan with the sweetcorn and vinegar. Bring to the boil, then simmer for 15 minutes.

2 Add the sugar, chillies, mustard seeds, salt, and peppercorns. Stir until the sugar has dissolved. Simmer, stirring frequently, for 50–60 minutes, until most of the liquid has evaporated and the mixture is thick.

3 Remove from the heat and stir in the mint. Ladle into the hot sterilized jars, then seal. The chutney will be ready in 1 month but improves with keeping.

I tend to make this delightfully fresh-tasting chutney in winter and sometimes add a combination of pawpaw, kiwi fruit, and lychees to the kumquats, apples, and sweetcorn.

Hot Mango Chutney

 DEGREE OF DIFFICULTY EASY **COOKING TIME** 1–1¼ HOURS **SPECIAL EQUIPMENT** NON-CORROSIVE PRESERVING PAN; SPICE MILL OR COFFEE GRINDER; STERILIZED JARS WITH VINEGAR-PROOF SEALANTS (SEE PAGES 12–13) **YIELD** ABOUT 1.5KG (3LB) **SHELF LIFE** 2 YEARS **SERVING SUGGESTIONS** SERVE WITH POPPADOMS OR WITH PLAIN BOILED RICE FOR A LIGHT SUPPER DISH

INGREDIENTS

2kg (4lb) unripe mangoes, peeled and cut into 2.5cm (1in) chunks (see page 224)

2 limes or lemons, sliced into semi-circles

3–4 fresh red chillies, deseeded and coarsely chopped

750ml (1¼ pints) white wine vinegar or distilled white vinegar

500g (1lb) light soft brown sugar

1 tbsp salt

1 tbsp green cardamom pods

1 tsp cumin seeds

1 tsp chilli powder (optional)

½ tsp saffron strands or 1 tsp ground turmeric

1 Put the mangoes, limes or lemons, chillies, and vinegar in the preserving pan. Bring to the boil, then reduce the heat and simmer for 10–15 minutes or until the mango is just tender. Add the sugar and salt, stirring until they have dissolved. Simmer for 50–60 minutes, until most of the liquid has evaporated and the mixture is thick.

2 Grind the cardamom and cumin to a powder in the spice mill or coffee grinder. Add to the chutney through a sieve, with the chilli powder, if using. Soak the saffron strands in a little hot water for a few minutes. Stir into the chutney, or add the turmeric.

3 Ladle into the hot sterilized jars, then seal. The chutney will be ready to eat in 1 month.

This recipe is from Bihar in India, and it produces a hot, richly flavoured, golden preserve. Turmeric can be used, but saffron gives the chutney a unique flavour.

Date Blatjang

☆ **DEGREE OF DIFFICULTY** EASY 🍲 **COOKING TIME** ABOUT 15 MINUTES 🍴 **SPECIAL EQUIPMENT** NON-CORROSIVE PRESERVING PAN; FOOD PROCESSOR; STERILIZED BOTTLES WITH VINEGAR-PROOF SEALANTS OR CORKS (SEE PAGES 12–13) 🫙 **YIELD** ABOUT 1 LITRE (1¾ PINTS) 🫙 **SHELF LIFE** 2 YEARS ✎ **SERVING SUGGESTIONS** SERVE WITH RICE OR OILY FISH; IT IS ESPECIALLY GOOD WITH GRILLED MACKEREL

INGREDIENTS

150g (5oz) tamarind block

350ml (12fl oz) boiling water

500g (1lb) pitted dates,
coarsely chopped

5cm (2in) piece fresh ginger root,
peeled and chopped

8 garlic cloves, chopped

3–4 dried red chillies, deseeded
and chopped

1 litre (1¾ pints) red wine vinegar

2 tsp salt

1 Soak the tamarind in the boiling water for 30 minutes. Strain, then pour the liquid into the preserving pan with the rest of the ingredients. Bring to the boil, simmer for 10 minutes, then cool.

2 Purée in the food processor. Return to the cleaned pan and boil for 1–2 minutes. Pour into the hot sterilized bottles, then seal. The sauce is ready immediately but improves with keeping.

> **TIP**
> **Other fruit – such as fresh or dried apricots, peaches, and mango – can be used instead of dates.**

I came across this recipe in South Africa, where it had been introduced in the 17th century by Malay slaves. It has a hot, sharp, sweet flavour.

Pickled Limes

 ☆☆ **DEGREE OF DIFFICULTY** MODERATE **COOKING TIME** ABOUT 5 MINUTES **SPECIAL EQUIPMENT** SPICE MILL
OR COFFEE GRINDER; NON-CORROSIVE PRESERVING PAN; STERILIZED JARS WITH VINEGAR-PROOF SEALANTS (SEE PAGES 12–13)
 YIELD ABOUT 1KG (2LB) **SHELF LIFE** 2 YEARS **SERVING SUGGESTIONS** SERVE AS A RELISH WITH
A SELECTION OF APPETIZERS, OR SPREAD OVER WHOLE FISH OR FISH FILLETS BEFORE BAKING

INGREDIENTS

1kg (2lb) limes

100g (3½oz) salt

1 tsp cardamom pods

1 tsp black cumin seeds (kalajeera)

1 tsp cumin seeds

½ tsp cloves

*500g (1lb) soft light brown
or white sugar*

1 tbsp chilli powder, or to taste

*75g (2½oz) fresh ginger root,
finely shredded*

1 Put the limes in a bowl and cover with cold water. Leave to soak overnight, then drain. Top and tail them, and cut into slices 5mm (¼in) thick. Put in a glass bowl and sprinkle with the salt. Mix well, cover with a clean cloth, and leave to stand for 12 hours.

2 The next day, place the spices in the spice mill or coffee grinder, and grind to a powder.

3 Drain the limes and put the liquid they have produced in the preserving pan with the sugar and ground spices. Bring to the boil, stirring until the sugar has dissolved, and boil for 1 minute. Remove from the heat, stir in the chilli powder, and leave to cool.

4 Add the limes and ginger to the cooled syrup, and mix well. Pack into the sterilized jars. Poke the limes with a wooden skewer to ensure there are no air pockets, then seal. Leave in a warm place, such as a sunny windowsill, for 4–5 days before storing. The pickle will be ready in 4–5 weeks.

This recipe produces a sharp, hot pickle from the Punjab in India. You can also prepare lemons or oranges in the same way.

Pickled Okra

☆ **DEGREE OF DIFFICULTY** EASY 🍲 **COOKING TIME** ABOUT 10 MINUTES 🍴 **SPECIAL EQUIPMENT** STERILIZED JARS WITH VINEGAR-PROOF SEALANTS (SEE PAGES 12–13) **YIELD** ABOUT 2KG (4LB) **SHELF LIFE** 6 MONTHS 🔪 **SERVING SUGGESTIONS** SERVE ON ITS OWN OR AS A PICKLED SALAD TO ACCOMPANY COLD MEAT

INGREDIENTS

750g (1½lb) crisp, young okra

1 tbsp salt

275g (9oz) carrots, cut into thick matchsticks

6 large garlic cloves, sliced

3–4 fresh red chillies, deseeded and sliced (optional)

small bunch of mint, coarsely chopped

FOR THE PICKLING MIXTURE

1 litre (1¾ pints) cider vinegar

4 tbsp sugar or honey

1 tbsp salt

2 tsp ground turmeric

1 Trim any dark bits from the stalk end of the okra, but leave the stalks attached. Prick each okra in a few places with a wooden cocktail stick.

2 Lay the okra out on a large baking sheet, and sprinkle with the salt. Leave to stand, preferably in the sun, for 1 hour.

3 Rinse the okra well under cold running water and dry on paper towels. Blanch the carrots in boiling water for 2–3 minutes (see page 21).

4 Mix together the garlic, chillies (if using), and mint. Arrange the okra and carrots in layers in the hot sterilized jars, evenly distributing the garlic mixture between the layers. The jars should be full but loosely packed.

5 For the pickling mixture, put the vinegar, sugar or honey, and salt in a non-corrosive pan. Bring

to the boil and skim well. Add the turmeric, and return to the boil for a few minutes.

6 Pour the hot vinegar into the jars, filling them to the top and making sure that the okra are covered. Poke the vegetables with a wooden skewer to ensure there are no air pockets, then seal. They will be ready to eat in 2 weeks.

This pickle is based on a traditional Iranian recipe. Do not be alarmed if the pickling liquid thickens – it is due to the okra's glutinous sap.

Potted Cheese

☆ **DEGREE OF DIFFICULTY** EASY ❙❙ **SPECIAL EQUIPMENT** 3 x 175ML (6FL OZ) STERILIZED RAMEKINS OR A 500ML (16FL OZ) EARTHENWARE DISH (SEE PAGES 12–13) **YIELD** ABOUT 500G (1LB) **SHELF LIFE** 6 WEEKS, REFRIGERATED

SERVING SUGGESTIONS SERVE AS A FIRST COURSE WITH HOT TOAST, OR USE TO FILL SANDWICHES

INGREDIENTS

500g (1lb) mature Cheddar or Cheshire cheese, or a mixture, finely grated

75g (2½oz) softened unsalted butter

1 tbsp pale dry sherry

1 tsp English mustard

¼ tsp finely grated lemon rind

large pinch freshly grated nutmeg

large pinch cayenne pepper or chilli powder

150g (5oz) clarified butter (see page 47)

1 Put all the ingredients except the clarified butter in a large bowl. Beat together until smooth. Pack into the ramekins or dish, filling them to within 1cm (½in) of the rim. Smooth the top, and refrigerate for 2–3 hours.

2 Seal the top with the melted clarified butter (see step 4, page 47). Cover and refrigerate. The cheese will be ready in 2 days.

Potting is a wonderful way to use up odd bits of good leftover cheese. Blended with butter, the cheese makes a flavourful paste that keeps for more than a month. Any kind of mature hard cheese is suitable, including blue cheese.

Mushroom Ketchup

☆☆ **DEGREE OF DIFFICULTY** MODERATE  **COOKING TIME** 3½–4½ HOURS

SPECIAL EQUIPMENT FOOD PROCESSOR; STERILIZED JELLY BAG; NON-CORROSIVE PRESERVING PAN; STERILIZED

BOTTLES WITH SEALANTS OR CORKS (SEE PAGES 12–13)  **YIELD** ABOUT 750ML (1¼ PINTS) **SHELF LIFE** 2 YEARS,

HEAT PROCESSED **SERVING SUGGESTION** USE IN SMALL AMOUNTS TO FLAVOUR SOUPS AND STEWS

INGREDIENTS

2kg (4lb) large flat-cap mushrooms

60g (2oz) dried ceps (optional)

150g (5oz) salt

300g (10oz) shallots, unpeeled,
quartered

5cm (2in) piece dried ginger
root, bruised

125ml (4fl oz) port

1 tbsp cloves

2 tsp crumbled mace blades

1 Put the fresh mushrooms in the food processor and coarsely chop. Arrange in thin layers with the dried ceps (if using) in the casserole dish, sprinkling each layer with some of the salt. Cover and leave to stand for 24 hours.

2 Bake in an oven preheated to 140°C/275°F/gas 1 for 3 hours. Cool and strain through the jelly bag, squeezing to extract all the liquid. Put the liquid in the preserving pan with the remaining ingredients. Bring to the boil, then simmer for 45 minutes or until the mixture has reduced by a third.

3 Strain again, then return the liquid to the pan and bring back to the boil. Pour into the hot sterilized bottles, then seal. Heat process, cool, check the seals, and dip corks in wax (see pages 13–15). The ketchup will be ready to use in 1 month but improves with keeping.

TIP
This makes a flavoursome ketchup, but it is important to use only flat, fully matured mushrooms.

MUSHROOMS

Sweet and earthy, mushrooms can be pickled or used as the basis of a ketchup. However, they yield most of their flavour when dried, which makes them a convenient staple for the storecupboard. Dried mushrooms can be rehydrated and used in pasta sauces or risottos.

Mushrooms in Oil

 DEGREE OF DIFFICULTY EASY **COOKING TIME** ABOUT 45 MINUTES ❘❘ **SPECIAL EQUIPMENT** 1.5 LITRE (2½ PINT) STERILIZED JAR WITH VINEGAR-PROOF SEALANT (SEE PAGES 12–13); THERMOMETER **YIELD** ABOUT 1KG (2LB) **SHELF LIFE** 6 MONTHS ⊘ **SERVING SUGGESTIONS** SERVE AS AN HORS D'OEUVRE, OR USE WITH A LITTLE OF THE OIL FROM THE JAR AS AN INSTANT PASTA SAUCE

INGREDIENTS

500ml (17fl oz) white wine vinegar

250ml (8fl oz) water

3–4 garlic cloves, coarsely chopped

1 tsp black peppercorns

2 tsp salt

4–6 sprigs thyme

1kg (2lb) assorted mushrooms

1–2 strips lemon rind

1 bay leaf (optional)

good-quality olive oil, to cover

1 Put the vinegar, water, garlic, peppercorns, salt, and a few sprigs of the thyme in a deep non-corrosive pan. Bring to the boil, then reduce the heat and simmer for 30 minutes.

2 Add the mushrooms to the pan and simmer for about 10 minutes or until they are just cooked. Remove them with a slotted spoon and drain well. Remove the thyme.

3 Arrange the mushrooms, strips of lemon rind, bay leaf (if using), and remaining thyme sprigs in the hot sterilized jar.

4 Heat the olive oil in a pan to 75°C (167°F) and pour it carefully into the jar, making sure the mushrooms are completely covered. Poke the mushrooms with a wooden skewer to ensure there are no air pockets, then seal. The mushrooms will be ready to eat in about 2 weeks.

TIP
Mushrooms soak up water like a sponge, so do not wash them unless absolutely necessary. Just trim them, brush off any dust and dirt, and wipe clean with a paper towel.

For me, mushrooms bring back memories of cool autumn days and the haunting scent of wood and rotting leaves. Oil is the best way to preserve a glut of mushrooms.

Spiced Vinegars

☆ **DEGREE OF DIFFICULTY** EASY   🍲 **COOKING TIME** ABOUT 12 MINUTES   🍴 **SPECIAL EQUIPMENT** MUSLIN; STERILIZED BOTTLES WITH VINEGAR-PROOF SEALANTS (SEE PAGES 12–13)   🫙 **YIELD** ABOUT 2 LITRES (3½ PINTS)

INGREDIENTS

2 litres (3 ½ pints) vinegar

SIMPLE SPICED VINEGAR

2 tbsp peppercorns

2 tbsp mustard seeds

1 tbsp cloves

2 tsp crumbled mace blades

2 nutmegs, broken into pieces

2–3 dried chillies, crushed (optional)

1 cinnamon stick, crushed

2–3 bay leaves

1 tbsp salt

HOT AND SPICY VINEGAR

90g (3oz) shallots, chopped

75g (2 ½oz) fresh ginger root, crushed

5–6 dried red chillies, crushed

1 tbsp black peppercorns

1 tbsp allspice berries

2 tsp cloves

1 cinnamon stick, crushed

2 tsp salt

PERFUMED VINEGAR

5cm (2in) piece fresh ginger root, sliced

2 tbsp coriander seeds

1 tbsp black peppercorns

1 tbsp cardamom pods

1 tbsp allspice berries

2 cinnamon sticks, crushed

2 nutmegs, broken into pieces

1 tsp aniseed

a few strips of lemon or orange rind

1 tbsp salt

MILD EUROPEAN VINEGAR

1 tbsp black peppercorns

1 tbsp juniper berries

1 tbsp allspice berries

1 tbsp caraway seeds

2 tsp dill or celery seeds

2–3 bay leaves

2–3 garlic cloves, crushed

2–3 dried red chillies (optional)

2 tbsp salt

SPICY EUROPEAN VINEGAR

100g (3 ½oz) shallots or onions, coarsely chopped

small bunch fresh tarragon

4 garlic cloves, crushed

2 tsp black peppercorns

1 tsp cloves

2 tbsp salt

MELLOW TRADITIONAL BRITISH VINEGAR

90g (3oz) fresh horseradish root, sliced

1 tbsp black peppercorns

1 tbsp mustard seeds

1 tbsp allspice berries

2 tsp cloves

2 pieces dried ginger root

1 cinnamon stick, crushed

2 tbsp salt ingredients

2 litres (3 ½ pints) vinegar

1 For each vinegar, tie all the flavourings except the salt in a piece of muslin (see Spice Bags, page 31). Place in a non-corrosive pan with the salt and vinegar. Bring to the boil, and boil for about 10 minutes.

2 Leave to cool, then remove the spice bag. Filter the vinegar if it is cloudy (see page 21). Pour into the sterilized bottles, then seal. The vinegar is ready immediately but improves with keeping.

These basic flavoured vinegars are very easy to make, and they mature and mellow with time. Any type of vinegar can be used, but make sure it has an acidity of no less than 5 per cent.

Biltong

☆ **DEGREE OF DIFFICULTY** EASY 🍲 **COOKING TIME** 8–16 HOURS, OVEN-DRIED

🍴 **SPECIAL EQUIPMENT** STRING AND LARDING NEEDLE, OR MEAT HOOKS 🫙 **YIELD** ABOUT 1KG (2LB)

🫙 **SHELF LIFE** 3 WEEKS, SEMI-DRIED; 2 YEARS, FULLY DRIED 🔪 **SERVING SUGGESTION** SERVE AS A TASTY SNACK

WARNING THIS RECIPE CONTAINS SALTPETRE; SEE PAGE 12

INGREDIENTS

2kg (4lb) piece of top side, sirloin, or silverside of beef or venison

250g (8oz) coarse salt

3 tbsp soft brown sugar

1 tsp saltpetre

3 tbsp coriander seeds, toasted and crushed

2 tbsp black peppercorns, crushed

4 tbsp malt vinegar

IMPORTANT INFORMATION

- The rules of proper hygiene should be followed strictly at all stages of preparation and storage (see page 12).
- The meat should be marinated in a cool place, preferably the bottom of the refrigerator.
- Discard the meat if it starts to smell off at any time during the drying process.
- Check the stored meat regularly; if it goes mouldy or starts to smell off, discard it at once.

1 Using a sharp cook's knife, slice the meat along the grain into long strips about 5cm (2in) thick. If the meat was partially frozen, leave the slices to defrost.

2 For the marinade, put the salt, sugar, saltpetre, lightly toasted coriander seeds, and crushed black pepper into a glass bowl, and mix until evenly blended.

3 Sprinkle an earthenware baking dish with a layer of the salt mix. Add the meat and cover it with the remaining mix, rubbing it in well.

4 Spoon the vinegar evenly over the meat and rub the salt mix into both sides of the meat again. Cover the dish and leave to marinate in the bottom of the fridge for 6–8 hours. Halfway through this resting time, rub the marinade into the meat again.

6 Press a meat hook through one end of the meat, or make a hole in each piece and tie a loop of string through it. Hang it up in a cool, dry, dark, airy place (6–8°C/42–46°F) for 1½ weeks. After this time, the biltong will be only semi-dry, so its shelf life will be limited. Wrap in waxed paper, refrigerate, and eat within 3 weeks.

The meat will be a lot paler when it has finished marinating

5 After the meat has marinated in the cure, it will become paler and stiffer. Lift the meat out of the cure and brush off any excess salt.

When the biltong is dark and bone-dry, it is ready to eat

7 For a longer-lasting product, dry the meat further. To speed up the drying, you could use an oven. First, line the bottom of the oven with aluminium foil to catch any drips. Place one of the oven shelves on the highest position and hang the meat from its bars. Dry the biltong at the lowest possible oven setting, for 8–16 hours, until it is fully dry and dark and it splinters when bent in two.

Chilli Salami

☆☆ **DEGREE OF DIFFICULTY** MODERATE **SPECIAL EQUIPMENT** MINCER; SAUSAGE MAKER OR SAUSAGE FILLER; MEAT HOOKS **YIELD** ABOUT 750G (1½LB) **SHELF LIFE** 4–5 MONTHS, REFRIGERATED **SERVING SUGGESTIONS** SLICE AND SERVE RAW, OR ADD TO BEAN STEWS AND CASSEROLES **WARNING** THIS RECIPE CONTAINS SALTPETRE; SEE PAGE 12

INGREDIENTS

1kg (2lb) pork shoulder, hand or blade, cut into large cubes

1½ tbsp salt

1 tbsp soft brown sugar

½ tsp saltpetre

75ml (3fl oz) brandy

350g (11½oz) pork back fat, cut into small, rough chunks

4–5 large, mild red chillies, very finely chopped

2 garlic cloves, crushed

2 tbsp sweet paprika

1 tsp chilli powder, or to taste

1 tsp aniseed

about 2 metres (2 yards) hog casing

IMPORTANT NOTE

Before starting this recipe, please read the information on pages 12 and 244.

1 Put the pork in a large glass bowl, and sprinkle with the salt, sugar, saltpetre, and brandy. Mix together with your hands. Cover and refrigerate for 12–24 hours.

2 Put the meat through the coarse disc of the mincer. Mix well with all the remaining ingredients except the casing. Prepare the casing (see steps 3 and 4, page 190). Stuff with the meat and divide into 50cm (20in) links (see step 5, page 191).

3 Tie the ends of each sausage together to form a horseshoe. Hang up in a cool, dry, dark, airy place (at 6–8°C/42–46°F) for 4–6 weeks or until they have lost about 50 per cent of their original weight. Wrap in greaseproof paper and refrigerate until needed.

VARIATION

SMOKED CHILLI SALAMI
Dry for 1–2 days or until the surface is just moist, then cold-smoke for 6–8 hours at 30°C/86°F. Dry as above. The smoked sausages will be ready to eat in 4–5 weeks.

TIP
You can mince the fat on the coarse disc of a mincer instead of chopping it by hand, but you will lose the sausages' wonderful marbled appearance.

These spicy sausages are similar to Spanish chorizo and can be used in cooking or eaten raw. To make milder sausages, simply reduce the number of chillies. Before serving raw, the sausages should be brought to room temperature.

Landjäger

☆☆ **DEGREE OF DIFFICULTY** MODERATE **SPECIAL EQUIPMENT** MINCER; SAUSAGE MAKER OR

 SAUSAGE FILLER; MEAT HOOKS; SMOKER **YIELD** ABOUT 1.5KG (2½ LB)

SHELF LIFE 4–5 MONTHS, REFRIGERATED **SERVING SUGGESTION** WONDERFUL FOR PICNICS

WARNING THIS RECIPE CONTAINS SALTPETRE; SEE PAGE 12

INGREDIENTS

*1.25kg (2½lb) lean beef, such
as chuck, shoulder, or rump, cut
into large cubes*

1kg (2lb) streaky bacon, rind removed

5 garlic cloves, crushed

1 tbsp salt

1 tbsp soft brown sugar

½ tsp saltpetre

2 tsp coriander seeds, finely ground

1 tsp freshly ground black pepper

2 tsp caraway seeds

75ml (2½fl oz) kirsch

*3.5 metres (3¾ yards) beef
runners (casing)*

a little groundnut oil

IMPORTANT NOTE

Before starting this recipe, please
read the information on pages 12
and 244.

1 Put the beef through the
coarse disc of the mincer and the
bacon through the fine disc.

2 Add all the remaining
ingredients except the beef
runners and oil, and mix well.
Pack the mixture tightly into
a bowl, making sure there are
no air pockets. Cover and
refrigerate for 48 hours.

3 Prepare the beef runners
(see steps 3 and 4, page 190).
Stuff with the meat and divide

into 15cm (6in) links (see step 5,
page 191). Place between two
wooden boards and weight down
(see page 166). Refrigerate for
48 hours.

4 Hang up in a cool, dry, dark,
airy place (at 6–8°C/ 42–46°F)
for 24 hours, then cold-smoke
for 12 hours at 30°C/86°F.

5 Rub the sausages with a little
oil. Hang up to dry as before for
2–3 weeks or until they have lost
50 per cent of their original
weight. To store them, wrap in
greaseproof or waxed paper and
keep refrigerated, or freeze for up
to 3 months.

TIP
**To speed up the
drying process, hang
the sausages in front of
an electric fan switched
to the cold setting.**

Landjäger *is the German word for hunter,
and these flat, spicy sausages used to be the
favourite food to take on a hunt. If possible,
use cherry tree chips when smoking them.*

Pastrami

☆☆ **DEGREE OF DIFFICULTY** MODERATE 🍲 **COOKING TIME** 4–6 HOURS, SMOKING; 2½–3 HOURS, SIMMERING
🍴 **SPECIAL EQUIPMENT** MEAT HOOK; SMOKER 🧂 **YIELD** ABOUT 2–2½KG (4–5LB) 🏺 **SHELF LIFE** 4–6 WEEKS,
REFRIGERATED; 6 MONTHS, FROZEN 🔪 **SERVING SUGGESTIONS** SERVE HOT OR COLD, OR AS A SANDWICH FILLING
WARNING THIS RECIPE CONTAINS SALTPETRE; SEE PAGE 12

INGREDIENTS

3kg (6lb) lean beef brisket

250g (8oz) coarse salt

6 garlic cloves, crushed

4 tbsp soft brown sugar

4 tbsp coarsely ground black pepper

2 tbsp coriander seeds, coarsely ground

1 tbsp ground ginger

1 tsp saltpetre

IMPORTANT NOTE

Before starting this recipe, please read the information on pages 12 and 244.

1 Put the beef in a deep glass dish. Rub 100g (3½oz) of the salt into the meat. Cover and leave for 2 hours, then rinse the meat and dry well.

2 Mix the remaining ingredients together, including the rest of the salt, and rub well into the meat. Return the meat to the cleaned dish. Cover and refrigerate for 1½–2 weeks, turning the meat every few days.

3 Lift the meat out and pat dry. Insert a meat hook into the beef, and hang up to dry in a cool, dry, dark, airy place (at 6–8°C/42–46°F) for 1 day. Cold-smoke below 50°C/100°F for 4–6 hours.

4 Cook the pastrami in simmering, unsalted water for 2½–3 hours or until it is tender. Remove from the cooking liquid, drain well, then serve. To serve cold, drain well and weight down (see page 166). Leave to cool, then refrigerate until needed.

TIP
Traditionally, pastrami is lightly smoked for 4 hours. Smoke it for up to 12 hours over some fragrant fruit wood for a more intense flavour.

New York just wouldn't be the same without pastrami on rye. This lightly smoked, deliciously piquant cured meat originated in Romania, but its roots probably lie in Turkey.

Gravad Lax

☆ **DEGREE OF DIFFICULTY** EASY **YIELD** ABOUT 1KG (2LB) **SHELF LIFE** 1 WEEK, REFRIGERATED; TO KEEP LONGER, SEE HERRINGS IN SPICED OIL (PAGE 64) **SERVING SUGGESTION** SERVE WITH A DILL AND MUSTARD SAUCE, ACCOMPANIED BY A POTATO OR BEETROOT SALAD

INGREDIENTS

1kg (2lb) middle-cut of salmon, filleted, all bones removed (see steps 1 and 2, page 250)

4 tbsp coarse pickling salt

3 tbsp soft brown or white sugar

1 tbsp coarsely ground black pepper

1 large bunch dill, coarsely chopped

2–3 tbsp aquavit or vodka

1 Place one fillet of the salmon skin side down on a large piece of aluminium foil. Mix together the salt, sugar, and pepper. Sprinkle half of the salt mixture evenly over the salmon.

2 Sprinkle with the chopped dill, remaining salt mixture, and the aquavit or vodka. Place the other fillet of salmon skin side up over the top. Fold the foil over and wrap well.

3 Put the foil-wrapped salmon in a shallow dish. Cover with a board or plate and weight down (see page 166). Refrigerate for 24–36 hours, turning the parcel over every 12 hours.

4 Unwrap the salmon and carefully remove each fillet from the foil. Gently brush off all the salt, dill, and spices. To serve the salmon, cut it into very thin slices with a long-bladed, serrated knife, angling the knife at 45 degrees.

This delicious Scandinavian recipe is the simplest and most enjoyable way to cure fish. Trout, mackerel, and even very fresh halibut can be prepared in the same way. Alcohol is not a traditional ingredient, but it adds flavour and helps preserve the fish.

TIP
Brown sugar gives the fish a delightful flavour and an appetizing dark colour.

Smoked Salmon

☆☆ **DEGREE OF DIFFICULTY** MODERATE 🍲 **COOKING TIME** 3–4 HOURS, COLD-SMOKED; 2–3 HOURS, HOT-SMOKED
🍴 **SPECIAL EQUIPMENT** SMOKER 🧂 **YIELD** 1.5–2KG (3–4LB) 🫙 **SHELF LIFE** 3 WEEKS, REFRIGERATED;
3 MONTHS, FROZEN 🔪 **SERVING SUGGESTIONS** SERVE HOT-SMOKED SALMON THICKLY SLICED, WITH A GREEN
SALAD AND BREAD, AS A LIGHT MAIN COURSE; CUT COLD-SMOKED SALMON INTO PAPER-THIN SLICES AND
SERVE WITH CREAM CHEESE IN BAGELS; OR USE TO MAKE PÂTÉ OR MOUSSE

INGREDIENTS

2–3kg (4–6lb) fresh salmon, cleaned

375g (12oz) sea salt

125g (4oz) light soft brown
or demerara sugar

1–2 tsps whisky

1 To fillet the salmon, cut around the head on one side, using a sharp filleting knife. Slide the knife between the flesh and the backbone, keeping it as close to the bone as possible, and slice off the fillet in one piece.

2 Turn the salmon over and repeat the filleting procedure on the other side. Run your fingers along each fillet to locate all the remaining bones, then remove them with tweezers. Rinse the fillets and dry well.

3 Sprinkle some of the sea salt and sugar into a non-corrosive container to form a 5mm (¼in) layer. Lay one fillet skin side down on top, then sprinkle with another layer, about 1cm (½in) thick, thinning it towards the tail end.

4 Put the second fillet skin side down on top of the first, and sprinkle the remaining salt mix over the fish. Cover the dish with clingfilm and leave to stand for 3–3½ hours in a refrigerator or cool place.

5 Remove the salmon from the salt mix and rinse under cold running water to remove the excess salt. Dry well with paper towels. Push a wooden skewer through the back of each fillet at the head end.

6 Brush both sides of each fillet with the whisky, and hang up to dry in a cool, dry place for about 24 hours or until the sides of the fish are almost dry to the touch and have developed a shiny salt glaze.

The salmon will have a glaze by the time it is ready to be smoked

7 Put the fillets on a rack in the smoker and either cold-smoke at 28°C (82°F) for 3–4 hours or hot-smoke at 55°C (130°F) for 2–3 hours. Remove the salmon from the smoker and allow to cool completely. Place the salmon on a piece of foil-covered card, then wrap it in waxed paper to store.

Foil-covered card makes it easier to lift the salmon

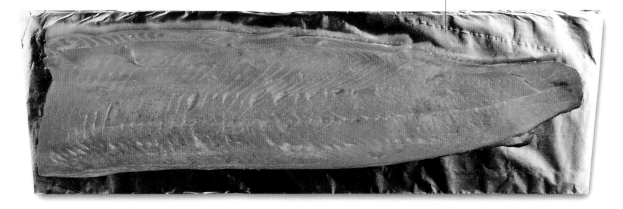

Trouble-Free Preserving

Because so many factors affect the preserving process, it is possible that the end product may not look, smell, or taste as you expected. If this is the case, you need to know what went wrong and, more importantly, whether the food is safe to eat. The most common problems that are encountered during preserving are listed below, with clear guidelines on when a product should not be eaten.

PICKLES	JAMS AND SWEET PRESERVES	SWEET AND SAVOURY PRESERVES	SALAMI AND CURED MEAT
The pickles are not crunchy • The vegetables were not salted for long enough beforehand. • The vinegar or salt solution was not strong enough. **The pickles are hollow** • The raw ingredients were too mature or kept for too long before use. **The pickles are dark** • Iodized (table) salt was used. • Too many spices were added. • Iron or copper utensils were used. • A dark vinegar was added. • The brine was made with hard water; try filtered or bottled water. **The pickles look pale or bleached** • The jar must have been exposed to light during storage. **The pickles are soft and slippery** • The salt or vinegar solution was not strong enough. • The jar had a poor seal. *Discard the product immediately.* **Garlic looks green** • Fresh garlic may turn a harmless but unappetizing shade of green when steeped in vinegar; blanch in boiling water before using.	**The jam or jelly is not setting** • There is too little pectin. Add pectin stock or commercial pectin and re-boil until the setting point is reached (see page 16). Note: frozen fruit contains less pectin than fresh fruit. • There was an incorrect balance between pectin and acid. Add lemon juice and re-boil. **The fruit looks too dark** • The preserve was cooked for too long, and the sugar started to caramelize. (The traditional advice is to warm the sugar before adding it, to shorten the cooking time, but this makes little difference.) **Fruit has risen to the top of the jam** • The jam was not allowed to settle. Leave it until cold, fold in the fruit evenly, then pot. Cover with waxed paper discs dipped in brandy, and seal. • The syrup is too thin. Drain it off and return to the pan with more sugar. Boil rapidly until the setting point is reached (see page 16). **The jam has crystallized** • Too much sugar was added. • The storage temperature was too cold. This is harmless and does not affect the flavour of the product.	**There is mould on the surface** • A result of a fungus contamination. *Discard the product. Moulds send out a network of invisible threads and produce spores that may be harmful.* **The preserve has fermented** • If a sweet preserve ferments, too little sugar was added. • For a pickle or chutney, the brine or vinegar solution was too weak. • Storage conditions were too warm. • Equipment or containers were not sterilized thoroughly. • Cooking time was too short. *Discard the product immediately; this fermentation may produce harmful toxins. Note: some pickles are fermented as part of a recipe.* **Unpleasant odours have developed** • *Any product that develops an off-putting smell should be discarded immediately.*	**There is a white powdery mould on salamis or cured meat** • This naturally occurring mould is encouraged by the right storage conditions. It is harmless and adds to the flavour of the product. **There is green or black mould on salamis or cured meat** • The salt solution was too weak. • The meat was not cured properly. • The storage atmosphere was too damp and warm. *Discard the product immediately.* **White salt burns appear on drying cured meat** • The salt solution used was too strong. **The dried cured meat has a powdery texture** • Too much vinegar in the cure. **The curing liquid turns syrupy** • Not enough salt was added. • Storage temperature was too high. *Discard the curing liquid and make up a new batch.* Re-sterilize the container. Wash the meat well with cold running water, then rub with vinegar. Dry the meat thoroughly with paper towels, and immerse in the new cure.

Index

ACKNOWLEDGMENTS

Author's Appreciation
This book is the fulfilment
of a lifelong obsession with
preserving and would not have
been possible without the help
of hundreds of passionate
picklers, recipe writers,
recorders, housewives, grocers,
farmers, and taxi drivers, who
shared with me their culinary
secrets. Without good-quality
raw ingredients, pickling is
impossible, and I would like
to thank my local suppliers,
especially Graham and David
at Graham Butchers, Pedro at
Pedro Fisheries, Green Health
Food Store (Finchley), and Gary
at Ellinghams, for their help
and advice.

As always I would also like
to thank Saul Radomsky for
his patience and support, and
the many friends who have
helped, schlepped, tasted, and
commented: Trudy Barnham;
Jon, Ann, and Marjorie Bryent;
the Blacher family; Iris and
John Cole; the Hersch family;
Jill Jago; Dalia Lamdani; Joy
Peacock; Bob and Ann Tilley;
Eric Treuille; and Jo Wightman;
and a special thanks to Rosie
Kindersley, who made this
book possible.
  Finally, many thanks to my
agent, Vicki McIvor; to my
assistant Alison Austin;
photographer Ian O'Leary and
his assistant Emma Brogi; and

Jane Bull, Jane Middleton,
Kate Scott, and all at Dorling
Kindersley, whose enthusiasm,
help and expert eye made the
writing of this book such a
happy experience.

**Dorling Kindersley would
like to thank:**
Susannah Steel for the contents
list for this edition; Tables Laid
for props; Tate & Lyle for the
supply of preserving sugar;
Graham Brown at Meridian
Foods for the supply of fruit
concentrate; Cecil Gysin at the
Natural Casing Co Ltd for the
supply of sausage casings.
  Special thanks to Ian Taylor
at Taylor Foodservice for the

supply of a smoker; Barry
Chevalier from Aspall Cyder
for the supply of cider vinegar;
and Maureen Smith at SIS
Marketing Ltd for the supply
of a food dehydrator.

Picture Credits:
Alan Buckingham, pp.86–7.
All other images © Dorling
Kindersley.